GENDER

Gender Talk provides a powerful case for the application of discursive psychology and conversation analysis to feminism, guiding the reader through cutting-edge debates and providing valuable evidence of the benefits of fine-grained, discursive methodologies. In particular, the book concentrates on discourse and conversation analysis, providing a full account of these methodologies through the detailed study of data from a variety of settings, including focus groups, interviews and naturally occurring sources. Providing a thorough review of the relevant literature and recent research, this book demonstrates how discourse and conversation analysis can be applied to rework central feminist notions and concepts, ultimately revealing their full potential and relevance to other disciplines. Each chapter provides an overview of traditional feminist research and covers subjects including:

- Sex differences in language: conversation and interruption
- Reformulating context, power and asymmetry
- Gender identity categories: masculinity and femininity.

This unique and thought-provoking application of discursive and conversation analytic methodologies will be of interest to students and researchers in social psychology, sociology, gender studies and cultural studies.

Susan A. Speer is a Lecturer in Language and Communication at the University of Manchester School of Psychological Sciences. She is currently Principal Investigator on a three year project 'Transsexual Identities: Constructions of Gender in an NHS Gender Identity Clinic', which is part of the ESRC Social Identities and Social Action Research Programme. Susan was previously a Lecturer in Sociology and Communication at the Department of Human Sciences at Brunel University.

WOMEN AND PSYCHOLOGY
Series Editor: Jane Ussher
School of Psychology
University of Western Sydney

This series brings together current theory and research on women and psychology. Drawing on scholarship from a number of different areas of psychology, it bridges the gap between abstract research and the reality of women's lives by integrating theory and practice, research and policy.

Each book addresses a "cutting edge" issue of research, covering such topics as post-natal depression, eating disorders, theories and methodologies.

The series provides accessible and concise accounts of key issues in the study of women and psychology, and clearly demonstrates the centrality of psychology to debates within women's studies or feminism.

The Series Editor would be pleased to discuss proposals for new books in the series.

Other titles in this series:
THIN WOMEN
Helen Malson
THE MENSTRUAL CYCLE
Anne E. Walker
POST-NATAL DEPRESSION
Paula Nicolson
RE-THINKING ABORTION
Mary Boyle
WOMEN AND AGING
Linda R. Gannon
BEING MARRIED DOING GENDER
Caroline Dryden
UNDERSTANDING DEPRESSION
Janet M. Stoppard
FEMININITY AND THE PHYSICALLY ACTIVE WOMAN
Precilla Y. L. Choi
GENDER, LANGUAGE AND DISCOURSE
Ann Weatherall
THE PSYCHOLOGICAL DEVELOPMENT OF GIRLS AND WOMEN
Sheila Greene
THE SCIENCE/FICTION OF SEX
Annie Potts
JUST SEX?
Nicola Gavey
WOMAN'S RELATIONSHIP WITH HERSELF
Helen O'Grady
BODY WORK
Sylvia K. Blood
BEAUTY AND MISOGYNY
Sheila Jeffreys

GENDER TALK

Feminism, Discourse and Conversation Analysis

Susan A. Speer

LONDON AND NEW YORK

First published 2005 by Routledge
27 Church Road, Hove, East Sussex BN3 2FA

Simultaneously published in the USA and Canada
by Routledge
270 Madison Avenue, New York, NY 10016

Routledge is an imprint of the Taylor & Francis Group

Copyright © 2005 Routledge

Typeset in Sabon by Garfield Morgan, Rhayader, Powys
Printed and bound in Great Britain by TJ International Ltd, Padstow, Cornwall
Paperback cover design by Anú Design

All rights reserved. No part of this book may be reprinted or reproduced or utilized in any form or by any electronic, mechanical, or other means, now known or hereafter invented, including photocopying and recording, or in any information storage or retrieval system, without permission in writing from the publishers.

This publication has been produced with paper manufactured to strict environmental standards and with pulp derived from sustainable forests.

British Library Cataloguing in Publication Data
A catalogue record for this book is available from the British Library

Library of Congress Cataloging-in-Publication Data
Speer, Susan A.
Gender talk : feminism, discourse, and conversation analysis / Susan A. Speer.
p. cm.
Includes bibliographical references and index.
ISBN 0-415-24643-1 – ISBN 0-415-24644-X
1. Language and sex. 2. Feminism. 3. Discourse analysis. 4. Conversation analysis.
5. Gender identity. I. Title.
P120.S48S568 2005
306.44–dc22
2005008320

ISBN 0-415-24643-1 hbk
ISBN 0-415-24644-X pbk

CONTENTS

Acknowledgements	vi
Preface	1
1 Introduction: feminism, discourse and conversation analysis	7
2 Gender and language: 'sex difference' perspectives	30
3 Gender and identity: poststructuralist and ethnomethodological perspectives	60
4 A feminist, conversation analytic approach	90
5 Reconceptualizing gender identity: 'hegemonic masculinity' and 'the world out there'	126
6 Reconceptualizing prejudice: 'heterosexist talk' and 'the world in here'	151
7 Questions, conclusions and applications	178
Postscript: the future of feminist CA: methodological issues	193
Appendix: transcription conventions	199
References	200
Index	229

ACKNOWLEDGEMENTS

This book has been four years in the writing. During that time, many friends and colleagues have sustained and inspired me, and helped to shape the ideas presented here. I must extend my thanks, first of all, to those colleagues who read early drafts of the book, and who provided comments that helped me to keep going, and to look at the manuscript afresh. Special mention must go to Deborah Cameron, Victoria Clarke, Jakob Cromdal, Ian Hutchby, Elizabeth Stokoe and the series editor, Jane Ussher. The Discourse and Rhetoric Group in the Social Sciences Department at Loughborough University provided the intellectual environment during my PhD research from 1996 to 2000, during which time many of the ideas presented here were formulated. Particular thanks must go to Charles Antaki, Malcolm Ashmore, Mick Billig, Derek Edwards, Celia Kitzinger, Jonathan Potter and Sue Wilkinson. The ESRC provided the grant that funded the PhD (Award no. R00429634314), without which I wouldn't be in a position to write this book at all. When I moved to take up my first lectureship at Brunel University in 2000, where the book was actually written, Ian Hutchby was my intellectual sounding board. Anna Gough-Yates provided warmth, friendship and collegiality through some difficult times. Special thanks must go to Jonathan Potter, who has been a constant supporter throughout the past nine years, and an important influence on the development of my career to date. Lucy Farr at Routledge has been especially patient and helpful. My sanity has been maintained throughout by Gillian Bloxham and Victoria Clarke, both of whom will appreciate, perhaps more than anyone else, just what getting this book done and dusted represents for me.

I would like to thank Sage Publications for granting permission to use sections of copyright material from Speer, S. A. (2001b) 'Reconsidering the concept of hegemonic masculinity: Discursive psychology, conversation analysis, and participants' orientations', *Feminism and Psychology* 11(1): 107–35; Speer, S. A. (2002d) 'What can conversation analysis contribute to feminist methodology? Putting reflexivity into practice', *Discourse and Society* 13(6): 801–21; and Speer, S. A. and Potter, J. (2000) 'The management of heterosexist talk: Conversational resources and prejudiced claims', *Discourse and Society* 11(4): 543–72.

PREFACE

Our identities are multifaceted. For instance, I am a white woman, a brunette, a daughter, a sister, an aunt, a 32 year old, a driver, a feminist academic, and so on. At any point in an interaction, any one or more of these identities may become relevant, and influence what I or others do and say. Sometimes our gender and sexuality will be brought to focused attention, through the use of explicitly gendered or marked terms. To use some recent experiences by way of example, a number of service personnel have called me 'Mrs.' Speer, and an ex-colleague told me, 'Talking to you is like the argie-bargies I have with my wife'. It's relatively easy for me as a feminist on these occasions to point to what is said and say 'Look! There's a "gender thing" going on'. The first utterance – an address term – rests on, and makes explicit, assumptions which position me as a married, heterosexual woman. The latter utterance makes my gender identity explicit as part of a 'put-down', which relies for its insulting effect on the direct comparison that is drawn between my ex-colleague's experience of interacting with me, and his experience of interacting with his wife. Part of what is insulting about the comparison is that these interactions are constructed by my ex-colleague as *heterosexual* interactions, and he evaluates my behaviour in terms of his heterosexual *relationship*. Neither I nor my ex-colleague's wife fare particularly well. In both examples, the gendered nature of what is said is tied closely to the terms that are used, the comparisons that are made, and the assumptions about gender and sexuality that are embedded within them.

On other occasions, however, the 'marking' of gender and sexuality is less explicit. Take, for example, instances where strangers have said to me 'Morning darling' and 'Smile love', and where the same ex-colleague who I cited above told me 'You're a tough cookie aren't you', and 'Don't be paranoid'. On such occasions, even while I may know instinctively that there is a 'gender thing' going on, that what is said is based in patriarchal understandings of women as 'objects' who belong to men (as in the first two examples), or assumptions about normative feminine behaviour (as in the second two examples), it is, nonetheless, harder for me as a feminist seeking to 'unpack' these claims, to point to what is said and find evidence that will help me say so with certainty.

One factor that makes this second class of utterances so insidious and elusive (indeed – so effective) is that gender is not explicitly 'indexed' (Ochs 1992), or brought to the focused attention of the participants. It is, as it were, 'bubbling under the surface' of the interaction, and its power lies in what is *not* said, just as much as what is said. Indeed, some of these things could be said by different people under a different set of circumstances, and I may not feel that something gendered has taken place at all. In this sense, our feminist interpretation of these utterances, and our response, rests less on the specific meaning we attach to the words themselves, and more on our knowledge about, and interpretation of, the context in which the words are uttered. It is precisely because meanings are context sensitive, and shaped during the course of an interaction, that if one complains about the gendered nature of an utterance, then one risks being told that the person was 'just trying to be kind', 'funny', 'speaks that way to everybody' or, worst of all, that one is 'taking things too personally' (proof, perhaps, that one is indeed 'paranoid'!). As the above examples illustrate, it is not always clear precisely 'what counts' as gender talk, and by what criteria we might judge – and thus prove to those who may be sceptical of our feminist claims – that a piece of discourse is indeed gendered.

Many of us bypass these thorny linguistic and contextual problems altogether, by adopting the view that we must venture beyond an examination of the minute details of talk, and the local interactional context, to the external, 'extra-discursive' context or 'broader socio political reality' in which that talk is embedded, in order to adequately interpret what is going on, and be able to say anything politically effective. This situation suits us, partly because it allows us to interpret our respondents' utterances in ways that support our feminist theories *no matter what they say*.

One theorist who encourages us to engage directly with the question of 'what counts' as gender talk, and who provides a clear set of criteria for judging whether a piece of discourse is indeed gendered, is the conversation analyst, Emmanuel Schegloff. In his 1997 article 'Whose text? Whose context?', Schegloff poses a provocative theoretical and analytic challenge. Put simply, Schegloff suggests that we should not assume, in advance of an analysis of a piece of discourse, that demographic features of social context such as gender, will be relevant to what is going on within it, or that such things will automatically influence what gets said. Instead, we should bracket our politics and begin by looking at what we have in front of us in our transcript on the page, exploring what the interaction is 'demonstrably about' for the parties within it.

For Schegloff, this entails a close examination of 'each successive contribution' (1997: 165) that our participants make to a spate of talk, and an analysis of whether the participants themselves 'orient toward' (that is, make relevant, or bring to focused attention) gender in the interaction. Schegloff suggests that, if the participants *do* orient to gender, then that gives us grounds, as analysts, for making the claim that gender is 'procedurally consequential' for (that is – has a direct influence on) what is going on. Conversely, if they do *not* orient to gender, then we do not have grounds for claiming that gender is relevant or consequential for the participants in the interaction at that moment.

Schegloff's article has had a significant impact on feminist theorizing around gender and language. Indeed, his argument that we should not presume the a priori relevance of the speaker's sex has problematized the vast majority of variationist and sociolinguistic research since the mid-1970s, which searches for sex differences in language, and which concludes that 'women talk like this' and 'men talk like that'. Likewise it has problematized any approach to discourse which prioritizes the analyst's 'politicized' agenda.

Not surprisingly, Schegloff's article generated a number of vociferous counter-arguments and challenges. Many feminists, and others with a critical agenda, argue that although Schegloff's exclusive focus on participants' orientations may be 'extremely revealing' (Wetherell 1998: 404), such an approach is, nonetheless, 'unbearably limiting' (Kitzinger 2000a: 171; 2002), it is restrictive and impractical (Wetherell 1998), it is sexist (Lakoff 2003), and it cannot account for what is not oriented to (Frith 1998; Stokoe and Smithson 2002) or the pervasive, 'omnirelevance' of gender (Weatherall 2000). Finally, some researchers suggest that, contrary to Schegloff's injunction that the analyst must bracket their politics, conversation analysis (CA) is already ideologically loaded (Billig 1999a, 1999b; Edley 2001b; Stokoe and Smithson 2001, 2002) and 'imbued with politics' (McIlvenny 2002b: 18).

In my own work, by contrast, I have tried to take Schegloff's challenge seriously, to avoid presupposing that a focus on participants' orientations will necessarily be limited, or apolitical, and to set about exploring just how far an approach which *begins* with an analysis of what is relevant to the participants, can take us in advancing our understanding of gender talk. More specifically, I have combined insights from feminism, conversation analysis, and the closely related perspective of discursive psychology (DP), to develop a feminist analytic toolkit which will allow me to explore and rethink 'what counts' as gender talk.

Aims of the book

This book is intended to make a contribution on three levels. First, it will map out and clarify the complex and sometimes confusing terrain at the intersection of feminism, discourse analysis (DA) and conversation analysis. It will define some of the themes and concepts at the heart of the feminism, CA and DA interface, and chart the relationship between them.

Second, the book will report the distinctive details of the feminist analytic approach that I have developed in my own work, and how it relates to, and challenges a range of other perspectives on gender and language. In particular, it will argue for and demonstrate the radical potential that a *strongly CA-aligned* discursive approach can bring to feminism. It will enter debates that are currently taking place among feminists, discourse and conversation analysts, with a view to developing and extending them.

Third, the book is concerned to demonstrate to feminists and others with a critical agenda how, contrary to common assumptions, a fine-grained, data-driven form of analysis which draws on insights from the sociological perspective of CA, and the psychological perspective of DP, can be used to rethink the relationship between the 'macro-social' structural realm of gender norms, ideology (that is, belief systems that come to be accepted as common sense) and other such large-scale feminist issues and concepts, on the one hand, and the cognitive-psychological realm of thoughts, feelings, identity, and prejudicial attitudes and beliefs, on the other. I show how the purportedly 'external' social structural context (the macro realm) and the purportedly 'internal' psychological context (the cognitive realm) are constituted, oriented to, and reproduced in the 'micro-interactional', discursive realm. In the course of doing so, I aim to transcend the artificial distinction that separates these three realms (as they are commonly formulated in sociological and psychological work), and the abstract theoretical framework upon which such distinctions rest. Together, these aims reflect a broader concern to refresh and reinvigorate the field of gender and language research, and take it in new directions.

Audience for the book

This book covers a broad terrain. It brings together ideas and concepts from a range of disciplines, including feminist linguistics, psychology and sociology. As such, it should prove useful to a wide social science readership. Nonetheless, this book is written with a number of specific audiences in mind:

It is intended for feminist social scientists, critical psychologists, and lesbian and gay psychologists and their students, who either already have an interest in DA and CA (be that as a sceptic or a proponent), or who would like to find out more about some of the key debates between feminists, discourse and conversation analysts and what such approaches can offer them. It is for researchers who have an interest in the construction of gender and prejudice, and who seek alternative ways to access and illustrate the constitution of gender and prejudice in talk. Finally, while the substantive concerns that guide this book are feminist ones, it is intended for discourse and conversation analysts more broadly – particularly those with an interest in how insights from CA and DP can be combined to rethink the relationship between macro, cognitive and micro realms (the structure–agency debate) and the implications of such analyses.

Although it deals with a complex body of work, and I make an argument for a distinctive analytic approach throughout, the style and organization of the book is driven by a concern to make it accessible to advanced undergraduates and postgraduate students. Each chapter is intended to provide a stand-alone argument, which should make it accessible for teaching on a range of courses in conjunction with other texts, at undergraduate level and beyond.

There are a number of things that this book is not. This book is not intended as a textbook or a definitive overview of different approaches to gender and language. I aim to provide readers with an overall sense or 'map' of how I believe the field fits together, rather than a detailed, in-depth account of different research studies (see Weatherall 2002a for such an account). Nor is it intended as a methodological 'how to do it' guide to analysis. This book is not about the intricacies of how to analyse conversation using a CA or DP perspective (although I hope it will be illustrative in this respect). Interested readers should consult Hutchby and Wooffitt (1998), Potter and Wetherell (1987), ten Have (1999) and Wood and Kroger (2000) for introductory overviews. Finally, just as we must recognize that discourse is not neutral, so too we must accept that this book will not offer a neutral, value-free rendering of research on gender and language, but one which very much reflects the field as I see it at present, and my own background in the disciplines of sociology and social psychology. It provides a focused snapshot of what I see as the key approaches and debates at the interface of feminism, discourse and conversation analysis, and outlines some possible avenues for the field's development.

A note on data and transcription

This book is based on and dramatized with a range of data from a variety of social science, media and 'everyday' (or 'naturally occurring') sources. Many of the examples I use come from the published research of other authors. I have drawn on research and data collected and published by feminist linguists, conversation analysts and discursive psychologists. The source of each extract is indicated in the extract header.

Most of the data examples in Chapters 5 and 6, and selected extracts in other chapters, derive from a corpus of data that I collected as part of my research on gender, sexuality and leisure. This corpus was made up of informal interviews, focus groups and mealtime discussions with participants selected from among friends and relatives. The remaining data were drawn from television documentaries covering a variety of topics relevant to gender, sexuality and leisure.

Because the data examples are taken from a range of different sources, they are not all transcribed using the same conventions. Each transcript reflects the authors' 'hearing' of the tape at the point where it was transcribed or subsequently developed, as well as their decision about what details will be important for the analysis. As a number of feminists have shown, such choices inevitably have theoretical and political implications (Bucholtz 2000; Coates and Thornborrow 1999; Ochs 1979). The majority of my own data were transcribed using a simplified version of the conventions developed in CA by Gail Jefferson (see Appendix). Identifying information has been replaced with pseudonyms.

1
INTRODUCTION
FEMINISM, DISCOURSE AND CONVERSATION ANALYSIS

These are exciting times for the feminist study of gender talk. Since the mid-1970s there has been a rapid growth in the number and range of approaches that have set about exploring the relationship between gender and language. This is, in part, a consequence of the postmodern 'death of the subject' and 'turn to discourse' in the social and human sciences, in which language is seen, not simply as a neutral means of expression, a passive vehicle through which we report on events and experiences – but instead, as something that is central to the construction and reproduction of gendered selves, social structures and relations (Gergen 1985; Shotter and Gergen 1989).

Few feminists would dispute that discourse is often gendered, and that it forms one of the primary means through which patriarchy and oppressive norms and social practices are instantiated and reproduced. Indeed, we are, as feminists, increasingly aware of the fundamentally *political* nature of discourse. When we use discourse to communicate we 'naturalize' and perpetuate oppressive understandings of gender and 'gender role behaviour' – that is, we present them as timeless, rational and natural. These understandings become deeply ingrained in our commonsense views about the world, and become regarded as normative and expectable.

Likewise, we're aware that the politics of discourse is not onedimensional. Discourse can be used to expose and 'denaturalize', commonsense understandings of gender (through the use of humour and irony, for example) and to challenge ideas which create and sustain sexist and heterosexist social practices. By studying gender and discourse, and by exploring how dominant or prejudicial ideas about gender are created or resisted in discourse, we can acquire knowledge that can be used to inform social change for the better.

Research on gender and language is diverse, spanning a range of disciplines. Just as there is no one feminist theory or method, but rather multiple 'feminisms', so too there is no one approach to the study of gender and language. The field is characterized by epistemological and methodological diversity. It draws on approaches ranging from the phenomenological and experiential to the positivist and experimental, each revealing different, and often competing, theoretical and political assumptions about the way discourse, ideology and gender identity should be conceived and understood.

There now exist numerous books on gender and language, gender and discourse, feminism and discourse, sexuality and language, gender and conversation, and gender and interaction (for some recent examples, see Cameron and Kulick 2003; Eckert and McConnell-Ginet 2003; Fenstermaker and West 2002; Holmes and Meyerhoff 2003b; Hopper 2003; McIlvenny 2002c; Weatherall 2002a). Likewise, there are an increasing range of books on DA and CA (for some widely used examples, see Atkinson and Heritage 1984; Hutchby and Wooffitt 1998; ten Have 1999; Wetherell et al. 2001a, 2001b). However, the problem that faces feminists and other researchers new to the field of gender and language research is how to go about identifying and choosing between the numerous approaches to discourse that now exist. When one reads these books, as the students on my level three elective module, Feminism Discourse and Conversation, will testify, it is rather difficult to establish precisely what the theoretical and methodological 'boundaries' of the various approaches are, where they diverge and overlap, and what approach or combination of approaches might prove most productive (both empirically and politically) for feminism. It's easy to get bogged down in the detail of the different studies that are reported, at the expense of gaining a broader understanding of how the diverse theoretical and methodological models that are represented relate to each other, and a sense of their possibilities and problems.

The purpose of this introductory chapter is to provide an overview of the field of research on gender and language, and to situate my own approach in relation to it. In order to provide the reader with a sense of how my particular analytic approach fits within the broad terrain of research on gender and language, I want first to describe what I see as the main perspectives that dominate the field today. I outline some of the problems with the field as I see it at present – in particular, the reluctance on the part of many feminists and critically oriented researchers to adopt the kind of fine-grained form of analysis associated with CA. I describe five key features which distinguish the analytic perspective I argue for in this book, and which illustrate how I think the relationship between gender and language should be conceptualized. These five features serve as an organizing framework throughout the book, and provide a template for the reader to understand my particular analytic approach, and the criteria that I use to evaluate a range of other perspectives.

Feminist research on gender and language: mapping the terrain

For the purposes of this book, I group feminist research on gender and language into four broad organizing frameworks or traditions: sexist language; interactional sociolinguistics and the ethnography of communication; 'critical' discursive approaches informed primarily by (one or more of) critical theory, poststructuralism and psychoanalysis; and finally, discursive approaches informed primarily by ethnomethodology and CA. Research conducted within these four frameworks will be discussed in more detail in specific chapters as I work through the book. It must be emphasized that any attempt at categorization will caricature a far more complex terrain. There are no neat boundaries separating these frameworks from each other. Their boundaries are 'leaky', precisely because there is much cross-fertilization of ideas. While some researchers work in more than one tradition, others have adopted new frameworks and have moved into new research areas as their approaches have developed over time.

Sexist language

Research on gender and language has traditionally been divided into two strands: the study of how gender is represented *in* the language (the *form* of language) and the study of how men and women *use* language (the *function* of language). The study of how gender is represented *in* the language is a vibrant body of work which starts from the assumption that language is an 'ideological filter on the world' (Ehrlich and King 1994: 60). From this perspective, language reflects and perpetuates a sexist and heterosexist version of reality. Examples of sexist language include the purportedly generic pronouns 'he' and 'man', words such as 'mankind', job titles ending in '-man', and the asymmetry of address terms for men ('Mr') and women ('Mrs' / 'Miss'), where women are defined – not in their own right – but in terms of their relationship to a man. Some of the earliest work by feminist linguists such as Robin Lakoff (1973, 1975) set about demonstrating a range of ways in which language is sexist, while the radical feminist, Dale Spender (1980), explores the development of what she calls 'he/man' language. I discuss Lakoff and Spender's work in more detail in Chapter 2 (see also Henley 1987; Miller and Swift 1976).

There now exists an extensive body of research on sexist linguistic forms, and a range of sexist forms have been identified (see Mills 1995; Weatherall 2002a for examples). Commentators have diverse views about how sexist language should be conceptualized and remedied. According to some feminist reformers and the writers of 'non-sexist language guidelines', for example, sexist talk can be eliminated through the development of linguistic innovations which replace sexist with non-sexist words (see Doyle 1995; Miller and Swift 1980). Examples of such reforms include substituting the masculine 'generics' 'he' and 'man' with neutral terms such as the singular 'they' and 'he/she', replacing job titles ending in '-man' with neutral titles such as 'chairperson', 'chair' or 'spokesperson', creating neutral address terms for women such as 'Ms', and developing new categories that give meaning to experiences that have hitherto been ignored, such as 'sexual harassment' and 'date-rape' (Ehrlich and King 1994: 61; for a comprehensive account of feminist linguistic reform, see Pauwels 1998, 2003).

Although the English language is certainly evolving to contain fewer sexist forms (Weatherall 2002a: 12), some feminist linguists, most notably Deborah Cameron (1992, 1998b), have written extensively on the problems that are associated with linguistic reform efforts. In particular, Cameron is critical of any approach which implies that sexist meanings reside in, or come attached to certain words. For her, it is deeply problematic to imply that there are a limited number of context-free, derogatory terms that are 'essentially' sexist, and that by pinpointing them and substituting them with 'non-sexist' words, one can somehow rid the language of sexism. As she states, 'we cannot simply change a word's meaning for the whole community by *fiat*' (1992: 110, emphasis in original). According to Cameron, many institutional reform efforts and attempts at what has been termed 'verbal hygiene' (Cameron 1995) treat sexist talk as a linguistic rather than as a social and a contextual problem, and ignore the 'context sensitivity' of actual language *use*. Thus, arguments underlying linguistic reform work by stripping talk of its contextual subtleties and by caricaturing what might count as sexism to a significant degree (see also Cameron 1998b).

For many feminists, discourse analysts and sociolinguists, including Cameron, the meaning of words is not fixed but fluid. Linguistic meanings are socially constructed, contextually variable and continually subject to negotiation and modification in interaction. It follows that specific words need not always be sexist or egalitarian in their function. If the meaning of words is (at least partially) dependent on their context of use, then the whole idea that we can legislate 'non-sexist' language into existence – essentially fixing the meaning of 'approved' versus 'sexist' words, must be questioned.

As Speer and Potter (2000, 2002) and Speer (2002b) show in their research on the discursive construction of sexism and heterosexism, just as purportedly derogatory words (e.g., 'dyke', 'queen', 'queer') can, under certain circumstances (e.g. when they are reclaimed by lesbians and gay men, or used humorously or ironically), be invested with new meanings, and used to non-derogatory purposes, likewise seemingly benevolent, non-sexist or practically oriented descriptions and evaluations which do *not* index sexist words (for example, the claim that 'women should not play rugby because they might get injured') can be built and used in order to justify inequality and sexism (see also Gill 1993; Wetherell et al. 1987). For these researchers, the precise meaning of what is said can be established only by exploring what utterances are *doing* in specific contexts. As many discourse analysts now show, in contemporary society, there may even be a norm against explicit forms of prejudice, such that we are all apparently – overtly at least – 'politically correct' (Suhr and Johnson 2003) and hence 'liberal in our views' (Clarke 2005). Thus, speakers can frequently be heard to preface some arguably prejudiced claim, with a disclaimer (e.g., 'I'm not sexist but . . .', or 'I've got nothing against gay people, my best friend is gay but . . .) (Stokoe and Smithson 2002: 91; see also Potter and Wetherell 1987; van Dijk et al. 1997). This body of work highlights the problems that derive from any study which confines itself to the analysis of discrete word forms, and how linguistic meanings are more malleable, and more 'context-sensitive' than many researchers have hitherto assumed. I discuss this work further in Chapter 6.

Other gender and language researchers, while acknowledging that linguistic meanings are not fixed, are nonetheless concerned that, if taken to its logical conclusion, such 'linguistic relativity' may be taken to imply that the meaning of words is infinitely malleable, and that we can take them to mean whatever it is that we want them to mean. A 'communities of practice' perspective works to address this concern by locating sexism, not in specific words or individuals, but in distinctive social and political contexts – or 'linguistic communities' (see Eckert and McConnell-Ginet 1992; Ehrlich and King 1994; Holmes 1999; McConnell-Ginet 1989). Here, 'communities of practice' are defined as 'an aggregate of people who come together around mutual engagement in an endeavour. Ways of doing things, ways of talking, beliefs, values, power relations – in short, practices – emerge in the course of this mutual endeavour' (Eckert and McConnell-Ginet 1992: 464). For proponents of this approach, the meaning of an utterance 'is a matter not only of individual will but of social relations embedded in political structures' (McConnell-Ginet 1998: 207). Thus, linguistic meanings can be fully understood only when one considers the nature of the social context and, specifically, the background social knowledge and 'mutually accessible cultural beliefs' (Ehrlich and King 1994: 60) available to the linguistic community in which words are uttered. From this perspective, linguistic reform efforts will not always succeed, because 'terms initially introduced to be non-sexist and neutral may lose their neutrality in the mouths of a sexist speech community and/or culture' (Ehrlich and King 1994: 59; see also Ehrlich and King 1992; McConnell-Ginet 2003).

Although there are problems associated with the application of this 'communities of practice' approach (for example, how might one decide where a 'community' begins and ends, or account for variable, or contradictory linguistic meanings within the same community?), its value, nonetheless, lies in the way in which it helps to account for how linguistic meanings can 'congeal' or 'sediment' through time in specific institutional and cultural contexts, and how some non-sexist linguistic innovations may take hold in certain groups in society, among some individuals (e.g., young feminist women, gay men) and not others. It deals, in other words, with the perennial problem of how to account for how individuals are neither totally determined by language, nor totally free to make words mean whatever it is that they want them to mean.

Interactional sociolinguistics, and the ethnography of communication

The study of how men and women *use* language (the *function* of language) has its roots in linguistics and anthropology. Interactional sociolinguistics developed in the work of John Gumperz (1982a, 1982b) and focuses on the relationship between gender, language and culture. Sociolinguists are of the view that variations in patterns of language use are not random but are conditioned by macro-social and demographic features such as a person's gender or class, and the situation or context in which they find themselves. Unlike their variationist and quantitative sociolinguistic colleagues who use statistics to explore male–female patterns of linguistic (that is phonological and grammatical) variation (for an overview see Romaine 2003), proponents of interactional sociolinguistics use predominantly qualitative methods to study male–female variation in patterns of interaction and communicative *style*. These communication patterns are learnt during socialization, or emerge as a result of gender-segregated play during childhood. Examples of this approach can be found in the work of Coates (1986), Fishman (1978), Holmes (1995), Maltz and Borker (1982) and Tannen (1990, 1994b, 1997). Their findings have been buttressed by a range of work on children and child development in feminist psychology (e.g., Gilligan's (1982) theory of women's moral development). I discuss Tannen's work in more detail in Chapter 2.

A complementary approach – the 'ethnography of communication' (previously termed the 'ethnography of speaking') was developed in the work of Dell Hymes (1962, 1974) and describes research which uses ethnographic methods to explore how language using is done and understood differently by men and women in different cultural groups. Typically critical of the 'separate worlds hypothesis' developed in interactional sociolinguistics, and the 'polarizations of gendered norms of social interaction and communication' associated with it (see Goodwin 2003: 231; Kyratzis 2001), proponents of this approach deem ethnicity, social class, and context to be central to an analysis of gender talk. Focusing primarily on language use in either non-western, non-industrialized societies, or in culturally distinctive small groups within western societies, proponents of this approach focus on the 'ways of speaking' and the 'discourse genres' that are exhibited by the members of the culture being studied, and the diverse forms of social organization that are possible within that group. They are also concerned to explore cultural variability in gendered patterns of language use or communicative style, and this sets their work apart from that associated with many other approaches to discourse mentioned later in this chapter. This perspective is closely associated with the work of Marjorie Harness Goodwin (1990, 2001, 2002, 2003), who combines ethnographic methods with CA, and Elinor (Ochs) Keenan (1989; Ochs 1992; Ochs and Taylor 1995; see also Danby 1998; Kyratzis 2001; Sheldon 1990; Thorne 1993).

So far I have described research which explores how gender is represented *in* the language (the *form* of language), and how men and women *use* language (the *function* of language). Although both strands continue to be pursued as somewhat separate forms of inquiry, the field has developed such that many now regard them as part of the same process: the social construction of gender (Cameron 1998a; Crawford 1995). As some of the research discussed above highlights, meaning is not necessarily tied to specific words. Likewise, patterns of variation in our use of language or communicative style are not straightforwardly determined by the sex of the speaker, or by one's membership of a cultural group. Instead, sexism, gender and cultural difference are constructed in and through our interactions with one another. Central to this new understanding is the view that gender and sexism is 'best analysed at the level of discourse' (Cameron 1998c: 87). It is discourse rather than individual words, which, it is argued, constitutes the 'main locus' (Cameron 1998a: 962), or the key site, for the reproduction and resignification of gendered meanings. This focus on discourse has, in turn, led to a gradual shift away from research which analyses sexist word forms and 'decontextualized sentences', or which searches for the linguistic or cultural correlates of gender difference, toward an analysis of more extended sequences of language use, and its role in naturalizing specific understandings of gender.

Discourse analysis is a collective term for a diverse body of work spanning a range of disciplines. It is now possible to identify a broad variety of different types of DA, which derive from widely varying theoretical traditions (see Cameron 2001; Wetherell et al. 2001a, 2001b, for overviews). Feminist applications of DA are equally diverse: the first text on feminism and DA from a psychological perspective contains exemplars of a range of different approaches (Wilkinson and Kitzinger 1995). What does not help matters, of course, is that the label 'discourse analysis' tends to be applied uniformly, regardless of differences in theoretical focus and the level of analytic specificity exemplified across different studies. Moreover, some discourse analysts appear inconsistent in their approach, shifting between different perspectives in different papers, thus making it hard to identify coherent discourse 'types'; compare, for example, the different styles of analysis in Wetherell and Potter (1992) and Antaki and Wetherell (1999). The recent move by some discourse analysts to embrace the perspective that some are now calling 'feminist CA' has only served to exacerbate this lack of clarity (see, for example, the special issue of

INTRODUCTION

Discourse and Society on 'Gender, language, conversation analysis and feminism': Stokoe and Weatherall 2002; see also Kitzinger 2000a, 2002).

Many of the sociolinguistic researchers whose work I mentioned above pursue, or have gone on to pursue, questions about the relationship between gender and language by conducting some form of DA. Although it is widely acknowledged that such a distinction oversimplifies matters somewhat, and that the different types of DA overlap in many important respects, it is nonetheless common nowadays to divide the field into two different 'camps' (Edley and Wetherell (1997), 'strands' (Widdicombe and Wooffitt 1995) or 'styles' (Wetherell 1998) of discourse analytic work (for a range of perspectives on the 'two strands' debate, see Burr 2003; Parker 1997; Widdicombe 1995; Willig 2001). For the purposes of this book, and for the sake of clarity, I divide the field into 'critical' discursive approaches informed primarily by (one or more of) critical theory, poststructuralism and psychoanalysis, and discursive approaches informed primarily by ethnomethodology and CA.

'Critical' discursive approaches informed primarily by (one or more of) critical theory, poststructuralism and psychoanalysis

The first strand of DA incorporates work which applies ideas from a range of disciplines. Intellectual precursors to this work can be traced variously to poststructuralism (e.g., Foucault 1971, 1972; Kendall and Wickham 1999; Weedon 1997), feminist theories of the performative constitution of gender (Butler 1990a, 1993), positioning theory (Davies and Harré 1990; Harré and Moghaddam 2003), the Frankfurt School of critical theory (Habermas 1984), critical linguistics (Fairclough 1989, 1992, 1995; Fairclough and Wodak 1997; Kress 1985; van Dijk 1993), philosophy (Derrida 1976; Wittgenstein 1953) and psychoanalysis (Lacan 1989). Feminists have combined one or more of these approaches to develop their own distinctive brand of DA.

Although individual studies differ slightly in their precise analytic emphasis, advocates of this strand of DA tend to conduct broad-based, topic or theme-focused analyses focusing on power, ideology and the self. They explore the 'constitutive' power of discourse, and seek to identify the 'broad meaning systems' invoked in talk, variously termed 'global patterns in collective sense-making', 'interpretative repertoires', 'practical ideologies' and 'psycho-discursive' resources. Drawing on relatively lengthy excerpts of talk from both spoken and written texts, researchers working within this framework commonly transcribe data to a level which represents the general content of the words spoken, as opposed to the dynamics of turn-taking or the characteristics of speech delivery. Since advocates of this approach tend to focus on how gendered subjects are *positioned* through or by discourses, and how powerful social structures, norms, ideologies and conventions shape and constrain individuals' actions 'from above' or 'outside' the text, critical forms of DA are commonly referred to as 'top-down', 'macro-level' forms of analysis. Proponents of this approach are influenced strongly by political aims. Indeed, this form of DA is commonly referred to as *critical* DA (or CDA), because researchers have a 'leftist' or 'socialist' political and analytic stance, and their primary goal is to examine texts which naturalize unequal power arrangements and ideologies. Researchers are driven by a belief that insights gained from the analysis of discourse and 'engaged scholarship' will help us to change society for the better.

Feminists who employ this approach, who have backgrounds in sociolinguistics, and who are influenced primarily by poststructuralism or theories of performativity, include Baxter (2002, 2003), Bucholtz et al. (1999), Cameron (1997a), Coates (1996, 1997, 1999), Hall and Bucholtz (1995) and Sunderland (2004). Feminist 'critical discourse analysts' who are influenced primarily by research in the Frankfurt School and critical linguistics include Talbot (1997, 1998, 2000) and Wodak (1989, 1997, 2003). Within psychology, feminists influenced primarily by theories of social positioning or psychoanalysis, include Frosh et al. (2003), Gough (2004), Henriques et al. (1984), Hollway (1989, 1995, 1998) and Kulick (2003). Finally, proponents of a feminist 'critical discursive psychology' (or CDP), who are informed by an eclectic mix of poststructuralism, theories of social positioning, social constructionism, linguistic philosophy and ethnomethodology, include Burman and Parker (1993), Crawford (1995), Edley and Wetherell (1997, 1999, 2001), Gavey (1989), Korobov and Bamberg (2004), Weatherall (2002a), Wetherell (1998, 1999a, 2003) and Wetherell and Edley (1998, 1999).

Discursive approaches informed primarily by ethnomethodology and CA

The second strand of discourse work takes its primary influence from ethnomethodology and CA. Ethnomethodology developed in the work of Harold Garfinkel (1967) and takes as its topic for study 'members' methods' for producing their everyday affairs. Members' methods consist of the routinized, taken-for-granted procedures individuals employ as they go about their everyday lives and tasks. CA was developed in the pioneering lectures of the American sociologist, Harvey Sacks, between 1964 and 1972 (Sacks 1995), and has its roots in Garfinkel's (1967) ethnomethodology, Goffman's (1983) theory of the interaction order and linguistic philosophy (Austin 1962; Wittgenstein 1953). Harvey Sacks and his colleagues, Emmanuel Schegloff, Gail Jefferson and Anita Pomerantz, were among the first to translate ideas from these perspectives into an empirically grounded, data-driven, and highly systematized research agenda.

Building on the ethnomethodological critique of the structural functionalist, Parsonian idea that order is achieved because individuals act on the basis of an internalized system of constraining social norms (Parsons 1937), conversation analysts instead theorize members as active participants who produce and orient to social order as they interact with one another and engage in ongoing, interpretative, meaning-making work Thus, for conversation analysts, the interest is in the *in situ* organization of conduct, and the *local* production of order (for more on the relationship between ethnomethodology and CA, see Heritage 1984, 2001). Drawing on analyses of first-hand, transcribed examples of everyday interactions, CA is primarily concerned to describe the methods speakers use to coordinate their talk to produce orderly and meaningful conversational actions. It studies the design of both individual utterances or 'turn constructional units', as well as the organization of turns into sequences of utterances. Finally, it seeks to explicate how talk is implicated in broader forms of social organization at the 'institutional' or 'social structural' level.

While CA developed primarily in sociology in the United States in the 1960s, the related approach of discursive psychology (DP) was developed in social psychology in the United Kingdom in the 1980s by Potter and Wetherell (1987; see also Gilbert and Mulkay 1984). DP has developed an angle which applies principles from ethnomethodology, CA, linguistic philosophy and the sociology of scientific knowledge, to rethink a distinctive set of concerns around cognition, and a range of other psychological concepts, processes and questions. Thus, where CA respecifies the dominant sociological concept of social structure, DP respecifies the dominant psychological notion of cognition. Indeed, DP has a very distinct way of conceiving of the psychological world and research into it. Discursive psychologists are critical of the idea that mental entities such as 'attitudes' or 'feelings' can simply be 'read off' from talk, or that talk is a relatively transparent 'window' on our inner worlds. Instead, they are interested in what people *do* with attitude talk and feeling talk, and how a whole range of 'mentalist notions' are constructed and used discursively by participants in interaction. This focus on action, not cognition, entails a reformulation of traditional 'theories of the subject', or identity, in practical, discursive terms (for examples of this 'anti-cognitivist' approach, see Edwards 1997; Edwards and Potter 1992; Potter 1996b; Te Molder and Potter 2005). Indeed, within both DP and CA, identities are treated, not as demographic facts or variables that condition or constrain behaviour, and which people just 'have' (cf. much sociolinguistics). Rather, features of identity (including gender), are treated as locally occasioned resources, whose relevancies may or may not be oriented to, or 'procedurally consequential' for talk (Antaki and Widdicombe 1998a).

Although the relationship between CA and DP is a contentious point for those who are concerned with defining, defending and policing their disciplinary boundaries – see, for example, the debate between Hammersley (2003a, 2003b, 2003c) and Potter (2003a, 2003b) – CA and DP are becoming increasingly hard to separate on methodological and conceptual grounds. As David Silverman (1998: 193) points out, since there is evidence that some discursive psychologists 'pay considerable attention to the turn-by-turn organization of talk . . . we may end up in a pointless debate about whether such work is DA or CA!' Indeed, Silverman (1998: 193) notes that the distinction between DP and CA often rests on whether the author pays their 'disciplinary dues' to psychology or sociology (see also Wooffitt 2005). Moreover, although Margaret Wetherell – one of DP's central proponents – has shifted more firmly toward the more 'eclectic' understanding of discourse associated with CDP, other key DP figures, including Jonathan Potter and Derek Edwards, have moved strongly towards the CA end of the analytic spectrum, and have recently come together with the conversation analysts John Heritage, Paul Drew, Anita Pomerantz and others, to write about the relationship between talk and cognition (Te Molder and Potter 2005).

Proponents of this CA strand of DA align with Harvey Sacks' (1995) view that much of what is going on in interaction occurs in its particulars: in the details of pauses, turn taking organization, hesitations, word choices, repairs and overlaps. CA has developed a comprehensive system for transcribing such features, and a simplified version of these transcription conventions are included in the Appendix. Analyses are typically conducted using a number of short extracts, transcribed and analysed to a high level of technical detail. Sometimes researchers analyse longer stretches of talk – or 'single cases' – to explore how a range of conversational devices figure in its production.

Finally, since advocates of this approach tend towards more finegrained, action-driven analyses which stick closely to an analysis of participants' orientations and what is happening within the data – from 'ground level', so to speak – it is commonly referred to as a 'bottom-up', 'micro' (and, more controversially for the perspective developed in this book), 'non-critical' approach.

Neither CA nor DP are explicitly feminist in orientation. However, there is a long tradition of feminist work utilizing ideas from both perspectives to study a variety of topics relevant to feminist concerns. For example, a number of feminists have used CA to explore how patriarchy and male dominance 'is realized at the micro-level of interaction' (Stokoe 2000: 556; see Ainsworth-Vaughn 1992; Davis 1988; Fisher 1986; Fishman 1977, 1978; Todd 1989; West 1979, 1992; West and Garcia 1988; West and Zimmerman 1983; Zimmerman and West 1975). Others have used CA to highlight a range of gendered interactional patterns, for example, women's conversational competence (West 1995) and men and women's use of directives (Goodwin 1990; West 1998). What is interesting about this work, however, is that even while these studies demonstrate clearly how 'the inspection of authentic conversational materials might reveal more about women's and men's speech than armchair speculation (cf. Lakoff 1975)' (McIlvenny 2002c: 15), they are nonetheless guilty of using CA for predominantly 'non-CA purposes' (Stokoe 2000: 556; ten Have 1999). As Elizabeth Stokoe (2000: 556) points out, since 'these studies link gender to, for example, interruption, talk time, topic initiation and topic maintenance', then they retain the idea that on some level, talk can and should be mapped onto demographic variables or gendered attributes.

Wary of such shortcomings, more recently, a critical current has developed among feminists with backgrounds in feminist psychology, which has set about treating gender, sexuality and prejudice as emergent phenomena that are made relevant in interaction, and which are constructed and oriented to as participants' concerns (see, for example, Kitzinger 2000a; Kitzinger and Peel 2005; Speer 2001b, 2002d, 2005; Speer and Potter 2000; Stokoe 1998; Stokoe and Smithson 2001, 2002; Weatherall 2002b). A related strand of work has begun to merge this focus on participants' orientations to gender, with insights from Sacks' (1995) approach to membership categorization analysis (or MCA), in order to examine the construction of gender as a category in discourse, and how it is used and oriented to by members (see Edwards 1998; Fenstermaker and West 2002; Kitzinger and Wilkinson 2003; Speer 2002b; Stokoe 2003, 2004, in press; Stokoe and Edwards 2005; Wowk 1984).

Some problems with the field of research on gender and language

The analytic approach I argue for in this book is closely associated with this second strand of ethnomethodological and CA-inspired discourse work. However, while this approach is becoming more popular among feminists, many gender and language researchers have been sceptical of the value of CA for feminist work. For the most part, the majority of gender and language researchers, and others with a critical, political agenda, have favoured the broader forms of DA influenced strongly by critical theory, poststructuralism, and psychoanalysis.

There is, in Schegloff's terms, an 'impatience, and often intolerance, of close analysis' (1997: 180; see also Widdicombe 1995). This is primarily due to misgivings about the political efficaciousness and practical utility of a technical and fine-grained approach to feminist issues and concepts – an approach which many believe focuses on the mundane and the trivial aspects of social life, at the expense of an analysis of the more politically consequential aspects. As Kitzinger (2000a: 173; see also Kitzinger and Frith 1999: 311) observes, CA is often viewed 'as nit-picking, obsessively concerned with the minute details of in-breaths and hesitations, and as unable to see beyond the "micro-" level of the 0.2 second pause, to the "macro" level of oppression'. Critics often raise the objection that CA – as a 'micro' approach to talk-in-interaction that limits itself to the study of members' perspectives and the analysis of short extracts – cannot account for the ways in which gender norms and 'wider, macro power structures' exert a determining effect on action. Neglecting this 'top-down' or constraining feature of culture, society and context, some commentators argue, leads to apolitical and reductionist forms of analysis that leave us few opportunities to comment on patriarchal power or the oppressive constraints on women's lives. As such, this approach is not only unnecessarily limiting, but also has little practical relevance to feminism, or the world beyond academia (Billig 1999a, 1999b; Edley 2001a, 2001b; Weatherall 2000; Wetherell 1998).

For the majority of feminists, feminism is a politics which rests on the belief that women as a group are oppressed by men as a group. It is dedicated to social and political change. Since participants themselves might not be conscious of the impact of the broader social and ideological context within which their utterances are embedded, an approach which limits itself to an analysis of participants' orientations, and which relies on participants *explicitly attending to* the topic under investigation, offers little by way of resources to advance core feminist aims. As Hannah Frith (1998: 535) notes, it is highly doubtful whether all the dimensions relevant to a piece of interaction, such as participants' 'shared whiteness', will be 'interactionally displayed', or made explicitly manifest in the 'micro-interactional' – that is, the small-scale, discursive features of an interaction. This view has led some feminists to suggest that Schegloff's approach 'limits admissible context so severely that only the most blatant aspects of gendered discursive practice, such as the overt topicalizing of gender in conversation, are likely candidates for Schegloffian analysis' (Bucholtz 2003: 52). For some critically oriented researchers, neither CA nor DP should be treated as self-sufficient paradigms (Hammersley 2003a: 751). Rather, both need subsidizing with other methods.

Others argue that the 'symmetrical', seemingly 'neutral' form of analysis associated with a participants' orientations approach, is apolitical, 'invites missed opportunities' and 'risks a form of ideological complicity' (Edley 2001b: 137). Mick Billig (1999b: 554–6), for example, claims that CA's 'participatory rhetoric' encourages the analyst to treat participants' contributions equally, thus ignoring the power differential between – say – rapist and victim.

Finally, some assert that, contrary to the conversation analyst's injunction that we must stick closely to an analysis of 'participants' orientations', that CA analyses already involve – indeed rely on – the articulation of members' and analysts' cultural and commonsense knowledge as 'largely unacknowledged and unexplicated resources' (Stokoe and Smithson 2001, 2002). From this perspective, a 'pure' form of CA which does not go beyond the text and an analysis of members' perspectives is not only an inaccurate and unrealistic portrayal of the actual practice of CA, but is also impossible (Stokoe and Smithson 2001, 2002).

Thus, for most of these researchers, we must venture *beyond* the limits of the text and the micro-analysis of members' perspectives, in order to be able to observe, and say anything politically effective about, the 'constraining' or 'enabling' impact of a range of large-scale, 'extra-discursive', 'macro' social structural factors. Indeed, similar concerns do not just preoccupy feminists, but are part of a much broader and longstanding social scientific debate concerning the relative importance that we should give to the macro-social structural and micro-interactional realms, and which realm is primary or determinate of the other (Giddens 1981, 1984; Knorr-Cetina and Cicourel 1981).

How should the relationship between gender and language be conceptualized?

A view that I articulate in this book is that there is nothing *intrinsic* to a strongly CA-aligned discursive approach which would prevent feminists and others with a critical agenda from using it to ask politically motivated questions, or to reach politically efficacious outcomes. Indeed, I suggest that we should take seriously precisely those features of CA (for example, its focus on 'participants' orientations' and the fine-grained analysis of talk), which have frequently been dismissed as anti-feminist (see also Kitzinger 2000a). We should see how far we can get with such analyses, and what they can offer us in terms of advancing our understanding of the constitution of gender, sexuality and prejudice in talk, and in terms of 'grounding' our feminist politics.

I argue that an adequate feminist discursive approach that draws on insights from the sociological perspective of CA, and the closely related psychological perspective of DP, would be characterized by five key features: (i) a constructionist approach; (ii) discourse of mind and world as topic, not resource; (iii) language as a form of social action; (iv) analysts' claims are grounded in participants' practices; and (v) a relativist approach. These five features serve as an organizing framework throughout the book, and provide a template for the reader to understand my particular analytic approach, and the criteria that I use to evaluate a range of other perspectives. It's important to note that these criteria do not map onto some preexisting feminist discursive type, and that not all researchers who are influenced by CA or DP would agree with the criteria that I have chosen (for example, as I will show later in this book, many conversation analysts would reject the suggestion that their work can be described as constructionist, or even relativist in its focus). I have chosen to combine elements from both perspectives because I believe that combined, they provide the most productive and 'complete' framework for reconceptualizing the relationship between gender and language.

(i) A constructionist approach

In many social scientific studies, researchers adopt an *essentialist* approach to analysis, in which they treat people as having relatively fixed 'traits', 'attributes' or 'essences' residing inside them that condition what they do or say. Essentialist assumptions about sex and gender manifest themselves most clearly in the variationist and sociolinguistic studies of the type described earlier in this chapter. In sociolinguistic 'sex differences' research, for example, research participants are divided into groups of males and females, and sex differences in their use of language are mapped and measured accordingly. Sex and gender are treated as pre-given traits or 'natural facts', that reside in individuals and which determine the linguistic resources men and women use to speak.

Many feminists problematize essentialism on the grounds that it sustains and reproduces 'binary thinking' (Bing and Bergvall 1998; see also Ferree et al. 1999; Hare-Mustin and Maracek 1994; Hollway 1994; Kitzinger 1994b). Essentialist studies will always support arguments that men and women are fundamentally different, because they *start* from the assumption that the sex of the speaker both causes and accounts for male–female linguistic differences.

In order to avoid this kind of circular reasoning, the approach I adopt throughout this book, is, by contrast, a *constructionist* one (Burr 2003; Gergen and Gergen 2003). In a constructionist analysis, both sex and gender are treated as fluid accomplishments. Gender is something one *does* rather than as something that one *has* (see Bohan 1993; Cealey Harrison and Hood-Williams 2002; Harding 1998; Lorber 1994; West and Zimmerman 1987). Researchers who adopt a constructionist perspective focus on how gender identities are *achieved*, and treat the coherence of gender as something which is produced and reproduced in the course of social interaction.

In constructionist analyses, the focus of inquiry shifts away from studies which correlate linguistic variables with demographic variables, and which claim that 'men talk like this' and 'women talk like that', toward analyses of the dynamic '*processes* by which people come to describe, explain or otherwise account for the world (including themselves) in which they live' (Gergen 1985: 266, emphasis added). The focus is on how language users *produce* speakers as male and female, and construct, orient towards, and use gendered identities in their talk. This paves the way for a more detailed analysis of the ways in which people use language to *produce gender difference*, and to construct gender dualism as natural, inevitable and timeless (Cameron 1992; Fenstermaker and West 2002). I discuss the relationship between constructionist and essentialist theories of gender and language further in Chapters 2 and 3.

(ii) Discourse of mind and world as topic, not resource

Mainstream sociology and psychology (and their feminist derivatives) work with a model of the world that is divided into three realms: the macro-social structural realm, the cognitive-psychological realm, and the micro-interactional, discursive realm. In mainstream sociology, for example, explanations for activity, discourse and other social phenomena (such as crime and prejudice) tend to be sought in terms of the 'broader', 'extra-situational', 'macro-social' contexts within which they are embedded. These contexts may include social institutions (such as the family and marriage), social structures (such as the law, economy or education system) or the social norms and conventions which are learnt through socialization and which give rise to particular ideologies and patterns of social behaviour (ideas about appropriate 'masculine' and 'feminine' behaviours, for example) (Burr 2003: 8–9). Psychologists working within the dominant 'cognitivist' paradigm add a further level to this explanation, in that they treat such macro-social structural contexts as things which, in order to be perceived, experienced, and understood – that is, in order to have their effects – they must pass through the 'interior' cognitive psychological realm of mental states, cognitive structures and processes (Potter 1998c: 33).

From within this framework, macro-social structures ('the world') and cognitive-psychological processes ('the mind') are treated as primary 'inputs' to social action, while activity, discourse and other social phenomena (e.g. crime or prejudice) are treated as something secondary – a by-product or 'output' of the system (Edwards and Potter 2001: 15). In both cases, discourse – to the extent that it is studied 'first hand' at all – is treated as an analytic *resource* which, barring certain kinds of methodological bias and distortion or error, reflects the world and people's perceptions of it (Edwards and Potter 2001: 12).

The perspective I adopt in this book inverts this distinction. Instead of treating discourse as a secondary resource that can be used to access facts or information about the macro-social structural, and cognitive-psychological realms, world and mind (and their corresponding 'realms') are treated as phenomena that are constructed and oriented to by people in discourse as they go about their everyday lives and tasks (Edwards and Potter 2001: 15). It follows that discourses of mind and world become studiable as the primary *topic*, or domain for analysis in their own right (Edwards and Potter 2001: 15). I demonstrate what this approach looks like in Chapters 4 to 6.

(iii) Language as a form of social action

As I showed in my discussion of sexist talk above, some researchers have sought to isolate and remedy problematic linguistic terms, and treat 'discourses' as having fixed meanings. In this book, by contrast, I treat discourse as a social *practice* rather than a *thing* (Potter et al. 1990). One of the central tenets of both CA and DP is that talk and texts have an *action orientation* – that is, the precise way we construct the world, and the import of an utterance, depends on the specific action or business that talk is designed to achieve. 'Action' here can refer to a whole range of practical, technical and interpersonal tasks that people perform as they go about their everyday lives and tasks. For example, as both CA and DP researchers have shown, discourse can be used to constitute events and identities, to manage issues of responsibility and stake, to present oneself in a favourable light, to account for one's actions (to offer excuses, for example), to make invitations, requests, offers and assessments, to persuade and argue, and to achieve and manage justifications, mitigations and blamings. The analytic approach I adopt focuses on what discourse is doing, how it is constructed to make certain things happen, and the conversational resources that are drawn on to facilitate that action or activity (Potter 2004b).

The idea that language does things – that it creates rather than reflects meaning – is closely tied to the concept of indexicality. The notion of indexicality captures the ethnomethodological (Garfinkel 1967) idea that we settle or 'fill in' the meaning of an utterance on any given occasion, by noting information about the context in which the words are uttered. 'Context' here refers to the sequential or interactional environment of the talk itself, in which events unfold turn-by-turn, as well as the local context – the setting in which an activity takes place.

If the import of an utterance is tied to its context, then it follows that the same statement can be used to perform different actions, depending on the interpretative context in which it is uttered. For example, consider the evaluative phrase 'I love dancing': (a) when used in a conversation with a friend, the words 'I love dancing' may be an attempt to elicit an invitation to a night club (an implicit request); (b) when said to a friend who accuses you of dancing too much, and not spending enough time chatting to them in a night club, may be used as a justification or an excuse; and (c) when said to a partner who has just cancelled your ballroom dancing lesson, may be part of a blaming, or an attempt to make that person feel guilty. Thus, in order to understand what an utterance is doing, we need to analyse the local contextual and sequential environment in which it is situated. I flesh out what an 'action orientation' approach to discourse looks like, in Chapters 4 to 6.

(iv) Analysts' claims are grounded in participants' practices

Feminist research is epistemologically and methodologically diverse. However, a strong trend among second wave feminist writing on methodology has been a critique of mainstream social scientific methods. Many feminists reject 'masculine' notions of objectivity, value neutrality and scientific detachment, because they are thought to reinforce the objectification, exploitation and subordination of women (Cook and Fonow 1990: 72). Consequently, many feminists adopt data collection practices that foster egalitarian and non-hierarchical research relations. Methods are chosen that will minimize harm to respondents, and which will 'shift the balance of power and control toward the research participants' (Wilkinson 1999: 233). The overriding concern is to avoid imposing the researcher's own analytic categories and concepts on what respondents say, and to encourage them to 'assert their own interpretations and agendas' (1999: 233). In this way, the researcher gains access to participants' own language, meanings and vocabulary, their 'opinions and conceptual worlds' (1999: 233).

While the majority of feminists agree that data collection practices should cultivate non-hierarchical research relations, and that respondents 'must be in the driver's seat of research' (Campbell and Salem 1999: 67; see also DuBois 1983), the concern to adopt 'respondent centred' data collection practices in which the researcher's role is minimized, tends not to be translated at the analytic level, where the relative importance given to the perspective of the respondent over that of the researcher is reversed.

Indeed, many feminists argue that since women are not always in a position to see – and thus problematize – their own oppression, that when it comes to our analyses, our role is not simply to act as a 'neutral conduit' through which participants speak, or to uncritically accept and 'give voice' to the generally non-feminist, non-politicized arguments of our participants (Kitzinger and Wilkinson 1997; see also Kitzinger 2003). Instead, we are morally and politically obliged to 'go beyond' our data, to prioritize our feminist political agenda, and to treat our analyses as an occasion for *doing* politics. Rather than simply reflecting and validating 'whatever women tell us about their experience', many of us use our analyses specifically in order to challenge and criticize 'the way in which women's experience is constructed under (hetero) patriarchy' (Kitzinger and Wilkinson 1997: 573).

In the feminist analytic approach I advocate in this book, by contrast, I avoid producing analyses which are driven, in the first instance, by my politics, and by my assumptions about the constraining or enabling features of a range of 'extra-discursive', 'macro-structural' or 'cognitive-psychological' factors. Instead, following Schegloff (1997), I consider, first and foremost, what is going on from a member's perspective, and how the social and political is constituted and oriented to (if at all) in participants' talk. I explore the notion of participants' orientations further in Chapters 4 to 6.

(v) A relativist approach

Many social scientists working within the mainstream positivist and interpretivist paradigms adopt a realist approach which supports the view 'that there is a reality independent of the researcher whose nature can be known, and that the aim of research is to produce accounts that correspond to that reality' (Hammersley 1992: 43). From this perspective, providing that all sources of methodological bias and extraneous influences are eliminated from our data (through the control of 'contaminating' variables, for example), then the discourse that the researcher collects can be treated as a transparent medium through which they can gain unmediated access to facts about the world and respondents' perceptions of it, or the objectively measurable 'reality' that lies beyond or beneath talk. By contrast, the relativist approach I adopt in this book can be defined as:

> a stance of systematic and thoroughgoing doubt about objectivist, essentialist and foundational positions. It is not so much a position as an anti-position or a meta-position. Relativist arguments emphasise the inescapable role of rhetoric in constructing claims as objective and foundational, and the contingency of tests, criteria, rules, experimentation and other procedures that are claimed to guarantee objective foundations.
>
> (Potter 2004c: 951–2)

The relativist argues that all knowledge (including 'scientific facts') is historically and culturally relative. It follows that there are no independent means of determining what is 'true' (Edwards et al. 1995). There are infinite possible ways of constructing the world, and an infinite number of ways in which the same events can be recounted and constituted. As such, there is no way of knowing whether any particular version offers an accurate description of 'what really happened', or whether it corresponds to what took place 'in the real world'.

Since, as Wetherell and Potter (1992: 62) put it, 'there is no versionless reality', a relativist approach urges us to take a critical stance towards all knowledge claims. It encourages us to question our commonsense assumptions about the way the world works, and particularly about those objects, events and categories that are presented to us as 'naturally occurring givens' – including 'scientific facts' about biology, subjectivity and mind.

Indeed, this approach 'is fundamentally anti-intuitive: it specifically aims to deconstruct those things we 'just know' on the basis of personal experience or introspection' (Kitzinger 1992: 224).

Sex, for example, is one of our primary means for classifying and organizing the world, and sexual dimorphism, the idea that the world consists of two and only two sexes, is a distinction upon which *heterosexuality* depends (Butler 1990a). While it may seem obvious, or even sensible, that we divide the world up according to male–female 'reproductive differences', a relativist would question whether there is anything intrinsic to the nature of persons that requires us to divide the world up in this way – and to develop a whole host of institutionalized practices based on gender dualism (e.g., sex-demarcated toilet cubicles, sports teams, leisure pursuits, bicycle frames, gym shoe colours, dress codes, children's toys, and so on). The relativist might ask why we cannot equally organize the world on the basis of some other classification system based on categories of weight, height or eye colour, for example (see Burr 2003: 3). Thus, just because biological 'sex differences' are made to be important in modern western societies, it does not mean that they must inevitably be that way. Institutionalized gender demarcation is a choice rather than an inevitability. For the feminist relativist, the goal of social scientific inquiry is not 'truth-seeking'. Rather, the focus shifts to an examination of how certain truths, ways of seeing the world, or versions of reality are constructed, and the social practices that sustain some oppressive, sexist and heterosexist versions over others.

A relativist approach ultimately leads us to reflexivity, where the researcher must recognize that their own practice of constructing knowledge and studying the world is itself socially constructed and organized. From this perspective, the researcher must self-consciously acknowledge and pay attention to their own role in practices of knowledge construction – for example how the role of the researcher and their methods for collecting gender talk in part shape the nature of the gender talk obtained (Speer 2002d). I will explore these issues further in Chapters 4 and 7 and in the Postscript.

Together these five features generate a distinctive feminist analytic approach. My aim in the rest of this book is to demonstrate what this approach might look like, and how and why it offers the most productive form of analysis for feminism.

Chapter overviews

In Chapters 2 and 3 I introduce some important work on the relationship between gender, language and identity that has developed within sociolinguistics, poststructuralism and ethnomethodology. This research underpins, and forms a precursor to, much research on gender and language, and can be broadly divided into two strands or types: the first strand of research, which has been conducted primarily within sociolinguistics, explores sex differences in language. The second strand of research, which has been conducted primarily within poststructuralism and ethnomethodology, explores how gender identity is constituted – how people 'do' gender. Research conducted from within these two traditions represents often competing theoretical and methodological assumptions about the nature of the relationship between gender and language, and how it might best be grasped analytically. My aim in Chapters 2 and 3 is to provide a focused overview and critique of research conducted within both perspectives, with a view to illustrating the distinctiveness of my own position.

I begin, in Chapter 2, by interrogating the theoretical and methodological assumptions that underpin three classic studies within the sociolinguistic 'sex differences' paradigm. I argue that even while work within this tradition has had a significant impact on the field of research on gender and language, that the sex differences framework nonetheless suffers a number of problems when it comes to the empirical analysis of gender and language. Specifically, this research has a tendency to reinforce dualistic understandings about sex and gender, and take us further away from, rather than closer to, an understanding of how gender and sexism are constituted and reproduced in interaction.

In Chapter 3, I contrast the 'sex differences' approach to gender and language considered in Chapter 2, with some important work on 'doing' gender that developed concurrently outside linguistics within poststructuralism and ethnomethodology. This work, while concerned more with gender *identity* than with language, challenges us to see sex and gender as a performance, or an accomplishment, rather than an essence. Poststructuralism and ethnomethodology have had a significant impact on the development of the two discourse strands that I identified earlier in this chapter: the 'critical' discursive work informed by critical theory, poststructuralism and psychoanalysis on the one hand, and the discursive work informed by ethnomethodology and CA on the other. By inspecting the theoretical and methodological assumptions underpinning poststructuralist and ethnomethodological studies of gender identity construction, I begin to flesh out some of the similarities and differences that underpin these two discourse strands, and the rather different feminist analyses of gender and language that derive from them. I suggest that despite the radical political potential this poststructuralist and ethnomethodological work has offered feminism, that neither of these perspectives, in and of themselves, offer an adequate empirical programme for the analysis of talk-in-interaction. Instead, I argue that an approach which draws on insights from CA, and the closely related constructionist perspective of DP, is the most fruitful analytic framework for feminism.

In Chapter 4 I demonstrate how insights from CA and DP contribute theoretically and methodologically to the five criteria for the development of an adequate feminist analytic approach set out in this chapter. I show how feminists and others with a critical agenda have used insights from both perspectives to interrogate the relevance of gender in talk, and to explore 'what counts' as gender, or an 'orientation to gender' in an interaction. I suggest that these studies challenge both the essentialist gender-typing story associated with the vast bulk of variationist and sociolinguistic research conducted to date, and the 'broader' forms of analysis associated with poststructuralist, 'top-down' approaches to discourse. I argue that an approach which is concerned with the turn-by-turn analysis of taped and transcribed segments of talk, provides the tools with which we may begin to produce an empirically grounded form of feminism, and ultimately to rethink what we mean by 'gender-talk'.

This discussion sets the scene for Chapters 5 and 6, where I argue against the anti-CA critics, to show how an analytic approach which sticks closely to an analysis of participants' orientations, can be applied to, and used to rework our understanding of, the relationship between the purportedly 'external' macro-social structural context of gender norms, ideology and 'the world out there', on the one hand (Chapter 5), and the purportedly 'internal', cognitive-psychological context of gender identity, subjectivity, prejudicial attitudes and beliefs, and 'the world in here', on the other (Chapter 6). These chapters demonstrate how traditional sociological and psychological understandings of the relationship between macro-social and cognitive-psychological realms (particularly as they are formulated in 'critical' and poststructuralist approaches to discourse) can be rethought using a micro-interactional framework, and without losing a political thrust.

I make this case in Chapter 5 by reviewing Wetherell and Edley's (1999) critical discursive work on the widely used 'macro-analytic' concept of *hegemonic masculinity*. Using data from two informal interviews with men in their early twenties, I explore how participants construct masculinity and situate themselves and others in relation to those constructions. I ask whether participants *themselves* orient toward something that analysts have glossed – in more abstract, theoretical contexts – as hegemonic masculinity, and consider what such orientations may be doing interactionally. Specifically, I look to see just how far an approach which does *not* go beyond participant orientations can take us in our understanding of the discursive constitution of gender identity. I argue that even while participants may align with, and differentiate themselves from, a version of masculinity that they define in similar ways across extracts, that hegemony and hegemonic masculinity are *not* participants' categories, and that, in its particularities, masculinity is defined in variable ways that are appropriate for the local interactional context, and the work that needs to be done to invoke or manage a particular identity.

INTRODUCTION

In Chapter 6, I show how a participants' orientations approach can be applied to rethink 'cognitive-psychological' understandings of prejudice and – specifically – heterosexist talk. I begin by criticizing current psychological work on heterosexism, highlighting the way its operationalization tends to obscure flexible discursive practices and settle them into stable, causal attitudes within individuals. Then, drawing on extracts from a variety of sources where sexuality is made relevant, I examine whether participants themselves orient to their talk as heterosexist or problematic in any way, and consider what such 'attending to' may be doing interactionally. I suggest that speakers use various conversational and interactional resources to manage the potential trouble that their remarks may engender, and to foreclose possible counter-arguments and challenges. Importantly, I argue that it is in this very management – this attending to potential trouble – that we can find the constitution of what the participants take to be prejudicial, accountable 'heterosexist talk'. Finally, I show (cf. much critical discursive and 'sex differences' research) that heterosexist utterances do not have their negativity built into them, but become prejudicial, troublesome or otherwise for participants *in situ*, as their sense is produced and negotiated.

In Chapter 7 I summarize some of the main themes to come out of the book, and consider their implications. My discussion is framed in terms of several questions that readers may still have about the five key features of the feminist analytic approach I advocate. My responses to these questions point to some common misunderstandings of both CA and DP. I explain why I believe my approach is a theoretically and methodologically fruitful one for feminism, and how, contrary to popular belief, it may be politically and practically consequential.

Finally, in the Postscript, I consider some methodological issues that will influence the future development of feminist CA, and which researchers interested in using this perspective might usefully consider.

2

GENDER AND LANGUAGE

'SEX DIFFERENCE' PERSPECTIVES

My aim in this chapter and the next is to use the five criteria for a feminist analytic approach introduced in Chapter 1, to provide a focused overview and critique of some important work on the relationship between gender, language and identity that has developed within the fields of sociolinguistics, poststructuralism and ethnomethodology. This research spans a period of thirty years, and has formed a precursor to, and developed in parallel with, the CA and DP tradition.

I begin, in this chapter, by focusing on work conducted primarily within interactional sociolinguistics, and which explores *sex differences* in language. In Chapter 3, I focus on research conducted primarily within poststructuralism and ethnomethodology, and which explores how gender identity is constituted – how people 'do' gender. Even while such a categorization simplifies matters and obscures problematic areas of crossover and overlap, research conducted from within these two traditions represents often competing theoretical and methodological assumptions about the nature of gender and how it might best be grasped analytically. By focusing on the detail of some of these assumptions, I hope to begin to illustrate the distinctiveness of my own analytic position.

Introducing sex differences research

We are surrounded in our everyday lives with powerful commonsense ideas about speech which tell us that men and women communicate and use language in different ways. Men talk about sport and cars, women 'gossip', 'natter' or 'waffle' about relationships and trivialities; men like to talk about themselves, women like to 'nag' men; men talk a lot, women listen; men are assertive, women are submissive; men are logical, women are illogical. Such ideas circulate widely in society and culture, and in the broadcast and print media, and collectively have come to be known as 'folklinguistics' (Goddard and Patterson 2000).

Although folklinguistic ideas about male and female 'speech styles' stem from stereotyped beliefs about men and women, such ideas nonetheless constitute powerful forces in our lives, and offer revealing insights into the social positioning of men and women in society. Indeed, when translated in popular consciousness, folklinguistic ideas about difference become normative and expectable, with personal and political consequences. For example, historically, they have been translated (in etiquette books, for example) into definitive statements about how men and women *should* speak, and about 'appropriate' gendered behaviours. Phrases such as 'speaking like a lady', 'nice girls don't swear', 'boys don't cry' – all of these tell us not only that men and women act in different ways, but also that they *ought* to do so. To behave inappropriately for one's gender is seen as sanctionable, immoral or taboo. Thus, folklingusitic ideas have served to regulate and constrain the behaviour of men and women. Importantly, however, these ideas tend not to be applied to men and women in equal measure. Women's behaviour tends to be subject to more constraints than that of men's, and is frequently judged against a male 'norm'.

For feminists and linguists working within the 'sex differences' tradition, folklinguistics raises some pressing questions. For example, are these potentially restrictive and damaging stereotypes about language true? Are there really sex differences in language? Do men and women speak and use language in different ways? Moreover, if there *are* sex differences in language, then what can this tell us about the position of men and women in society, and how can we use such information to inform social change for the better (Kramer et al. 1978)?

One of the first academic studies to examine the relationship between gender and language was written in 1922 by the male linguist, Otto Jesperson. Jesperson's book, *Language: Its Nature, Development and Origin*, contained a chapter on sex differences in language called 'The woman' (reprinted in Cameron 1998c) in which he addressed the above questions from a male-centred viewpoint. Jesperson identified a range of male–female lexical variations. He claimed that women's language is more polite and more 'refined' than that of men, and that women are considerably less inventive and have a much smaller vocabulary than men. They have a fondness for 'hyperbole', favouring 'adverbs of intensity' like 'awfully pretty' and 'terribly nice' (Jesperson 1998: 236–7). Finally, women speak more quickly than men, frequently breaking off what they're saying mid-sentence as with 'Did you ever!' and 'Well, I never', for example (1998: 238).

Jesperson's study has been criticized by feminists because it is sexist, self-serving and patronizing. Based in folklingusitic stereotypes about women's language, it provides a purportedly 'scientific account of an already-assumed female inferiority' (Cameron 1992: 36). Feminist linguistic research began in the 1970s as part of feminism's second wave. Collectively, these studies have shown that language is not an equal opportunity phenomenon (McConnell-Ginet 1988, cited in Cameron 1992: 71). While most feminists agreed that there *are* sex differences in language, both in terms of the way men and women are represented *in* the language (the form of language) and the way they *use* language (the function of language), they differ in terms of what they perceive those differences to be, and in terms of how we might *account* for those differences.

Researchers in the gender and language field have interpreted male–female linguistic differences in three main ways: first, as evidence for women's powerlessness and subordinate status vis-à-vis men (the 'deficit' framework); second, as an example of male dominance and control of the language (the 'dominance' framework); or third, as an example of men and women's different but equally valid communicative styles (the 'difference' framework).

Most books on gender and language begin with an extensive summary of this work. Good examples can be found in Cameron (1992), Crawford (1995), Gibbon (1999) and Weatherall (2002a). It is not my intention to reproduce such a summary here, or to offer a definitive account of the findings of research conducted within the sex differences paradigm. Instead, what I want to do in this chapter is to provide an in-depth examination of three classic studies by Robin Lakoff (1975), Dale Spender (1980) and Deborah Tannen (1990). These studies are broadly representative of the 'deficit', 'dominance' and 'difference' frameworks described above. Although these studies span nearly two decades of feminist linguistics, and each attempts to rectify problems associated with prior studies, all three have been criticized over the years, from within, as well as outside of, linguistics. While I will refer to many of these criticisms as I proceed, my own discussion will be focused more closely on the extent to which studies conducted from within a sex differences framework meet the five criteria for a feminist, CA-inspired analytic approach set out in Chapter 1. I examine the procedures and techniques deployed in each study, as well as the assumptions those procedures and techniques bring into play.

The deficit framework: Robin Lakoff's *Language and Woman's Place*

The 'deficit' framework refers to any approach which interprets male–female linguistic differences as evidence for women's powerlessness and subordinate status vis-à-vis men. Robin Lakoff is widely regarded as the key proponent of this position. In her well-known book, *Language and Woman's Place* (1975; see also Lakoff 1973), Lakoff examines linguistic disparities in two facets of language: 'the ways women are expected to speak' (their *use* of language, or their language behaviour), and 'the ways in which women are spoken of' (how they are represented *in* the language, or the sexist and gendered nature of language) (Lakoff 1973: 45). I deal with each in turn.

Women's use of language

Lakoff identified quantifiable differences between the language use and speech styles of men and women:

- Women use a wider range of colour terms than men, and discriminate more precisely between different shades of the same colour. They use words such as *beige, ecru, aquamarine*, and *lavender* which are largely absent in the language of men.
- Women tend to avoid speaking in a way that conveys strong emotions and generally use 'weaker' expletives than men (e.g., 'Oh dear' as opposed to 'shit').
- Men and women use a different set of adjectives to convey their opinion on matters.

neutral	*women only*
great	adorable
terrific	charming
cool	sweet
neat	lovely
	divine

According to Lakoff, these features demonstrate that women's talk is confined largely to frivolous, non-serious matters that relate to their specific interests (e.g., matters of fine colour discrimination), which express approval of the trivial, and which convey a personal and emotional (rather than objective) reaction to their subject matter.

- Women use more 'tag questions' than men. Tag questions are declarative statements that have been turned into a question with the use of a tag, such as 'The war in Vietnam is terrible, isn't it?'
- Women use sentences with more rising intonations than men. Such sentences generally take the form of answers to questions, but have 'the rising inflection typical of a yes-no question' (1973: 55):

(2.1) [Lakoff 1973: 55]
(A)   When will dinner be ready?
(B)   Oh . . . around six o'clock . . .?

Tags and intonations require confirmation from others and act as requests for reassurance or approval.

- Women use more 'hedges' such as *well*, *y'know*, *kinda* than men. In doing so, they avoid making forthright statements. Women's use of hedging is evidence for hesitancy, making them appear less assertive than men.
- Women use 'hypercorrect grammar' and more 'superpolite forms' than men.
- Finally, women speak in 'italics'. That is, they give double force to certain words in order to convey the importance of what they are saying. Italics convey doubt about one's self-expression and one's fears 'that their words are apt to have no effect' (1975: 56). The speaker who uses tags, intonation, hedging and italics to excess may appear insecure and uncertain about what they are saying and lacking in self-confidence.

According to Lakoff, these linguistic disparities may be explained with reference to women's socialization into a subordinate status vis-à-vis men. Women sound inferior, not because they are naturally deficient in some way, but because they have been *trained* to be so. They are taught, through the use of various sanctions, what 'appropriate women's speech' consists of. Interestingly, however, women are not *rewarded* for learning to 'talk like a lady' by being accepted in society. If they embrace women's language, then their particular style of speech is used to ridicule them and justify their oppression – they are not forceful enough or do not express themselves precisely or seriously enough, for example. On the other hand, if they reject women's language and refuse to 'speak like a lady', then they are seen as unfeminine. The result is self-perpetuating:

> the behavior a woman learns as 'correct' prevents her from being taken seriously as an individual, and further is considered 'correct' and necessary for a woman precisely because society does *not* consider her seriously as an individual.
>
> (Lakoff 1973: 51)

Thus, linguistic disparities both reflect and perpetuate women's secondary status in society.

Representations of women in the language

Lakoff highlights a number of linguistic disparities in the use of purportedly parallel, or symmetrical terms that have taken on non-equivalent meanings for men and women:

- While a woman may be referred to as a 'cleaning lady' or a 'cleaning woman', a 'saleslady' or a 'saleswoman', there are no such alternatives

for men: a man cannot be referred to as a 'garbage gentleman' or a 'sales gentleman', only as a 'garbage man' or a 'salesman'.
- Women are more often referred to as 'girls', whatever their age, than men are as 'boys'.
- The terms 'master' and 'mistress' have taken on non-equivalent meanings: whereas 'master' is used to refer to a man who has acquired a comprehensive grasp of an object, activity, or field, 'mistress' is used in its sexual sense, and usually refers to a woman's relationship *to* somebody – typically a man.
- The same is true of the categories 'bachelor' and 'spinster': whereas the category 'bachelor' is considered a positive, desirable one, a status that may be chosen by men who do not want to marry, the category 'spinster' is, by contrast, a negative and undesirable one.
- There are different address terms for men ('Mr') and women ('Mrs' / 'Miss'), and women (and not men) are defined in terms of their marital status. In addition, most women take their father's name at birth and their husband's name on marriage.
- Finally, when it comes to 'professional naming' women are more likely to be referred to by their first name, or by their first name and last name, than men, who may be referred to by their last name alone, or by their title and their last name.

Just as with their *use* of language, the representation of women *in* the language reflects and perpetuates women's subordinate position within society. As Lakoff puts it, 'men are defined in terms of what they do in the world, women in terms of the men with whom they are associated' (1973: 64).

Lakoff's conclusions

Lakoff concludes by arguing that both facets of language cause women to experience 'linguistic discrimination':

> the overall effect of 'women's language' – meaning both language restricted in use to women and language descriptive of women alone – is this: it submerges a woman's personal identity, by denying her the means of expressing herself strongly, on the one hand ... and, when a woman is being discussed, by treating her as an object – sexual or otherwise – but never a serious person with individual views.
>
> (Lakoff 1973: 48)

Lakoff suggests that there are two main ways to remedy this situation, and create a context of greater linguistic equality. First, women can gain some authority and power by using men's linguistic strategies – or what Lakoff terms 'neutral language'. Second, linguists can pinpoint disparities in the language, highlight the damage certain forms do, and single out those areas which may be most receptive to change. Ultimately, however, since linguistic disparities are the symptom, rather than the cause of social inequality, Lakoff is of the view that linguistic change and social change must go hand in hand.

Summary and discussion of Lakoff

Language and Woman's Place is widely regarded as the first book in feminist linguistics. It has had a significant impact on the field of language and gender research, and, as Cameron (1998c: 216) asserts, 'it probably did more than any other text before or since to bring issues of language and gender to wider attention and to place them in the context of the post-1968 Women's Liberation Movement'. Indeed, such is the foundational and ongoing significance of *Language and Woman's Place* for the field of research on gender and language, that more than a quarter of a century later, it has been republished with additional commentaries from leading researchers in the field (see Lakoff 2004). In that book, Bucholtz (2004) suggests that without Lakoff, the disparate studies of language and gender available at the time she wrote *Language and Woman's Place* may not have converged into a coherent academic field at all.

Despite its lasting importance, Lakoff's work has been subject to a number of criticisms – from within as well as outside linguistics. The first criticism centres on Lakoff's theory and politics, and particularly on her assumption that women's language is a deficient variant of the purportedly more effective male or 'neutral' norm. Lakoff's research has been criticized for implying that there is something *wrong* with the way women use language, which is 'holding them back', and consequently, that it is their responsibility to put it right. The implication is that once these linguistic deficiencies have been remedied, then women will be treated more equally in society, and become more successful. Indeed, theories associated with the deficit framework have been particularly influential in the development of assertiveness training and other forms of 'language remediation' that are intended to make women become more effective communicators, and to speak more like men (see Cameron 1995; Crawford 1995). In many ways, therefore, it could be suggested that Lakoff's study reinforces many of the sexist, folklinguistic stereotypes that were evident in the work of Jesperson, before her, and yet which her study was initially designed to counter.

The second criticism of Lakoff centres on matters of empirical accuracy and methodological flaws. As Lakoff herself acknowledges (e.g., 2000: 135), many of her initial hypotheses about language and gender have subsequently been proven incorrect. Although one study supports her claim about women's greater differentiation of colour terms (Frank 1990, cited in Bucholtz 2004), a number of researchers have re-evaluated her claims about the linguistic vehicles of women's deficiency, and found them to be wanting. For example, Janet Holmes (1984) and Cameron et al. (1989) have found that men and women use similar numbers of tags, while others have found that men use *more* tag questions than women (Dubois and Crouch 1975). Similarly, many of the words that Lakoff claimed were 'empty' or redundant, and hedges such as 'sort of' and 'kind of', have been reinterpreted as important aspects of speech, which fulfil important functions like helping speakers to 'sound relaxed and informal' (Goddard and Patterson 2000: 98).

Despite these criticisms, Bucholtz (2004: 127) reminds us that Lakoff 'is not a failed feminist thinker, as some of her critics have alleged'. Instead, she lay the groundwork for much later work in gender and language scholarship, and continues to impact the field today. For example, in her subsequent writings, Lakoff has continued to develop and refine her ideas on the relationship between cultural ideologies of gender and linguistic practice, and how language using reflects and perpetuates the normative attributes that we expect from men and women (Lakoff 1990; see also Miller and Swift 1976). She has explored how women speak, and how they are spoken of, within male-dominated structures of power, and how women have started to challenge and undermine these structures (e.g., Lakoff 1995). More recently Lakoff (2003) has examined male academic discourse. Notable here is her analysis of Schegloff's (1997) article, 'Whose text? Whose context?', which, despite its claims to neutrality, Lakoff regards as an example of male dominance and sexism within the academy (see Stokoe 2005 for a critique).

The dominance framework: Dale Spender's *Man Made Language*

The second framework I want to consider here was developed five years later by the radical feminist, Dale Spender, in her book *Man Made Language* (1980). This book is often cited as an example of the 'dominance' framework (see also Thorne and Henley 1975). From this perspective, women are quite literally dominated by men in their talk, in terms of both the amount they talk, and their control over the topic.

Spender's critique of the deficit framework

Spender (1980: 8) is highly critical of the style of work conducted by Lakoff and others, which produces inventories of 'women's linguistic deficiencies'. According to Spender (1980: 32–3), not only has research on sex differences in language failed to find 'many of the hypothesized differences that have been tested', but the 'research procedures have been so embedded with sexist assumptions that investigators have been blinded to empirical reality'.

Spender (1980: 13) traces many of the 'inadequacies and inaccuracies' of the deficit framework to the tendency, evident in the work of Lakoff and others, to separate the form of language from its function – to treat language 'as an abstract system without reference to the context' (1980: 13). What is needed, according to Spender, is an explanation of the origin and function of sexist language, how it evolved, how it works, and how it can be changed. In other words, what is needed is an analysis of 'patriarchal order' (1980: 31). Spender claims that this kind of approach will pose questions that are not framed in terms of deficiency, and which will not, therefore, 'automatically lead to answers which support the case that there is something *wrong* with women, and their language' (1980: 8, emphasis in original). Once attention is turned towards 'the social context in which the language is used' (1980: 13), then it becomes apparent that both the form and the function of language are part of the same process – the *silencing* of women (1980: 51).

Man-made language

Spender argues that in order to give order and meaning to our world, and help us to interpret things, we need rules. However, the rules we live by are not natural or inevitable: Rather, our rules are 'man-made' (1980: 2). According to Spender, one of our most pervasive and insidious semantic rules is that of 'male-as-norm' (1980: 3). Spender (1980: 3) notes that 'while this rule operates we are required to classify the world on the premise that the standard or normal human being is a male one and . . . then those who are not of it are allocated to a category of deviation'. This rule operates chiefly through *language*. She notes, 'it is language which determines the limits of our world, which constructs our reality' (1980: 139).

For Spender, language is sexist because men, who are in a position of power, dominate and control it. Male grammarians, politicians, orators, philosophers and linguists have all had the power to name the world from their own perspective, and create a language that suits their own ends. It is precisely because men have a 'monopoly over language' that they are able to impose their worldview on everyone, and thereby ensure 'the myth of male superiority' (1980: 1). Indeed, men's 'monodimensional', linear view of the world has evolved because, unlike a multidimensional view of the world (in which there are multiple possible ways to experience the same phenomenon), this is a world that is controllable.

Examples of man-made language

Spender argues that women have had to express themselves in a language that is not their own, and which places limits on what they are able to experience and perceive. She provides a range of contemporary examples of the male naming of women's experience.

First, Spender discusses motherhood. According to Spender, in this society the legitimate meaning for motherhood is 'feminine fulfilment'. Spender argues that while this dominant, male definition, is not necessarily false, and may be true for some women, it is partial and it is not the only meaning available. Indeed, many women may not experience motherhood in such idealistic terms. However, since their meanings do not merge with the male (accepted and legitimized) view of motherhood, these women are frequently left feeling inadequate, confused, and that there must be something wrong with them. They may even come to doubt the validity or reality of their experiences (1980: 54). As Spender notes, 'if it is real, why has no one needed a name for it before?' (1980: 188). Denied the linguistic means to validate their own experience, they must either take on board a male reality, or remain silent, thus reinforcing 'their own muted position' (1980: 87). It is in this way that women become a 'muted' group. Alternative versions of motherhood are not legitimized or passed on through the generations, and women's meanings are lost.

A second example which illustrates how men have encoded sexism into the language, thereby ensuring their own primacy, is the use of what Spender terms 'he/man language'. Spender argues that even while they are often intended as 'generic' categories (that is, as 'inclusive' terms which apply to women *and* men), the use of the categories 'he' and 'man' actually makes women invisible by placing men at the forefront of our minds: 'people think *male* when they use the term *man*' (1980: 151). He/man language 'blinkers' us into seeing a male reality (1980: 154). As Spender (1980: 154) notes, 'it is not just that women do not see themselves encompassed in the symbol of he/man: men do not see them either' (see also Bodine 1975).

Finally, sexuality has been defined in male terms. To demonstrate this, Spender compared the names for sexually healthy adults and found that while men can be *virile* and *potent*, 'for women to engage in extensive sexual activity there is only repudiation: she is a *nymphomaniac*, a *baller*, a *bitch*' (1980: 175). Heterosexual sex has also been defined from a male perspective. Men emphasize their own role in the sexual act, so that women's contribution is 'omitted and rendered invisible' (1980: 177; see also Greer 1970).

Blocking women's meanings: research on interruptions

Spender suggests that one of the main ways in which men control language, is by 'blocking' women's meanings, and by insisting that women talk in a way acceptable to them. She says 'women are "queried", they are interrupted, their opinions are discounted and their contributions devalued in virtually all of the mixed-sex conversations that I have taped' (1980: 87). Drawing on research by Pamela Fishman (1977) and the early work of the conversation analysts Zimmerman and West (1975), Spender argues that women exert much of the effort in a conversation, by keeping it flowing smoothly, by drawing men out of themselves, and by suggesting topics which will cater to men's interests. By contrast, when men take up these topics, they 'often do so by interrupting and assuming control' (1980: 44).

Spender suggests that men use interruption as a mechanism by which to prevent women from talking, and to gain control of the floor for themselves (1980: 44). Thus, Spender is critical of research which purports to show that women are excessively talkative (1980: 41). Indeed, she accounts for this stereotype by arguing that in a patriarchal society, silence is the desired state for women. It is not that women talk too much in relation to men. Rather, they talk too much in relation to silence: 'when women are supposed to be quiet, a talkative woman is one who talks at all' (1980: 43; see also Spender 1989).

Spender's conclusions

Spender concludes by arguing that, if we want to create a different reality that gives more credence to women's meanings, and from which women can begin to 'deconstruct their muted condition' (1980: 93), then we need to change the semantic rule that denotes that males represent the positive and females represent the negative. We need, in other words, to liberate the language from male control and generate a new 'feminist reality'. In order to do this, Spender suggests that women must get together – in revolutionary and subversive forums such as consciousness-raising groups, in order to generate new, positive names for their experiences. Examples of feminist success in creating women-centred meanings include the terms *sexual harassment, phallocentrism, chauvinism, androcentric* and *patriarchal*. Women must generate new meanings from the basis of multi-dimensional (rather than a male, monodimensional) reality, which will allow experiences to be open to plural perception. Like Lakoff, Spender believes that linguistic change and social change go together as part of a dialectical and self-perpetuating process. Once women gain a voice, 'woman-centred meanings will multiply' (1980: 74–5), male supremacy will lose its legitimacy, and more women will gain the courage to end their silence.

Summary and discussion of Spender

Spender's work has been important on a number of levels. First, Spender was one of the first feminists to challenge the linguist's tendency – evident in the work of Lakoff and others – to separate the *form* of language from its *function*, or the study of how gender is represented *in* language from the study of how men and women *use* language. Spender's argument that both are part of the same process (the silencing of women), paved the way for later work which treats them as part of the *social construction of gender*.

Second, Spender's findings have proven influential in feminist politics. She demonstrates the importance of involving women in discussions about language, and of giving them a space to express their views and experiences. By encoding their own meanings, women can resist male power. These ideas are developed further in Spender's more recent work on gender and the internet. In this work, Spender (1995) argues that the internet provides a valuable space for women to communicate with one another. However, if we wish to avoid a situation where the World Wide Web becomes yet another site of male power, women must become prominent innovators and users of it.

Third, Spender's argument that men use linguistic resources to maintain their power and silence women, has become a popular theme for gender and language researchers in a range of fields, who have investigated the micro-interactional techniques that men use to dominate and control talk. For example, the conversation analysts, West, Zimmerman and colleagues, whose work Spender draws on, have gone on to develop their work on asymmetries in male–female interruption patterns and unilateral topic shifts (West 1992; West and Garcia 1988; West and Zimmerman 1983). Likewise, other researchers informed broadly by CA have explored how male physicians exercise power in consultations with female patients (Ainsworth-Vaughn 1992; Davis 1988; Fisher 1986; Todd 1989), and how men silence women in marital relations (De Francisco 1991). Although, as we saw in Chapter 1, these studies have been criticized for using CA to 'non-CA purposes' (Stokoe 2000: 556), since their findings are in keeping with a dominance framework, they do, nonetheless, give lasting validity to Spender's claims.

Despite its virtues, Spender's research has been widely criticized for its almost intractable linguistic determinism (Cameron 1992). Spender treats language as something that reflects male-centred meanings, and as something which men use to impose limits on what women can say, and what they can experience. As Goddard and Patterson (2000: 100) note, such an approach creates a picture 'of bullying men and meek, oppressed women... and... of men sitting round conspiring how to do women out of their linguistic inheritance'. Likewise, it offers a simplistic, 'monolithic' view of male power (Talbot 1998: 48; see also Black and Coward 1998), which ignores other dimensions of power, such as race and class – dimensions which may entail some women, in some circumstances, having *more* power than other groups.

The difference framework: Deborah Tannen's *You Just Don't Understand*

The third approach I consider here is the 'difference' framework. This perspective is most commonly associated with the work of Deborah Tannen. Tannen is a sociolinguist whose book *You Just Don't Understand! Men and Women in Conversation* (1990) has become a well-known manual for anyone interested in understanding male–female differences in conversational style, and who wants to improve their (heterosexual) communication to avoid conflict.

From dominance to difference

Like Lakoff and Spender, Tannen argues that men and women have different ways of talking. However, for Tannen, and other proponents of the difference framework, these differences cannot be explained with reference to either women's subordinate social status (Lakoff) or the male dominance of women (Spender). Tannen accepts that men are dominant within our society, but disputes the claim that conversations break down because men purposefully dominate women, arguing that 'the effect of dominance is not always the result of an intention to dominate' (1990: 18).

According to Tannen and proponents of the difference framework, men and women have 'different but *equally valid* styles' (1990: 15). Drawing on the work of the anthropologists Maltz and Borker (1982), Tannen argues that we learn these different styles as we grow up and use language with our peers. Boys and girls 'grow up in different worlds of words' (Tannen 1990: 43) and male–female linguistic style differences are akin to the differences one might expect to see between people from different cultures or subcultures. It follows that interaction between men and women is akin to cross-cultural communication (1990: 18) and 'instead of different dialects, it could be said that we speak different genderlects' (1990: 42). According to Tannen, although both styles are valid on their own terms, the differences can generate misunderstandings and tensions.

Tannen (1990: 24–5) argues that many men engage in the world 'as an individual in a hierarchical social order . . . Life, then, is a contest, a struggle to preserve independence and avoid failure'. Many women, on the other hand, approach the world 'as an individual in a network of connections . . . Life, then, is a community, a struggle to preserve intimacy and avoid isolation' (1990: 25). Even while men and women need both intimacy and independence, Tannen says that women are more focused on the former and men on the latter. It follows that since men and women focus on different aspects of communication, they can sometimes develop different views of the same situations.

The message and the meta-message

The differences between men and women can be explained further with reference to Tannen's idea that each act has two levels of meaning – a *message* and a *metamessage*. Take the example of the act of helping. The act of helping may be regarded as the *message*, 'the obvious meaning of the act'. But the act of helping also sends out a metamessage – that is information about the relationship between the participants and their attitudes toward one another. Each act can be interpreted as having two different metamessages, and these metamessages can be interpreted symmetrically or asymmetrically. So the act of helping may send a symmetrical metamessage of connection: 'a generous move that shows caring and builds rapport' (1990: 32). Alternatively it can send an asymmetrical metamessage of hierarchy or of differing status 'in which the person giving help is in a superior position with respect to the other' (1990: 32). According to Tannen, women tend to be attuned to metamessages of symmetry and connection with others – to their similarities, on whether 'the other person is trying to get closer or pull away' (1990: 38). Men, on the other hand, tend to be attuned to metamessages of asymmetry and status, on their difference from others, and 'on the jockeying for status in a conversation' (1990: 38). This model can be applied to a range of acts. So, in 'troubles talk', for example, women see their role symmetrically, as providing empathy and understanding, whereas men see their role asymmetrically, as problem solver and advice giver (1990: 53).

Tannen's conclusions

Given these very different orientations and sensitivities, Tannen claims that it is hardly surprising that men and women often end up 'talking at cross-purposes' (1990: 120). However, she suggests that if we reframe our gendered ways of talking as attempts to communicate across cultures, then we will cease blaming our relationships or each other for our communication problems, and the frustrations they engender. Tannen argues that men and women would both benefit from learning to use the others' style – not to adopt them entirely, but to equip them with additional strategies for communicating. As she says, 'understanding genderlect improves relationships' (1990: 298). So, women would benefit from assertiveness training just as men might benefit from sensitivity training. Tannen ends with the optimistic suggestion that once we have enhanced our understanding of gender differences in communicative style, that we are less likely to complain 'You just don't understand.'

Summary and discussion of Tannen

As the most recent of the three perspectives discussed here, Tannen's work overcomes many of the problems that feminists have identified in the work of Lakoff and Spender, above. Unlike Lakoff, Tannen does not present women's talk as a deficient variant of a male norm (Crawford 1995: 93). Moreover, unlike Spender, she does not offer a one-dimensional view of power, or present men as 'intentional bullies' and women as muted victims (Goddard and Patterson 2000: 101). According to the feminist psychologist, Mary Crawford (1995: 93), the 'two-cultures' model offers a 'no fault' approach to difference, which 'transcends' woman-blaming, and which 'is less likely to lead to woman-as-problem research programs or to widespread attempts to change women through therapy and skills training'. Moreover, the model allows us to 'positively revalue' aspects of talk thought to characterize women's language (Crawford 1995: 93). 'Gossip', for example, which is usually trivialized and treated in a negative fashion, can be seen as something which is important in 'establishing intimacy and rapport' (1995: 93).

A 'two-cultures' model has been taken up widely by feminist sociolinguists, who have sought to describe and explain a range of sex differences in communicative style (see, for example, Coates 1986; Fishman 1978; Holmes 1995; Maltz and Borker 1982). Moreover, in her more recent work, Tannen has gone on to elaborate her arguments about the discursive constitution of male–female communicative styles in the workplace, the family and in intimate relationships (Tannen 1994b, 1997, 1999, 2003), further specifying her understanding of the relationship between gender, power and solidarity.

One criticism of Tannen, however, is that she fails to contextualize her arguments against much of the feminist literature that would have been available to her at the time she wrote (Crawford 1995: 97). One of the consequences of this is that her ideas, and the difference framework more broadly, have often been used to support the commonsense, conservative idea that men and women are essentially different. Ideas about male–female differences in communicative style have been taken up in numerous 'pop psychology' advice books, which purport to diagnose and improve problems in male–female (heterosexual) patterns of relating, and create more mutually satisfying and fulfilling relationships (see, for example, Gray's (1992) *Men are from Mars, Women are from Venus* and Fein and Schneider's (1995) *The Rules*). Crawford (1995: 108) argues that such books deflect responsibility from men, excusing their bad behaviour as a 'stylistic quirk' (1995: 97; Freed 1992). They offer men 'a compelling rationale of blame-free difference' and women 'a comforting promise of mutual accommodation' (Crawford 1995: 98).

One particularly striking example of how Tannen's work has been used to the detriment of women, and of feminism, is Baron-Cohen's (2003: 55) widely acclaimed but controversial book, *The Essential Difference*. Baron-Cohen recruits Tannen's work to support the claim that male and female brains are essentially different. According to Baron-Cohen, 'the female brain is predominantly hard-wired for empathy. The male brain is predominantly hard-wired for understanding and building systems' (2003: 1). For him, these essential differences account for just the kinds of communicative style differences that Tannen identifies.

Finally, the two-cultures model has been criticized strongly for failing to acknowledge the role of structural inequalities in the maintenance and reproduction of gender differences at the interactional level (Crawford 1995: 96). For some, Tannen treats male–female differences as symmetrical, when in fact they are not. As Aki Uchida (1992) argues, even if men and women have equally valid styles, they still exist in a relationship with one another where men are culturally dominant. Cameron (1992: 43) makes a similar point, suggesting that 'so long as women are subordinate to men, their language will continue to be stereotyped as indicating natural subservience, unintelligence and immaturity'. In her defence, Tannen (1990: 235) does acknowledge that 'women as a class are dominated by men as a class', that women are often required to 'make more adjustments than men in mixed groups' (1990: 235), and that men's styles are often evaluated more positively and treated as the norm. However, the overall impression her book gives is of a sanitized world in which men and women's linguistic contributions are of equal status.

'Sex difference' perspectives: a focused evaluation and critique

So far I have described the three studies that are representative of the main theoretical perspectives within the sociolinguistic, sex differences framework, and some of the most common criticisms that each approach has engendered. What I want to do in the remainder of this chapter is to evaluate these three studies in relation to the five criteria for an adequate feminist analytic approach set out in Chapter 1, and bring out some of the problematic theoretical and methodological assumptions which they share. Thus, I explore the extent to which the sex differences framework adheres to the following five features: (i) a constructionist approach; (ii) discourse of mind and world as topic, not resource; (iii) language as a form of social action; (iv) analysts' claims are grounded in participants' practices; and (v) a relativist approach.

(i) A constructionist approach?

Theoretically, what 'sex differences' studies share is an *essentialist* understanding of gender identity. As we saw in Chapter 1, an essentialist approach is one which conflates sex with gender, and which treats gender as a relatively fixed trait or 'essence' that resides in male and female selves. Essentialist ideas are manifest in these studies' 'variables and effects' model of language. This model involves the researcher adopting methodological procedures and techniques that treat demographic features of social context, such as the speaker's sex, as an independent variable that is deemed to both cause and account for quantifiable differences between the language use or speech style of men and women. In other words, language use is treated as a direct reflection of one's sex and gender identity.

Although these studies are not quantitative in the traditional sense of that term, and they do not subject participants' talk to statistical tests and procedures, each, nonetheless, entails a form of 'linguistic survey'. This involves correlating linguistic forms (such as interruptions or tag questions) with pre-existing features of context, like sex or gender. So Lakoff's approach requires that she implicitly divide the speakers she refers to in her study into two discrete groups of men and women, and measure and 'map' sex differences in their (perceived) use of language accordingly. Likewise, Spender (1980: 46–7, 48–9) correlates gender with amount and type of talk, measuring the percentage of the time that the men talked compared to the women, who had control of topic, and who interrupted. Finally, Tannen argues that men and women approach their interactions from different 'vantage points'. In a strikingly essentialist claim, she suggests that their 'life-blood' runs in 'different directions' and 'they are tuned to different frequencies' (Tannen 1990: 26, 288).

There are a number of problems with this essentialist, 'variables and effects' model of language use. First, men and women are treated as belonging to two relatively homogeneous groups. Ideas about gendered speech styles are applied in a uniform way to *all* men and *all* women, which ignores differences *among* men and *among* women. Ultimately such studies serve to perpetuate notions of gender dualism, and reinforce 'a two genders agenda' (Stokoe and Smithson 2001: 219, 2002; and for related criticisms, see Crawford 1995).

Second, this approach has a tendency to 'reify' gender. To reify gender is to turn what is essentially an abstract and fluid *social construct* back into a fixed material or embodied 'thing'. Thus, in these studies, persons speak *as* coherently gendered subjects or *about* coherently gendered subjects. Gender – a social construct – is treated as something that is biologically determined and derived. It is precisely this act of reification which allows these authors to treat gender as a relatively fixed, invariant and determinate linguistic variable. None of these studies explore how sex or gender difference are constructed as natural and timeless givens in the first place, and in the course of participants' interactions.

Third, the 'variables and effects' model of language reinforces a 'container' theory of context, in which demographic variables such as gender, and the 'macro-social' contexts, structures or institutions within which they are embedded, are treated as independent variables which exist prior to, and outside language, and which contain or determine our actions. So, male–female linguistic disparities are caused by, and serve as a reflection of, women's deficiency as speakers and their subordinate status in society (Lakoff), a patriarchal, monodimensional reality (Spender) and the subcultural differences between men and women (Tannen). In each case, even while these authors accept that women have the power to generate alternative meanings, and thereby challenge existing social arrangements, they nevertheless have a tendency to imply that speakers have no agency. We are simply programmed from childhood to speak in normatively gendered ways, and to reproduce a gendered social structure as we talk. Here again, this ties us to an oppressively deterministic and fixed notion of gender.

Finally, since these researchers each *start* from the assumption that men and women are fundamentally different, and that their speech will vary along lines of gender, it is perhaps unsurprising that they do indeed find gender differences in talk. Indeed, the variables and effects model of gender, in which the researcher divides up talk according to the sex of the speaker, searches for and measures gender differences in talk, and then uses gender as the explanatory variable to account for those differences, leads to *circular* arguments where gender is deemed to both cause and account for what gets said. The speaker's gender is not only used to code what gets said, but it is also invoked as the explanatory (causal) variable. It is inevitable that this framework will prevent the researcher from seeing gender as anything other than a dualistic category.

(ii) Discourse of mind and world as topic, not resource?

The second problem these studies share is that they treat social structures and demographic factors such as gender 'out there in the world', and cognitive-psychological processes and structures 'inside the mind' as primary 'inputs' to social action, while language, activity, and other social phenomena (including sexism and heterosexism), are treated as something secondary – a by-product or 'output' of the system (Edwards and Potter 2001: 15). In each case, language is treated as an analytic *resource* which reflects the world and people's perceptions of it (Edwards and Potter 2001: 12).

This treatment of language is most evident in the way each study deals with talk about cognitive phenomena – that is, descriptions which invoke mental states and psychological processes of various kinds. For all three authors, language acts as an objective 'barometer' that tells the researcher what is going on inside the heads of men and women. It is through language that we can recover evidence of what men and women are thinking and feeling. For Lakoff, for example, there is a determinant, cause–effect relationship between cognitive processes such as feelings or knowledge, and linguistic forms. This idea that feelings drive language is wired into Lakoff's comments about what motivates us to speak:

> One makes a statement when one has confidence in his [sic] knowledge and is pretty certain that his [sic] statement will be believed; one asks a question when one lacks knowledge on some point, and has reason to believe that this gap can and will be remedied by an answer by the addressee. A tag question, being intermediate between these, is used when the speaker is stating a claim, but lacks full confidence in the truth of that claim.
>
> (Lakoff 1973: 54)

Thus, for Lakoff, the words we utter, and more specifically, our choice of linguistic form, can be explained with reference to our internal 'state of mind', and, in particular, the degree of 'knowledge' and 'confidence' we may possess.

Spender adopts a rather more complex, but equally cognitivist approach to the language–mind relationship. For her, there is a *dialectical* (that is, two-way) relationship between language and cognition. The language that we have available to us not only acts as a resource for accessing what is going on inside speakers' heads, but also determines, or places limits on, what we are able to perceive and experience. As Spender (1980: 14) says, language is 'the means of ordering and structuring experiences, knowledge, expectations and inner states'.

Finally, Tannen also treats language as a secondary resource that provides a direct route to a person's cognitions. For example, she claims to be able to show, on the basis of her analyses, what each party was *intending* to do or how each may have *felt* at the time they spoke. Indeed, her analyses are replete with descriptions of her participants' mental states, their 'feelings', 'distress', 'hurt', 'concern', 'discomfort' and 'annoyance', their 'wants', 'wills' and 'desires'. It is worth taking a closer look at one of Tannen's (1990: 40) examples of a 'recurrent and pivotal' conversation recollected by a woman who had just split up with her long-term partner. Tannen notes that the pair had agreed that they would both be free to see other people so long as it did not involve hurting each other. When he began sleeping with other women, the woman complained, and he was 'incensed':

(2.2) [Tannen 1990: 40]
SHE: How can you do this when you know it's hurting me?
HE: How can you try to limit my freedom?
SHE: But it makes me feel awful.
HE: You are trying to manipulate me.

In her analysis of this extract, Tannen argues that 'what he wanted conflicted with what she wanted' (1990: 40). She says that 'the key *issue for this man* was his independence, his freedom of action' while 'the *key issue for the woman* was . . . interdependence – *how what he did made her feel*'. Finally, Tannen suggests 'he *interpreted* her insistence on their interdependence as "manipulation": She was using her feelings to control his behavior' (1990: 40, emphases added). So, here, Tannen provides an almost literal translation of her data, treating what her respondents say as an outcome of, and evidence for, such complex and elusive internal cognitive and mental processes as 'issues', 'feelings' and 'interpretations'. Thus in all three studies, talk is treated as a straightforward reflection of what is going on inside the heads of male and female selves.

The problem with cognitivism, indeed with any approach which treats language as a resource which reflects the world beyond talk (whether that be the internal world beneath talk, or the external world outside it), is that it takes attention away from the activities that are *done* with descriptions of mind and world in specific contexts. In other words, it overlooks what such talk may be doing in the current interaction, in and for the local circumstances. As I argued in Chapter 1, talk can do much more than simply mirror our world. It can be used to manage issues of blame and responsibility, to account for one's actions, and to present oneself in a favourable light. Returning to the example from Lakoff (1973: 54), it is entirely plausible that a speaker *doesn't* just make statements when they feel *confident* about their knowledge and certain that they will be believed. Rather, it is equally likely that one will make a statement when one is *lacking* in confidence, and do so at exactly those moments where one is being held most accountable for having confidence (in an interview situation, for example). A speaker may make strong, assertive statements precisely so as to deflect the imputation that they lack confidence. Likewise, one may ask a question for a range of reasons, lack of knowledge being just one of them (because one is bored, perhaps, or because one wants to convey interest in someone). Consider the well-worn phrase 'Hi, how are you?' While it is entirely plausible that one may ask this question because one wants to find out the answer in a literal sense (for example, to enquire about the state of health of a friend whom one hasn't seen for a while), it is equally plausible, as conversation analysts have shown, that one might ask this question as a means of observing social mores or the ritual conventions of greetings. One may already know how the person is, or indeed, may not care much for the answer. There is no room for this kind of interactionally contextualized account within these three studies.

(iii) Language as a form of social action?

Each author starts out by understanding the notion of context in a similar way. Thus, they begin by asserting that words and linguistic forms do not have fixed meanings, and that their precise sense will depend on the context in which they are uttered. Lakoff says:

> it is a mistake to hope . . . that the acceptability of a sentence is a yes-no or non decision: rather . . . the acceptability of a sentence is determined through the combination of many factors: . . . the social context in which the utterance is expressed, and the assumptions about the world made by all the participants in the discourse.
> (Lakoff 1973: 76–7)

Likewise, Spender acknowledges that meanings are shaped by the social (patriarchal) context within which language is embedded. She claims, for example, that women's language is interpreted negatively, not because of something intrinsic to the words they use, but because women exist in 'negative semantic space' (1980: 20). Of the three authors, Tannen is the most explicit about the context sensitivity of meaning. She claims that 'much – even most – meaning in conversation does not reside in the words spoken at all', but 'is filled in by the person listening' (1990: 37). Indeed, in this and her later work (e.g., Tannen 1994c), she explores the relativity and multifunctional nature of linguistic forms, challenging the idea that interruptions, for example, are an automatic sign of male dominance.

However, despite first proclaiming that they are sensitive to context, each author simultaneously adopts practices, procedures and categories which strip talk of its contextual subtleties and which ignore the context-sensitivity of actual language use. They imply that, at least to some extent, gendered meanings do indeed reside in, and come attached to certain words and linguistic forms, regardless of the precise context in which such words are uttered.

Lakoff, for example, implies that there are a limited number of context free, problematic or derogatory terms which are 'essentially' damaging, and that by pinpointing them and substituting them with alternative words, one can begin to rid the language (and society) of sexism. This idea – that negativity can be attached to certain words, prior to their use in specific contexts, is explicit in Lakoff's claim that words like 'mistress' and 'spinster' are always more derogatory than 'master' and 'bachelor'. The meaning of these words appears to be, at least temporarily, fixed, and there is no room for the simultaneous possibility that in certain contexts these same words may be invested with alternative, or even conflicting meanings. As I argued in Chapter 1, words frequently used as terms of abuse, such as 'dyke', 'poof' and 'queer', have, in some contexts, been 'reclaimed' by lesbians and gay men, and invested with alternative, non-derogatory meanings (Speer and Potter 2000, 2002).

Lakoff has also been criticized for implying that linguistic forms like tag questions have only one meaning – they are vehicles of women's uncertainty, insecurity, and linguistic deficiency. A number of researchers dispute whether tags work in uniform ways (Cameron 1992; Spender 1980). Spender, for example, argues that there is some debate surrounding what a tag question is, and how one might 'differentiate grammatically the "tentative" ones from the "forceful" ones, as in, for example, "You won't do that again *will you?*"' (1980: 9). Likewise, Goddard and Patterson (2000: 97) claim that 'tag questions are complex items that can convey a range of different meanings where much depends on how they are said and the relationship between the interlocutors'. It is not the linguistic form (e.g., a tag question) that is the problem, but the sexist context in which that form is used.

Spender also undermines her own claims to be sensitive to context in her use of the rather vague and abstract notion of the 'semantic rule', which she applies in a very restricted way. This rule holds that 'the same word has negative connotations when applied to women and positive connotations when applied to men' (1980: 29). This implies that the gender of the recipient *determines* the meaning of the word or linguistic form. It follows that if we know the recipient's gender, then we will be able to predict whether the word or form that is uttered will have positive or negative connotations. While the notion of the semantic rule was initially used by Spender in order to capture the role of patriarchy in language use, this term, and her approach in general, does not allow for the indexicality and local production of linguistic meanings *or* gender. Meanings are still fixed – but they are fixed differentially and dualistically, along lines of gender. It is hard, within such a framework, to envisage a context in which the same word will be classified positively when applied to both men and women, or for words to switch their meanings in different interactional environments.

While Spender criticizes Lakoff for treating tag questions as having uniform meanings, her own work on interruptions (which in turn derives from the early CA work of Zimmerman and West 1975) can be subject to the same criticism. Indeed, there now exists an extensive body of work within both sociolingusitics and CA, which problematizes what we mean by 'interruption' (cf. 'overlap), and which casts doubt on any approach that maps interactional strategies, such as interruption, onto a speaker's gender (see, for example, Drummond 1989; Goldberg 1990; Jefferson 1986; Schegloff 1987, 1991, 2001; Talbot 1992; Tannen 1990, 1994a). It is worth detailing some of the criticisms here, as the issues they raise are highly pertinent to the concerns of later chapters.

Spender treats interruptions as a linguistic correlate of male dominance. However, just as with research on tag questions, there is some debate about the operational criteria that have been used to identify interruptions, and about whether interruptions work in uniform ways – as signs of male dominance and control of the language. Critics like Tannen (1990, 1994a) argue that studies of interruption tend to be based on rather mechanical operational criteria. She illustrates this point by re-analysing some data taken from Zimmerman and West's study of interruptions (1975).

(2.3) [Tannen 1990: 191]
FEMALE: So uh you really can't bitch when you've got all those on the same day (4.2) but I uh asked my physics professor if I couldn't chan[ge that]
MALE: [Don't] touch that
(1.2)
FEMALE: What?
(pause)
MALE: I've got everything jus' how I want it in that notebook, you'll screw it up leafin' through it like that.

Tannen notes that researchers typically identify interruptions by searching transcripts of conversations for evidence of 'overlap' – places where more than one person speaks at a time. The overlapping talk in the above extract is indicated with square brackets. Zimmerman and West (1975) argue that this overlap provides an instance of interruption because the male speaker started his turn while the female speaker was in the middle of saying the word 'change'. However, for Tannen (1990: 192), interruption, unlike overlap, 'is not a mechanical category'. It is a far more loaded concept:

> Interruption is inescapably a matter of interpretation regarding individuals' rights and obligations. To determine whether a speaker is violating another speaker's rights, you have to know a lot about both speakers and the situation. For example, what are the speakers saying? How long has each one been talking? What has their past relationship been? How do they feel about being cut off? And, most important, what is the content of the second speaker's comment, relative to the first: is it a reinforcement, a contradiction, or a change in topic? In other words, what is the second speaker trying to *do*?
>
> (Tannen 1990: 190)

So an 'overlap – two voices talking at once' is not necessarily an interruption, in the sense that it violates another person's speaking rights (1990: 195). Likewise, one may feel interrupted and that 'one's rights have been violated . . . when there is no overlap' (1990: 192). Indeed, for Tannen (1990: 195), the claim that an interruption is an automatic sign of male dominance is based on the erroneous assumption that conversations usually consist of one person speaking at a time. However in practice, in regular conversations, we often hear more than one voice speaking at once, and engage in simultaneous speech. So, Tannen suggests that the example from Zimmerman and West (1975) is not an interruption, because the intervention of the man's 'Don't touch' 'is justified in terms of interactional rights' (Tannen 1990: 190). The first speaker's rights to talk were not violated because the second speaker was interrupting in order to prevent her from ruining the organization of his notebook. Thus, some researchers have argued that rather than being 'a hostile act, a kind of conversational bullying' (1990: 189), a means to gain control of a conversation, or an automatic sign of male dominance, interruptions may mark affiliation or alignment (James and Clarke 1993; Tannen 1990). In sum, for Tannen (1990: 195), 'it is not the interruption that constitutes dominance but what speakers are trying to do when they talk to each other'.

Tannen's critique of research that ignores the multifunctional and relativistic nature of linguistic strategies, is a prominent and well-regarded one. However, Tannen herself can be criticized for implying that 'intimacy', 'hierarchy', 'symmetry' and 'asymmetry' have identifiable linguistic correlates that determine male–female linguistic styles, which are, in turn, relatively fixed and unchanging. Just as with the notion of 'interruption', it is unclear how intimacy, symmetry and so on, should be operationalized, and whether, once operationalized, their linguistic correlates won't be found to do different things in different contexts. Even while Tannen has been, in her later, discursive work (2003), at pains to point out that the relation between hierarchy and solidarity, power and connection, consists of a 'multidimensional grid' (2003: 181) and that both are 'at play in every moment of interaction' (1999: 237), on the whole, she does not seem consistent or clear in her conceptualization of how social context mediates the role of gender in establishing the meaning of an act.

(iv) Analysts' claims are grounded in participants' practices?

One of the main problems the Lakoff, Spender and Tannen studies share is that they rely on methodological procedures, data and analytic techniques which actually serve to distort or caricature their subject matter. Such an approach inevitably gives primacy to the perspective of the analyst, over and above that of the participants', thus preventing an analytically tractable analysis of gender.

For example, the data Lakoff uses are gathered via rather artificial and haphazard means, through 'introspection' (i.e. by examining anecdotal examples from her own speech and the speech of her friends, acquaintances and colleagues) and from fictional data that she has heard in commercials and situation comedies (1973: 46). The majority of her extracts appear to be made up: hypothetical examples of what people 'might' say in a range of hypothetical situations. For example, she says 'imagine a man and a woman both looking at the same wall, painted a pinkish shade of purple. The woman may say . . . The wall is mauve' (1973: 49). In each case, Lakoff's analysis amounts to her hypotheses or predictions about hypothetical individuals' hypothetical assumptions or conclusions about the hypothetical sentences of hypothetical men and women! Lakoff's analysis is, in fact, not so much based on her own intuitions, as she claims, but on what she assumes others will intuit about 'men's language' and 'women's language'. Her 'data' and 'analyses' have undergone multiple degrees of abstraction. This is politically problematic because it simply relies on others' stereotyped *assumptions* about male–female speech, thereby reproducing sexist assumptions about gender (see also Cameron 1992: 70; Spender 1980: 34). Indeed, these data have essentially undergone a form of analysis twice. First, the data have been 'recollected' or 'scripted' by Lakoff, as an example of how 'real-life' talk works (analysis 1), and second, they have been subject to an analysis by Lakoff, and 'interpreted' for what they can tell us about how 'real-life' talk works (analysis 2). Thus, none of Lakoff's data can be relied upon to provide accurate or convincing empirical examples of everyday talk that can be subject to (and validated by) an independent reanalysis.

In principle, there is nothing wrong with using these kinds of data for analysing one's own remembered or hypothetical experience of the world, or for exploring the way fictional language is used in commercials and situation comedies. Indeed, while Bucholtz (2004: 123) commends Lakoff's use of an 'introspective methodology' and desire to 'locate herself so squarely within her text' as an example of feminist 'reflexivity', Livia (2003: 147) argues that the use of constructed dialogue or scripts, can 'allow us to see . . . what expectations speakers have of patterns of speech appropriate for each sex' (for contemporary examples of the use of fictional data, see Cameron 1998d; Hopper 2003). The use of such data becomes problematic, however, if one intends to treat anecdotal, hypothetical or fictional data as *an appropriate substitute for actual talk*, and as something which can reveal how that talk works. For example, anecdotal, reported utterances are largely 'second-hand', filtered through the less-than-perfect memory of one or more individuals, and then reconstructed by Lakoff on the page as examples of 'how talk gets done'. There is no way of knowing how accurate such recollections and reconstructions are, nor what details of talk – which may prove essential to the analysis – they miss out. Likewise, hypotheses about how talk works are, by their very nature, the author's preconceived 'imaginings' and assumptions about talk, which necessarily caricature what happens in practice. Interestingly, Lakoff justifies not using 'real-life' recordings by referring to the pragmatics of obtaining and accessing such data. She argues that:

> random conversation must go on for quite some time, and the recorder must be exceedingly lucky anyway, in order to produce

evidence of any particular hypothesis, e.g. that there is sexism in language. If we are to have a good sample of data to analyze, this will have to be elicited artificially from someone; I submit I am as good an artificial source of data as anyone.

(Lakoff 1973: 47)

It is useful to take a step back and consider the assumptions about sexism that underpin this claim. Lakoff seems to be suggesting that recordings of 'random conversation' are not a reliable source of data because one would have to wait a long time – perhaps too long – to produce a sizeable enough sample of sexist talk. This is a common view held by gender and language researchers, and it has two problematic assumptions built into it. First, it assumes that sexism occurs rarely in mundane talk. This assumption actually serves to undermine Lakoff's argument that there is sexism in language – or at least that there is enough of it to warrant our concern. Second, it assumes that sexism consists of something 'obvious' and readily identifiable to the analyst, and that, given a long enough transcript, we would be able to pick out a sample of 'sexist instances' from it. In other words, Lakoff believes she *already knows* what sexism in 'random conversation' looks like, and how to identify it, *before collecting and analysing any data or examples of it*. For her it consists of a limited set of sexist 'words' or 'linguistic forms'.

In a sense, then, Lakoff imposes her own, analyst's definition and assumptions about the linguistic correlates of sexism on her data. What this neglects, however, is that sexism may be both more prevalent and more subtle in its linguistic manifestations than her approach allows. As I began to argue in Chapter 1, it is entirely plausible, for example, that in 'sexist talk', sexist terms may not always be explicitly named or mentioned. However, since Lakoff does not include any examples of data of sexism *in action*, taken from real-life situations, she is unable to comment on the production and management of sexist descriptions and practices which do *not* 'index' sexist words or linguistic forms (Ochs 1992). Nor is she able to comment on what members themselves might *treat as* sexist in different interactional contexts, where what counts as sexism may be negotiable and 'up-for-grabs'. We can see here how the problem of decontextualizing language, and the failure to explore participants' orientations, reinforce and confound one another.

Spender's approach is rather more sophisticated than Lakoff's. Where the majority of Lakoff's data consist of anecdotal, hypothetical or fictional examples of talk, the majority of Spender's data consist of records of interactions drawn from real life. This data includes detailed transcripts of recordings of single and mixed-sex talk, obtained from a range of formal and informal gatherings – from feminist conferences, feminist research groups, private social gatherings, consciousness-raising groups, and seminars. Even while Spender, like Lakoff, does not give details of her analytic approach, or specify how she selected extracts or coded her data, these data do give us reason to have more confidence in her findings. Since Spender provides the reader with detailed examples of 'real' talk, it is much easier than it was with Lakoff to grasp how she analysed her data and arrived at her conclusions. The reader does not have to rely solely on the author's judgement or interpretation about how talk works, but can go back and assess the adequacy of the analytic claims against the transcripts. In other words, the analysis can be independently validated, and this lends credibility to Spender's findings.

Although Spender's approach allows us to get closer to the details of what is happening in talk, her data can also be problematized. For example, of the thirty-nine excerpts in the book, the majority consist of individual female speakers talking at length about how women are excluded or marginalized by language, how men dominate talk, how men do not listen, and what happens when they interrupt men. Thus, the overwhelming majority of Spender's excerpts consist of monologic accounts of women talking *about* talk, their experiences, or the talk and behaviour of others. This in itself needn't be a problem. Like Lakoff's analysis of anecdotes and fictional data, it is perfectly feasible to analyse such data for what it can tell us about how people *talk about* talk, experiences and behaviours. However, just as Lakoff's use of idealized data becomes problematic when she attempts to use it as an appropriate substitute for actual talk, likewise, Spender's use of participants' talk about talk and second-hand reports and reflections on how language works, becomes problematic when she attempts to treat them as first-hand, unreconstructed evidence for how talk works.

Of the three authors considered here, Tannen uses the widest variety of data. She illustrates her argument using a combination of anecdotal, fictional and real-life talk from a wide range of sources, including personal anecdotes and recollected conversations gathered from relatives, friends, students and colleagues, audio and videotaped adult dinner conversations (often with Tannen herself as a participant), conversations between young children, and scripted dramatic dialogue from novels and plays.

Intriguingly, even while Tannen had access to such a rich data corpus, the vast bulk of the data she uses in her book are based on anecdotal sources similar to those used by Lakoff some fifteen years earlier. The majority of these anecdotes are presented as descriptive summaries of particular incidents involving heterosexual couples. Others are set out as transcripts of recollected conversations. Both sets of data are subject to the same problems as they were with Lakoff. Tannen, like Lakoff, treats such data as an appropriate substitute for actual talk. Indeed, she does not comment on, or distinguish between, the different analytic possibilities associated with her anecdotal and fictional data on the one hand, and her more 'naturally occurring' audio and videotaped data on the other.

All three researchers adopt materials, procedures and analytic techniques which are driven by the analyst's assumptions and folklinguistic stereotypes about the talk of men and women. The risk is that the analyses will prioritize the analyst's own political agenda, and actually serve to overlook, distort or caricature their subject matter, and the concerns and orientations of the participants. Consequently, this leads us to doubt the validity of their analyses and findings, and takes us further away from, rather than closer to, detailed insights into the constitution of gender talk.

(v) A relativist approach?

A final problem with the studies considered here is that they each adopt a *realist* approach to their data. As we saw in Chapter 1, the realist treats language as a transparent window through which they can gain unmediated access to the objectively measurable reality that lies beyond or beneath the talk. From this perspective, talk reflects rather than constructs reality. This realist orientation is manifest partly in these researchers' cognitivist treatment of language (described earlier) in which a person's talk about thoughts and feelings, for example, is treated as a straightforward reflection of what they are thinking and feeling. An additional way in which realism is manifest in these studies, is in the way the authors treat participants' talk *about talk* (that is, their second-hand reports and descriptions of how talk works), or reflections on the act of talking, as having a literal, 'mapping' relationship with reality, and as an unproblematic source of evidence for how talk gets done.

It is possible to get a sense of this analytic realism by looking more closely at how Lakoff, Spender and Tannen treat their data. In Lakoff's study, when her participants report that a hypothetical sentence is part of women's language, then Lakoff treats this as evidence that it is indeed part of women's language. Likewise, when Spender's female participants report to her that that they are considered 'hostile . . . dominating and bitchy' (1980: 45) when they try to interrupt men, Spender treats this as evidence that women are indeed seen as 'rude and ungracious' if they try to interrupt men (1980: 45). Finally, although she does occasionally treat talk as something that is action oriented and constructive, Tannen nonetheless argues that 'the ways that women and men talk about events in their lives *reflect* and create their different worlds' (1990: 176, emphasis added). She asks a 16-year-old girl 'whether boys and girls both talk about problems' (1990: 53). She treats the girl's answer, 'Yes . . . they both do . . . The girls go on and on. The boys raise the issue, one of them comes up with a solution, and then they close the discussion', as providing support for her claims about asymmetries in troubles-telling.

This realist approach seems to serve an important function for these researchers, in that it allows them to tell a particular kind of story in which their own, politicised versions of the world are 'naturalized'. Interestingly, for example, Spender appears to apply an analytic double standard to her data (a criticism similar to the one she made about Lakoff's approach to tag questions), apparently shifting between realist and constructionist analyses. Thus, when she analyses women's talk about men, she treats what they say (about male dominance or the male control of women's meanings) from within a realist framework, as an *accurate* reflection of reality. However, when she analyses men's talk about women (e.g. men's claim that women talk too much, for example), she treats what they say as a fundamentally *inaccurate* reflection of reality. While this may be *politically* consistent within her framework, and allows her to bolster her claims about how male dominance at the macro-social level is reflected at the micro-interactional level, Spender must be analytically inconsistent in order to make her politics work.

Here again, Spender, like Lakoff and Tannen, does not so much analyse her data extracts in order to 'discover' something about gender talk, so much as use her data to support her pre-established theory about the male control of language. Spender's feminist ontology of the world means that she has *already decided* that men dominate talk, and her analysis consists of searching for, and using examples of talk which support that theory. It is as though the 'findings' come first, the 'data' are merely exemplars – gold plating on a pre-established theory, not a source of new insights.

Chapter summary

In this chapter, I have provided a focused overview and critique of three key studies associated with the sociolinguistic, sex differences framework. Sex differences research has had a significant impact on the field of language and gender research. The work considered in this chapter was among the first to take seriously the relationship between gender and language, and the role of language in the reproduction and maintenance of sexism. Nevertheless, sex differences research also suffers a number of problems when it comes to the empirical analysis of gender and language.

First, sex difference researchers adopt procedures and techniques which encourage an essentialist, 'variables and effects' model of language. They reify gender, reinforce gender dualism, and take us further away from, rather than closer to, insights into how gender and gender differences are constituted and reproduced in everyday life. Second, sex difference studies treat language as a resource for accessing facts about macro-social and cognitive-psychological realms, rather than as a topic. This results in a cognitivist treatment of discourse, in which people's talk *about* thoughts and feelings is treated as a literal expression *of* those thoughts and feelings. Third, these studies offer a decontextualized understanding of gender. They imply that gendered meanings reside in certain words and linguistic forms (e.g. tag questions) and adopt practices, procedures and categories which strip talk of its contextual subtleties, and which ignore the context-sensitivity of actual language use. Fourth, they adopt analytic procedures and techniques which serve to distort or caricature their subject matter. These techniques give primacy to the perspective of the analyst, over and above that of the participants, thus preventing an analytically tractable analysis of gender. Finally, they adopt a realist approach, in which they treat participants' *talk about talk*, or reflections on the act of talking, as having a literal 'mapping' relationship with reality, and as an unproblematic source of evidence for how talk gets done.

The problems I have identified in this chapter are by no means unique to the three studies described here, but are applicable to the vast proportion of work – both within and outside sociolinguistics – which is conducted using a sex differences framework today. If we continue to use such models, we will reproduce just the kind of stereotyped assumptions about gender upon which patriarchy and heteronormativity depend.

Gender difference can never be an adequate explanatory *end point* for our analyses, because it is a social construction that needs studying in and of itself (see also Cameron 1992: 61). Thus, in order to develop a politically productive approach which moves beyond an essentialist framework, we must 'bracket' or suspend our belief in the idea that gender is a dualistic category that exists prior to and outside talk, and explore the myriad ways in which gender, and gender difference, are constructed, oriented to and *used* in language. As we saw in Chapter 1, by viewing gender in this way, the focus shifts away from studies that correlate linguistic variables with demographic variables, and which chart the linguistic differences between women and men, toward a more detailed analysis of the ways in which people use discourse to naturalize or challenge specific understandings of gender. In Chapter 3 I will outline what this alternative, constructionist approach to *performing, doing* or *accomplishing* gender might look like.

3

GENDER AND IDENTITY
POSTSTRUCTURALIST AND ETHNOMETHODOLOGICAL PERSPECTIVES

In Chapter 2 I provided a focused overview and critique of three key studies within the sociolinguistic, 'sex differences' paradigm. I argued that even while work within this tradition has had a significant impact on the field of gender and language research, that sex difference perspectives nonetheless suffer a number of problems when it comes to the empirical analysis of gender and language – these problems centring primarily around their *essentialist* account of gender difference.

Although work of the type discussed in Chapter 2 continues apace today, in the 1990s many feminist psychologists and gender and language scholars influenced by postmodern thinking, began to challenge the binary thinking associated with sex differences research (see, for example, Bing and Bergvall 1998; Ferree et al. 1999; Hare-Mustin and Maracek 1994; Hollway 1994; Kitzinger 1994b). These researchers moved away from an essentialist framework that treats gender as a relatively fixed trait residing in the individual speaker, to a constructionist one, where gender is theorized as a complex and fluid social construct located in interaction. As I argued in Chapter 1, a constructionist approach entails asking questions about gender which do not automatically tie it to embodied or sexed selves (Bohan 1993; Cealey Harrison and Hood-Williams 2002; Crawford 1995; Harding 1998; Lorber 1994; Lorber and Farrell 1991). From a constructionist perspective, our gender identities are not ready made, nor are they ever perfect or complete. As the feminist philosopher Simone de Beauvoir (1952) once said, 'one is not born a woman, one becomes one'.

In this chapter, I contrast the essentialist, sex differences framework set out in Chapter 2, with an alternative, constructionist approach to *performing, doing* or *accomplishing* gender, as it is played out in the work of the poststructuralist feminist theorist, Judith Butler (1990a, 1993, 1997a) on the one hand, and the ethnomethodologists, Harold Garfinkel (1967) and Kessler and McKenna (1978), on the other. Although these two approaches derive from radically different theoretical traditions – Butler's work is rooted in French poststructuralism and Lacanian psychoanalysis, while ethnomethodology is 'distinctively sociological' (West and Zimmerman 1987: 126) – there is, nonetheless, much overlap between them in terms of their critique of previous theories of gender, and their approach to gender identity (see Maloney and Fenstermaker 2002: 192; Smith 2002: x). In addition, poststructuralism and ethnomethodology have had a significant impact on the development of the two discourse strands I identified in Chapter 1: the 'critical' discursive work informed by critical theory, poststructuralism and psychoanalysis on the one hand, and the discursive work informed by ethnomethodology and CA on the other. Thus, a close inspection of the theoretical and methodological assumptions underpinning poststructuralist and ethnomethodological studies of gender identity construction, will allow me to begin to flesh out some of the similarities and differences that underpin these two discourse strands, and the rather different feminist analyses of gender and language that derive from them. Just as I did in Chapter 2, I will evaluate work conducted from within both perspectives, in relation to the five criteria for an adequate feminist analytic approach set out in Chapter 1.

Poststructuralist approaches: the work of Judith Butler

Judith Butler is a remarkable social theorist who has had a profound impact on the development of feminist poststructuralism and on our understanding of the relationship between sex, gender and desire. Indeed, Butler's work represents a dense and complicated system of ideas, which, in part, reflects her ambitious combination of a variety of theoretical influences. However, it is also immensely challenging and illuminating. I cannot possibly capture the subtleties and complexities of Butler's arguments here. However, what I do want to do is to give the reader a flavour of her approach as it relates to two key themes relevant to the analysis of gender and discourse: her theory of performativity, and of hate speech.

Butler's theory of gender and performativity

Butler's most important ideas about gender are contained in her two books, *Gender Trouble* (1990a) and *Bodies that Matter* (1993). At the time she wrote these books, the majority of feminists understood the categories of 'sex' and 'gender' to be separate and distinct from one another. While 'sex' was typically used to refer to the biologically determined (male and female) aspects of a person, 'gender' was used to refer to the cultural and socially constructed (masculine and feminine) elements (Rubin 1975; Unger 1979). The sex/gender distinction was initially introduced in order to provide a counter to biological determinism – that is, the tendency on the part of many researchers to explain women's oppression exclusively in terms of their biology. The distinction was intended to focus attention instead on the social and cultural processes surrounding what it means to be a 'woman' or a 'man'. One of the unanticipated consequences of the sex/gender distinction, however, is that in practice, the terms 'sex' and 'gender' are regularly conflated and used interchangeably. Masculine and feminine gender are treated as reducible to, and derivative of, male and female sex – and as equally dichotomous.

Butler is famous for challenging the idea that sex and gender are ontologically distinct from one another. By this I mean that she did not conceive of sex and gender as having different 'realities' or as belonging to different 'realms' – a primary, independent, biological realm (sex) and a secondary, dependent, cultural realm (gender). Rather, in Butler's framework, *both* sex and gender are socially constructed:

> perhaps this construct called 'sex' is as culturally constructed as gender; indeed, perhaps it was already gender, with the consequence that the distinction between sex and gender turns out to be no distinction at all.
>
> (Butler 1990a: 7)

The idea that sex is just as constructed as gender was (indeed, still is) considered a radical view. If sex is socially constructed, it follows that the 'naturalness' of the male–female dualism that underpins all sex difference research, must itself be open to question. In addition, this idea has far-reaching consequences for theories of sex, gender *and* sexuality. For Butler, gender and sexuality are mutually reinforcing categories. The notion of 'heterosexuality', for example, depends for its existence on the idea that the world is naturally divided into two (and only two) sexes. If this belief is shown to be false, then heterosexuality is, like sex, exposed as a discursive production 'an effect of the sex/gender system which purports merely to describe it' (Jagose 1996: 84). Like the male–female dualism, the hetero/homo binary collapses.

So, if sex is not a biologically determined given, then how are sex and gender constructed – and what accounts for their appearance as naturally occurring givens? Drawing on a Foucauldian (1972: 49) definition of discourse as 'practices that systematically form the objects of which they speak', Butler (re)conceptualizes both gender and heterosexuality as a discursive practice. For Butler, gendered subjects are constituted in and by discourse – a discourse which precedes them historically.

In both *Gender Trouble* and *Bodies that Matter*, Butler elaborates on the discursive mechanisms through which gender is constituted. According to Butler, the process of becoming gendered – of becoming a man or a woman – is never complete. Instead, we must continuously accomplish the 'naturalness' of gender through a performative display of gendered characteristics. Thus, for Butler, gender is not a singular act or event, but is 'the stylised repetition of acts through time' (1990b: 271) and the coherence of gender is achieved through 'the repeated stylisation of the body . . . within a highly rigid regulatory frame that congeal over time to produce the appearance of substance, of a natural sort of being' (1990a: 33).

Butler points out that the concept of performance should not be understood in too literal or 'dramaturgical' a sense. For her, there is no 'authentic' gender, no original referent or core beneath the performance of gender. In this sense, then, gender does not exist independently of its expression. Nor are gendered performances always wilful, deliberate, or freely chosen. It is not about 'trying on' or 'choosing' whatever gender one wants to be on a particular day (Jagose 1996: 87). Rather, gender is 'a performative accomplishment compelled by social sanction and taboo' (Butler 1990b: 271). Performative agency (the degree to which one can act volitionally) is both constrained and enabled through repetition, or the 'iterability' of signs.

The notion of 'iterability'

Iterability is a rather complex notion. Developed initially by the French philosopher, Jacques Derrida (1976), Butler uses it to highlight the importance of pre-existing discourse in the construction of gender. Broadly speaking, the notion of iterability captures the idea that discourse (talk – and especially writing) is not original but has a 'used again' or citational quality. As we speak, we use words and phrases that have been used repeatedly before. So, meaning is not created anew each time we speak about or 'do' gender. Rather, 'speakers "channel" previous speakers, as texts make intertextual reference to preceding texts' (Livia and Hall 1997a: 8). To illustrate this process, Livia and Hall use the example of the midwife's statement 'it's a girl', which they say 'is a performative that works through this power of citation' (Livia and Hall 1997a: 11). In Butler's (1993: 232) terms, such a statement 'initiates the process by which a certain girling is compelled'.

With the notion of iterability we can begin to see an implicit notion of social structure and causation in Butler's work. Since discourse is not original, it will always escape the complete control of the intentional, speaking subject. Discourses shape gendered subjects and place limits on what can be said and by whom. Indeed, statements of gender like 'it's a girl' do not just describe a state of affairs. They are also prescriptive: they bring into play a whole host of pre-existing and normative ideas about what a girl is and how a girl should behave, thus requiring the recipient to act in gender normative ways. Thus a performative 'accumulates the force of authority through the repetition or citation of a prior and authoritative set of practices' (Butler 1995: 205).

Such a framework may, like some of the work discussed in Chapter 2, sound rather determinist. The speaker appears to have no agency – no room to challenge, resist or transform the discourses which created them, and within which they are embedded. However, Butler is keen to point out the citational nature of the utterance, and the discursive practices that produce gendered subjects, do not just constrain an individual's behaviour. For Butler 'speech is finally constrained neither by its specific speaker not its originating context' (1997a: 40). Instead, the repetition that is central to the construction and maintenance of gender is always 'repetition with a difference' (Lloyd 1999: 200). It is inevitable that each subsequent citation will diverge slightly from the previous one, and it is this which makes 'gender transformation' and 'critical agency' possible (1999: 200–1). What Butler (see Bell 1999: 164) stresses, then, is that the constitution of subjects 'in and by discourse' is not a 'unilateral' or 'unnuanced' process (as Butler argues Foucault's rather mechanistic and one-sided account of subject constitution seems to imply). Rather, an agent is only partially constituted, or constituted in ways that are tenuous, vulnerable, and subject to failure (for more on Butler's understanding of performativity, agency, and social structure, see her dialogue with Benhabib et al. 1995). Having established this, the issue for Butler becomes one of grasping precisely how it is that 'a subject who is constituted in and by discourse' is able to 'recite' the same discourse to another purpose, to 'resignify' it and give it new meaning (Bell 1999: 165). In other words, Butler is concerned to identify the juncture at which resistance and the resignification of gendered meaning is possible.

In order to provide an approach which can explicate the processes through which resistance and the resignification of meaning may come about, Butler turns to psychoanalysis. By combining the notion of iterability with a theory of the 'psyche', the internalization of norms and 'psychic excess' (Bell 1999: 164; Butler 1997b), Butler works to produce an account of discourse and gendered subject formation that captures a sense of both structure and agency, constraint and creativity. For Butler, resistance is treated as the outcome of agentive psychic and social processes made possible through the internalization and displacement of constraining social norms. She notes 'the psyche, which includes the unconscious . . . is precisely what exceeds the imprisoning effects of the discursive demand to inhabit a coherent identity to become a coherent subject' (Butler 1997b: 86). In other words, the unconscious works as a 'destabilizing force' (McNay 1999: 175, 184), enabling agency and resistance.

Butler argues that subjects can resignify normative gender models and contest the naturalization of heterosexuality by staging gender in a way that exposes its discursive as opposed to its essential character. Although she does not want it to be taken as a paradigmatic example of subversion (Butler 1999: xxii), one strategy of resistance advocated by Butler is the 'parodic repetition of gender norms' through Drag. Drag imitates gender, and in so doing, 'implicitly reveals the imitative structure of gender itself – as well as its contingency' (Butler 1990a: 137). Importantly, for Butler (1990a: 138), Drag is not an imitation of some *original*, but a parody of the whole notion of an original – a parody of a parody.

Butler's theory of 'hate speech'

Butler's concern to theorize both structure and agency, but at the level of the utterance, is taken forward in her more recent work on 'hate speech', in her book *Excitable Speech* (1997a). Hate speech is a concept that developed primarily in the US context. Initially used to refer to 'any form of expression deemed offensive to any racial, religious, ethnic, or national group', it has, more recently, been widened in some US campus speech codes, to include gender and sexual preference (Walker 1994: 8; see also Fish 1994). Although there have been recent proposals to regulate against hate speech on US campuses and in the workplace, hate speech is more firmly protected constitutionally under the US First Amendment (which allows 'freedom of speech'), than it is elsewhere in the world.

Butler, like many others, is sceptical of a law in which hateful speech (which is deemed to be distinct from 'action') is protected. Although hate speech is typically thought to refer to explicitly uttered verbal expressions of hatred toward minority groups (the insulting use of the words 'queer', 'dyke' and 'faggot', for example), what counts as hate speech is by no means straightforward. As Butler (1997a: 2) argues, it is not just the words but also the mode of address that may result in 'linguistic injury'. For Butler, the problem of defining hate speech is particularly acute in legal contexts, where it is a political and moral matter. Indeed, part of her concern in *Excitable Speech* is to consider the consequences of legal definitions of speech as action, and to determine what is at issue for legal practitioners in particular cases. For example, one way in which an instance of hate speech may be legislated against, is to prove that it was not speech at all, but an action which incites violence or is harmful. However, part of the difficulty for courts and jurors in the US context is in deciding what counts as 'just' speech, and what counts as an action. Therefore, Butler argues that any legislation based on attempts to separate speech from its effects is inherently problematic.

Butler (1997a: 2) deals with important issues around context and the discursive construction of meaning when she considers what it means to be 'wounded' by language, and how we might identify 'which words wound, which representations offend'. She argues that the power to wound – to cause linguistic injury or offence – is not located in, or determined by the words themselves. Instead, according to Butler, which words wound will depend on the context or manner in which those words are deployed.

However, she notes that one cannot change a word's meaning simply by manipulating the context: it does not follow that any word can wound given its appropriate deployment. Moreover, some words seem to have a greater power to wound than others. Indeed, for Butler, it is the *failure* of certain words to wound which can help us to understand how we can change a word's meaning and use it in a critical way.

Just as she had used the notion of iterability to understand how gender can be resisted and 'resignified', in *Excitable Speech*, Butler (1997a: 13) uses the notion of iterability to explore 'how the offensive utterance can be restaged'. She asks, how do we exploit the 'ritual' or 'iterable' function of speech 'in order to undermine it . . . what would it mean to restage it, take it, do something else with the ritual so that its revivability as a speech act is really seriously called into question' (Bell 1999: 166). Central to this endeavour is Butler's critique of the linguistic philosopher, John Austin's (1962) notion of the illocutionary speech act. Austin had a tendency to treat the meaning of an utterance as bound up with the speech act and its grammatical organization. Instead, following Derrida (1976), Butler argues that the iterable, open nature of the utterance means that meaning is not fixed but fluid. With each successive use, words take on a slightly different meaning, and come to be resignified. The very possibility of resignification undercuts the conflation of speech with its effect – the idea that the same word(s) will always produce the same outcome (McNay 1999: 178). It is this fluidity which, Butler suggests, makes it possible to theorize 'how words might, through time, become disjoined from their power to injure and recontextualized in more affirmative modes' (Butler 1997a: 15). Terms such as 'queer', for example, 'can be reclaimed, or "returned" to the speaker in a different form', used to produce different, positive, or politically consequential effects (1997a: 14).

Butler argues that the theory of speech acts has some important legal and political consequences. Since no speech act (including violent and oppressive forms of hate speech) *necessarily* produces injury, then no simplistic conceptualization of the speech act will produce a legalistic yardstick against which 'the injuries of speech might be effectively adjudicated' (1997a: 15). According to Butler, it is this gap between speech and its effect – the idea that a word's meaning is iterable, resignifiable, and therefore at least partially shaped by its context of use – which allows for a theory of linguistic agency, and which offers an alternative to the unrelenting search for legal remedy.

Summary and discussion of Butler

Widely regarded as 'revolutionary' (Cealey Harrison and Hood-Williams 2002: 191), Butler's work has had a profound impact on feminism, and on our understanding of the role of discourse in the construction of gender and prejudice. Indeed, there is much in Butler's work that resonates with the concerns of gender and language researchers. Although Butler does not talk about language using in this way, as Cameron (1997b: 29) suggests, 'it is easy to see how speech in particular might be analysed as a "repeated stylization of the body"'. Indeed, a number of feminist researchers have sought to apply Butler's poststructuralist model of discourse and her theory of performativity, in their own empirical investigations of the relationship between gender, sexuality and language (see, for example, Cameron 1997a; Coates 1996, 1997, 1999; Bucholtz et al. 1999; Livia and Hall 1997b; Speer and Potter 2002). What is striking however, as McIlvenny (2002c: 9) contends, is how 'more often than not the work of Butler and other queer theorists has had only a superficial influence on language and gender studies'. According to McIlvenny (2002c: 29), the turn to performativity in much contemporary feminist thought, has 'missed an opportunity to ground its theorising in an . . . empirical account of conversational practice and action'. This is an important point, and one I will go on to elaborate later in this chapter. For the moment I want to note that it is extremely difficult to apply Butler's theory of gender performativity and hate speech to an analysis of discourse, because its remains largely abstract in its focus, and bereft of just the kinds of examples of members' practices and actions that would enable us to translate her theory into a discourse analytic programme. We can find a more viable model for the study of the interactional constitution of gender, in a body of work overlooked by Butler, that developed within ethnomethodology, some twenty years earlier.

Ethnomethodological approaches

Garfinkel's study of an intersexed person called Agnes

One of the earliest studies to shed light on the situated accomplishment of gender, was conducted by the ethnomethodologist, Harold Garfinkel (1967). Ethnomethodology, as I noted in Chapter 1, takes as its topic for study 'members' methods' for producing their everyday affairs. According to Garfinkel, members' methods consist of the routinized, taken-for-granted procedures individuals employ as they go about their everyday lives and tasks.

It is precisely because such methods are routinized and taken-for-granted that Garfinkel refers to them as '"seen but unnoticed" backgrounds of [our] everyday affairs' (1967: 118). For Garfinkel, gender (what he called 'sex status') is one such 'invariant but unnoticed' (1967: 118) background in everyday life. It is omnirelevant, and yet its organization is something that, for most individuals who can take their sex status for granted, remains hidden. What interested Garfinkel was that for some members, such as intersexed persons ('individuals born with anatomy or physiology which differs from contemporary ideals of what constitutes "normal" male and female': The UK Intersex Association: http://www.ukia.co.uk), this is not the case. Far from being able to take their sex status for granted, intersexed persons are engaged in the constant 'work of achieving and making secure their rights to live in their elected sex status' (1967: 118). For them, the work of passing as a 'normal' or 'natural' male or female is an 'enduring practical task' (1967: 118), which requires constant work and 'active deliberate management' (1967: 139) on their part. Garfinkel believed that by studying their situation, the ethnomethodologist can uncover what culture makes invisible – 'the accomplishment of gender' (West and Zimmerman 1991: 18).

Introducing Agnes

The specific case Garfinkel researched was that of a pre-operative intersexed person called Agnes. Agnes presented as a 19-year-old woman who had fully developed breasts and normal appearing male genitalia (1967: 117). She had a male chromatin pattern, 'moderately high' female hormone activity, but no uterus or ovaries. Born, raised and recognized as a boy, she developed 'secondary feminine sex characteristics' at puberty. At the age of 17 she assumed a female identity, several years prior to undergoing sex reassignment surgery. She also had a male partner, to whom she eventually disclosed her condition. Before she could undergo surgery, Agnes was referred to the Department of Psychiatry at the Medical Centre of the University of California, Los Angeles (UCLA). It was there, in October 1958, where she met with Garfinkel, a psychiatrist called Robert Stoller, and the psychologist, Alexander Rosen. In March 1959 Agnes underwent 'a castration operation' at UCLA in which the penis and scrotum were removed and a vagina and labia constructed in their place (1967: 121). Both prior to and after surgery, a concern for Agnes if she was to 'escape detection' – and avoid the 'status degradation' (1967: 117–18) that may result from the incongruity of her situation – was to pass convincingly as a 'normal', 'natural' female. Agnes became preoccupied with competent female sexuality, and passing became her chief priority.

In order to pass as a 'real' woman, Agnes had to produce patterns of behaviour that would be seen as normative female behaviour. She had to acquire certain skills and competencies, and display feminine feelings and appearances. Garfinkel argues that Agnes learnt how to 'act like a lady' by becoming a 'secret apprentice', learning from her friends, her partner, Bill, and his mother. It was on the basis of his study of Agnes's more and less successful experiences of passing that Garfinkel was able to produce a preliminary description of those features that make up our 'natural attitude' toward 'normally sexed persons' (1967: 122).

The 'natural attitude' toward 'normally sexed persons'

This consists of the belief among adult members of society that:

(1) Society is populated by two and only two sexes.
(2) The dichotomy of sex is morally legitimate.
(3) Everyone counts themselves as a member of one sex or the other.
(4) All members are invariantly (i.e., 'always have been, and always will be') either male or female.
(5) The essential identifying 'insignia' for males is the possession of a penis and for females a vagina.
(6) People will not wilfully or randomly transfer from one sex status to another.
(7) In the case of 'ambiguous' individuals whose sex status is not immediately obvious, it should still be possible, in principle, to classify them as either male or female (Garfinkel 1967: 122–8).

One of the paradoxes of Agnes's situation was that even while she (and others like her) did, by virtue of her ambiguous status, challenge the natural attitude, she too subscribed to these beliefs, and treated dichotomous gender as a 'moral fact' (1967: 122). Indeed, it was through her acts of passing that she strove to produce a sense of the objective existence of those facts, and reinforced and reproduced the natural attitude. For example, Agnes strongly insisted that she was to be treated as, and had always been, a 'natural, normal female' (1967: 122), that her status as female was 'ascribed' rather than 'achieved', and that the changes she elected to undergo as part of her surgery were simply to rectify 'nature's original mistake' (1967: 181). Thus, the surgery was the fulfilment of a life-long desire to become what she has always been.

Garfinkel's conclusions

Garfinkel argued that Agnes's practices demonstrate '*that* and *how* normal sexuality is accomplished through witnessable displays of talk and conduct' (1967: 180, emphasis in original). Indeed, Agnes learnt how to be a woman by studying behaviour and becoming highly attuned to, and aware of, conventions and expectations around gender, and the habitual but typically unnoticed workings of social structures. In this sense, Agnes had become a 'practical methodologist' (1967: 180), applying her findings to her own actions:

Her studies armed her with knowledge of how the organized features of ordinary settings are used by members as procedures for making appearances-of-sexuality-as-usual decidable as a matter of course. The scrutiny that she paid to appearances; . . . her sensitivity to devices of talk; her skill in detecting and managing 'tests' were attained as part of her mastery of trivial but necessary social tasks, to secure ordinary rights to live. Agnes was self-consciously equipped to teach normals how normals make sexuality happen in commonplace settings as an obvious, familiar, recognizable, natural, and serious matter of fact.

(Garfinkel 1967: 180)

Agnes's methodological practices led Garfinkel to conclude that 'normally sexed persons are cultural events' and that members' practices 'produce the observable-tellable normal sexuality of persons' (Garfinkel 1967: 181). It was on the basis of his study of Agnes that Garfinkel was able to demonstrate precisely how it is that 'over the temporal course of their actual engagements, and "knowing" the society only from within, members produce stable, accountable practical activities, *i.e.*, social structures of everyday activities' (1967: 185).

Summary and discussion of Garfinkel

In the appendix to the chapter in which the Agnes study was reported, Garfinkel reveals that eight years after the research took place, Agnes admitted that she had lied to the research team, and that the feminization of her body was not due to the intersex condition known as 'testicular feminization syndrome', but rather to her having ingested female hormones that were originally prescribed for her mother. Thus, Agnes was not an intersexed person at all, but a male-to-female transsexual (transsexualism is formally designated in DSM-IV (American Psychiatric Association 1994) as a 'Gender Identity Disorder', in which persons exhibit 'a strong and persistent cross-gender identification and a persistent discomfort with their sex or a sense of inappropriateness in the gender role of that sex': The Harry Benjamin International Gender Dysphoria Association 2001). Although there is some debate about the extent to which this revelation invalidates Garfinkel's findings (see Armitage 2001), the Agnes study has, nonetheless, been described as 'a groundbreaking work in sociology' (Bologh 1992: 199) and 'a profound analysis' (Heritage 1984: 181), which 'affords an unusually clear vision' of the workings of the social construction of gender (Zimmerman 1992: 197). Indeed, Garfinkel's analysis of 'the accomplished character' of what, at the time he wrote, was 'taken as a biologically given, ascribed by birth "sexual nature"' (Zimmerman 1992: 197), was path breaking, and has clear resonances with Butler's later, 'radical' work on the social construction of sex.

The lasting importance of the Agnes study is evidenced in the debates and discussions that took place more than two decades after its publication; see the exchange in *Gender and Society* between Bologh (1992), Rogers (1992a, 1992b) and Zimmerman (1992), and in *Sociological Theory* between Denzin (1990, 1991), Hilbert (1991), Lynch and Bogen (1991) and Maynard (1991). Part of this debate involves a wide-ranging feminist critique. Rogers (1992b), for example, argues that although the Agnes study furthers our understanding of how gender is accomplished, that Garfinkel can, nonetheless, be accused of 'androcentrism' and of 'methodological blind spots' (Rogers 1992b: 169, 170). First, Agnes lacked power in the research process and was manipulated by the all-male research team. Indeed, Agnes agreed to take part in the research in the hope that by doing so she would be granted surgery. Second, the text relies on and reproduces sexist stereotypes (1992b: 185) and commonsense understandings about the 'priorities and competences' of young (heterosexual) men and women (1992b: 180). Moreover, there is a voyeuristic feel to the text, in which Garfinkel repeatedly mentions Agnes's shapeliness, physical attractiveness and measurements. Rogers suggests that this reinforces the 'objectification of women as sexual objects' (1992b: 182). Finally, Rogers deems the study to be insufficiently radical. Garfinkel fails to acknowledge how he and his collaborators, in passing as men and as scientists, played a role in Agnes's passing as a woman. Thus, Garfinkel's own 'background expectancies' about gender were not only his topic, but also influenced and shaped the research situation and his own masculine, 'interpretive stance' (Rogers 1992b: 176). For Rogers, this means that Garfinkel fails in 'the ethnomethodological bracketing of commonsense understandings', and thus reproduces the 'orthodox sociology' that ethnomethodologists typically reject (1992b: 182). For feminists such as Rogers, ethnomethodology as it is applied in the Agnes study, is insufficiently reflexive to realize its radical potential.

Nonetheless, the publication of the Agnes study preceded the feminist revolution in the social sciences, and in this sense, it is hardly surprising that it 'bears the imprint of its age' (Rogers 1992b: 169). Certainly, Garfinkel is not a feminist, and the study was not written for or disseminated widely among a feminist audience. It is partly for these reasons that ethnomethodology initially remained obscure and marginal to the majority of feminists (though see Smith 1978; Stanley and Wise 1993). In fact, it was not until some eleven years later, with the publication of Kessler and McKenna's book *Gender: An Ethnomethodological Approach* (1978), that Garfinkel's ideas about the social construction of sex were taken up and applied for a feminist audience.

Kessler and McKenna's 'Gender: An Ethnomethodological Approach'

Kessler and McKenna develop and extend the ethnomethodological perspective exemplified in Garfinkel's study, in their detailed analysis of the *gender attribution process*. The gender attribution process describes the methodical procedures through which members come to identify others as unambiguously male or female. Like Garfinkel, Kessler and McKenna were not satisfied to accept the 'natural facts' or the 'just so story' of sex. Adopting the phenomenological technique of 'bracketing' – which involves temporarily suspending one's belief in the natural attitude, and the idea of the timeless and autonomous existence of objects (in this case, a world of two sexes) – Kessler and Mckenna chose to explore instead the ethnomethodological question of how it is that 'members of a group produce, in each particular situation, the sense of external, constant, objective facts which have their own independent existences, not contingent on any concrete interaction?' (1978: 5).

By exploring how members 'do' gender attributions, Kessler and McKenna hoped to find out how it is that in each instance of interaction, we produce the sense of dichotomous gender as an objective fact. They ask, 'what kinds of rules do we apply to what kinds of displays, such that in every concrete instance we produce a sense that there are *only* men and women' (1978: 5–6). Not satisfied to explore ordinary members' procedures for attributing gender, Kessler and McKenna set about demonstrating how gender is attributed in science and in everyday life, with a view to demonstrating how the former process (that is, the way gender gets attributed in 'scientific' contexts – for example, when gender is assigned at birth) is based in the latter, everyday gender attribution process.

Transsexualism and the gender attribution process

Kessler and McKenna argue that while the dichotomous nature of the gender attribution process is typically hidden, it comes to the fore in situations where members attempt to assign gender to 'ambiguous' individuals, or to make sense of seemingly contradictory 'gender cues'. Thus, following Garfinkel, they set about exploring what transsexualism can tell us about the gender attribution process, and about the everyday construction of gender by all members.

They explored four features of transsexuals' self-presentation which contributed to their being seen as members of the 'correct' gender: talk, physical appearance, the body and the personal past. While Kessler and McKenna shared Garfinkel's view that gender is omnirelevant in interaction and that 'gender "work" is required' (1978: 136), unlike Garfinkel, they did not believe that most of the work was needed by the person displaying gender. Instead, they believed that the majority of the work required was 'done for the displayer by the perceiver' (1978: 136) and that a gender attribution is the result of interaction between both parties. Thus, they note that although displayers create the first gender attribution, primarily through means of talk and physical appearance, once an attribution has been made, the perceiver's role is central to its maintenance (1978: 136–7).

The centrality of the perceiver's role is demonstrated persuasively in Kessler and Mckenna's 'ten question gender game'. This game was designed to resemble a form of Garfinkel's 'documentary method' of interpretation, which describes the procedure through which members come to assemble evidence, search for patterns and assign meaning, even when faced with incomplete or contradictory evidence. During the game an experimenter asks a respondent to identify the gender of a hypothetical person. The respondent is allowed to ask up to ten questions about the person which can be answered with 'yes' or 'no' (they are not allowed to ask 'are you male/female'?). At the end of the game they are asked to state their 'final decision on the person's gender' (1978: 142). What they do not know is that the experimenter is answering 'with a prearranged, random series of "yes's" and "no's"' (1978: 142).

Kessler and McKenna's conclusions

What Kessler and McKenna found was that once gender had been assigned, almost anything that person did would be seen as consistent with that gender attribution. Irregular details (e.g. a male-sounding voice) would be understood with reference to the original attribution and used to substantiate it (e.g., 'It is a husky-voiced female': 1978: 128). When faced with contradictory evidence, members would do anything to make sense of it, except, that is, to acknowledge that the person might be ambiguously gendered. It is in this way that members make sense out of inconsistencies, construct gender to be invariant, and reproduce a natural attitude which denotes a world of two, and only two, genders.

In a statement that echoes Garfinkel's conclusions about the relationship between gender, social structure, and members' practices, Kessler and McKenna describe the gender attribution process as 'simultaneously an *ahistorical* and an *historical* process'. It is *ahistorical* in the sense that gender attributions are made in particular interactional contexts. It is *historical* in the sense that once gender has been assigned, then it is no longer essential that one keeps 'doing male' or 'doing female' (1978: 159).

Summary and discussion of Kessler and McKenna

Kessler and McKenna's book has reached a much wider feminist audience than Garfinkel's study of Agnes. In a reappraisal of their work in the journal *Feminism and Psychology* (Crawford 2000b), it is described as 'an extraordinary book, a prescient work' (Denny 2000: 63), which provides a 'bold assault on the sanctity of the two-gender model' (Tiefer 2000: 36). Indeed, in many ways Kessler and McKenna offer a more reflexive approach than Garfinkel, which shows how *science* itself (including feminism) relies on the everyday gender attribution process. The radical potential of this argument is that our existing ways of organizing the world along lines of a gender dichotomy, is not inevitable, and may be otherwise. This approach, then, suggests grounded possibilities for change.

Kessler and McKenna's vision of the social construction of gender was taken up later by West and Zimmerman (1987) in the first explicit formulation of 'doing gender'. Drawing on insights from Goffman (1977, 1979), Garfinkel (1967) and Kessler and McKenna (1978), West and Zimmerman (1991: 13) develop 'an ethnomethodologically informed . . . understanding of gender as a routine, methodical, and recurring accomplishment'. Avoiding the essentializing tendencies associated with their earlier CA work (referred to in Chapters 1 and 2), which treats gender as an independent variable that can be correlated with linguistic practices such as interruption and unilateral topic shifts, in this study, West and Zimmerman (1991: 14) treat gender as 'an emergent feature of social situations'. They clearly note that 'gender is not a set of traits, nor a variable, nor a role'. Instead 'the "doing" of gender . . . involves a complex of socially guided perceptual, interactional, and micropolitical activities that cast particular pursuits as expressions of masculine and feminine "natures"' (1991: 13–14).

Although, as I will show below, there is a fraught relationship between ethnomethodology and some later empirical applications of it, ethnomethodological work by Garfinkel and by Kessler and McKenna, has proven to be better suited than the largely abstract, poststructuralist work of Butler, for an empirical analysis of how members construct and reconstruct gender in everyday life. For example, West, Fenstermaker and colleagues have gone on to produce a highly successful body of work that draws on ethnomethodology, membership categorization analysis and CA, to develop their theory of doing gender to specify how a range of social categories, including race and class, are accomplished in ways that reproduce inequality (for an overview of this work see Fenstermaker and West 2002).

Poststructuralist and ethnomethodological perspectives: a focused evaluation and critique

So far I have described three classic studies of gender identity, and some of the ways in which they have been taken up or criticized by feminist researchers. What I want to do in the remainder of this chapter is to evaluate these studies in relation to the five criteria for an adequate feminist analytic approach set out in Chapter 1. In doing so, I hope to tease out some of the similarities and differences that underpin poststructuralist and ethnomethodological approaches to gender identity construction, and the rather different feminist analyses of gender and language that they have inspired.

(i) *A constructionist approach?*

Butler's theory of the performative constitution of gender is widely credited for challenging essentialist understandings of gender, and for placing *constructionist* ideas about gender firmly on the feminist agenda (Alsop et al. 2002). What we see in Butler is a very clear move away from the 'variables and effects' model of gender discussed in Chapter 2. Criticizing any approach that 'understands gender as an *attribute* of a person who is characterized essentially as a pregendered substance or "core"' (Butler 1990a: 10), for Butler, 'gender is not a noun' or 'a set of free-floating attributes' (1990a: 25). Gender, like sex, does not have a natural biological basis or essence. It does not exist prior to and outside of discourse, and does not determine a person's actions. Instead, gender is a complex and fluid social construct that can, in principle, exist in multiple forms and transcend sexed boundaries.

In common with much constructionist thinking, Butler regards gender as a performance rather than as an essence, 'a practice rather than a category, an actively constructed performance rather than a pre-existing role' (Bucholtz 1999a: 7; see also Bucholtz et al. 1999; Hall and Bucholtz 1995). Since Butler conceives of gender as something that is performatively *achieved*, rather than ascribed, her work represents an implicit challenge to all 'sex differences' research that incorporates procedures based on an assumed gender dualism. Indeed, since Butler does not *start* with the assumption that men and women belong to fundamentally different groups, she does not produce circular arguments which explain gender difference in terms of gender difference. Her work also overcomes the implicit determinism associated with essentialism. Within Butler's framework we are not powerless automata condemned to rehearse the social and linguistic roles we were assigned at birth, but can resist and throw off the shackles of constraint, and in doing so, create new configurations of gender.

Finally, Butler does not reify gender, but provides a framework for the 'radical denaturalisation' of gender and heterosexuality (Jagose 1996: 125), drawing attention to the processes through which they are constituted and made to appear stable and natural. The idea that gender is not naturally dichotomous, that it is a process rather than a thing, has some far-reaching implications for feminism. For example, one consequence of

Butler's 'non-reified' theory of gender, is that she undermines the very categories around which feminists have traditionally mobilized. For Butler, if the category of 'woman' is a boundariless, disembodied construction, then it makes little sense to ground a politics of liberation around it. 'Woman', like 'gender', is a regulatory, cultural fiction, rather than a 'natural basis for solidarity' (Jagose 1996: 84). More than this, feminists who use the 'woman' category risk reinforcing those normative relations that work to legitimize heterosexuality (1996: 83–4). This poststructuralist approach is often called 'queer theory', precisely because it involves a persistent questioning and radical reworking of identity politics and the very categories upon which our politics rest (though see Butler 1994).

Although it is clear that there are elements of Butler's work which resonate with a constructionist agenda, to treat ethnomethodology as straightforwardly constructionist, is riddled with problems. Indeed, there is considerable debate surrounding whether ethnomethodology can be described as 'constructionist' in its focus. Some ethnomethodologists are adamant that ethnomethodology is *not* constructionist – it is, if anything, a-constructionist (Wowk forthcoming). Thus, Wowk (forthcoming) criticizes Celia Kitzinger's (2000a, 2002) appropriation of ethnomethodology for a constructionist, feminist CA, asserting that ethnomethodology 'rejects the term "social constructionist" as a relativising term' (Wowk forthcoming). According to Wowk, 'the notion of construction for Garfinkel has overtones of emphasis on *mere fabrication*' (emphasis in original), as though 'the sexuality of persons were simply a matter of "negotiated interaction"' (Garfinkel and Wiley 1980: 12, cited in Wowk forthcoming). So, for Wowk, although gender may be a production, or an achievement, 'the objective facticity which is attributed to gender is, as Garfinkel emphasises, a massively *obstinate moral fact*' (Wowk forthcoming; see also Watson 1994, for a comparison of ethnomethodological and constructionist accounts of a Canadian judiciary's judgement).

Notwithstanding these arguments, many feminists and ethnomethodologists *do* treat ethnomethodological claims about sex and gender as constructionist. As Zimmerman notes, 'one of the most notable features of Garfinkel's research was his demonstration of the specifically *social* reality of gender and, in that sense, *its socially "constructed" nature*' (1992: 197, latter emphasis added). Moreover, Bologh argues that the Agnes study 'represented a groundbreaking work in sociology with respect to *the social construction of gender*' (Bologh 1992: 199, emphasis added).

Like Butler, Garfinkel and Kessler and McKenna conceive of gender as an activity rather than an attribute – a belief system rather than a fact. Gender is not 'a property of individuals' but 'an emergent feature of social situations' (West et al. 1997: 136). As Kessler and McKenna explicitly state, '*gender is a social construction* . . . a world of two "sexes" is a result of the socially shared, taken-for-granted methods which members use to construct reality' (1978: vii, emphasis added). For the ethnomethodologist, then, gender is an accomplishment which (like the objective world itself) is given its 'sense of objectivity and reality through the course of social interaction' (Kessler and McKenna 1978: vii). By conceiving of gender in this way, ethnomethodologists also overcome the more serious 'essentializing' tendencies associated with the sex difference theorists' variables and effects model of gender considered in Chapter 2.

According to Garfinkel and Kessler and McKenna, 'sex difference' researchers have been asking the wrong questions. In asking 'how are girls different from boys?', they overlook the fact that in order to ask the question, they have already decided what boys and girls are (Kessler and McKenna 1978: ix). As Kulick (1999, cited in Stokoe 2004) puts it, these researchers 'start out "knowing" the identities whose very constitution ought to be precisely the issue under investigation'. Instead, Kessler and McKenna propose 'a paradigm change in the way gender is viewed' and 'a new focus for research' (1978: 163). Rather than assuming the prior and invariant status of everyday categories such as gender, and 'concentrating on the *results* of seeing someone as female or male' (1978: 163, emphasis in original), they suggest instead that researchers should examine how familiar categories such as gender come to be presented as invariant, independent variables, or natural, 'irreducible fact[s]' in the first place (1978: ix). Ethnomethodologists thus propose a radical shift in our focus of analysis, whereby gender itself becomes the *topic* of research. In his commentary on the Agnes study, the conversation analyst, John Heritage, provides a neat summary of this shift:

> In studies of gender, it has been traditional to treat the conventional categories 'male' and 'female' as starting points from which to portray the different outlooks, life chances and activities of the sexes in relation to social structure . . . Garfinkel, by contrast, wanted to treat sexual status as a produced and reproduced fact . . . The reproduced differentiation of culturally specific 'males' and 'females' is thus the terminus of his investigation rather than its starting point.
>
> (Heritage 1984: 181–2)

In many ways, this ethnomethodological approach not only predates Butler's, but is also far more radical and far-reaching. According to Lundgren (2000: 55), Kessler and McKenna were remarkably 'ahead of their time'. Likewise, Garfinkel's (1967: 181) claim that 'normally sexed persons are cultural events' can be considered a radical comment on the social construction of sex, more typically credited to Judith Butler (1990a) more than two decades later. Indeed, Garfinkel and Kessler and Mckenna do not just claim, but were also among the first to *demonstrate* that and how sex is a situated accomplishment. Unlike Butler, they draw attention to the interactional processes by which gender is constituted, and analyse the interpretative practices and taken-for-granted methods that enable us to create the 'fact' of a world of two sexes. As Dorothy Smith (2002: ix) puts it 'postmodern feminists reinvented the wheel' and 'it is tiresome to read contemporary feminist philosophers and literary theorists presenting as radically new discoveries ideas that are old hat to sociologists' (2002: ix).

(ii) Discourse of mind and world as topic, not resource?

One of the strengths of Butler's approach, indeed the reason why so many feminists have been attracted to her work, lies in her attempt to provide a balanced account of subject constitution which captures a sense of both structure and agency. By combining Foucault's poststructuralism with a theory of the psyche, Butler acknowledges both the constitutive power of discourse, and the agency and creativity of speakers. Indeed, Butler is keen to note that the psyche and the social are contingently related to one another (the psyche cannot be conceived as pre-social, nor the social as extra-psychic: Butler 1997b: 19). Although this represents a powerful counter to the determinist tendencies associated with sex-differences research, it is also the source of some significant problems.

Like sex differences research, Butler treats social structures ('the world') and psychological processes ('the mind') as primary 'inputs' to social action. In other words, world and mind shape people's behaviours. They come first, actions – like resistance – come second. However, both approaches differ in terms of where 'discourse' fits into this process, and in particular, in terms of how discourse relates to social structures and other such 'macro' contexts. Although they talk about language rather than discourse, sex difference researchers understand language to be observable and amenable to analysis. As we saw in Chapter 2, language is understood as both a secondary output or by-product of mind–world relations, and as something that provides an analytic *resource*, which reflects the world and people's perceptions of it (Edwards and Potter 2001). For Butler, by contrast, discourse takes on a rather more abstract and elusive role. The discourse in Butler's account is a vague, decontextualized and *reified* one which limits the suitability of her approach for feminist discursive work.

Butler reifies discourse by turning what is an essentially agentless, disembodied, *social practice*, into an agentive, embodied, *thing-like* subject, that has the power to *do* things to us, and that's on a par with macro-social structures and institutions. For Butler, it's as though these broad discourses exist outside gender and outside talk, but have tangible effects on and constrain both. These discourses are, like social contexts, structures and institutions, separate from identity, bearing down on it to create and constrain gendered selves, norms and actions. Gender identities are simply the outcome or effect of decontextualized 'performatives' or 'reiterative' acts.

We begin to see here the seeds of some deeply entrenched problems with the empirical application of a broadly poststructuralist conception of discourse, and the critical forms of DA associated with it. Like Butler, numerous feminists and critical discourse analysts reify discourse, treating it as a causal agent. In her book *Applied Discourse Analysis* (1999a), for example, the feminist psychologist, Carla Willig, following Foucault, defines discourse as 'a system of statements which constructs an object'. She is concerned with how discourses 'positioned participants', and how individuals can be 'constrained by available discourses because discursive positions pre-exist the individual' (Willig 1999a: 113–14). Similarly, in Nightingale and Cromby's (1999b) *Social Constructionist Psychology*, various authors suggest that discourses contain subject positions which 'constrain . . . experiences and practices' (Willig 1999b: 43). They 'regulate the conduct of individuals' (Burkitt 1999: 71), 'produce knowledge' and 'serve particular power relations' (Burr 1999: 114). Finally, in his book, *Critical Textwork*, Parker (1999b) argues that 'we are not entirely in control of meaning' (1999b: 6) and 'discursive practices . . . *position* us in relations of power' (1999b: 6, emphasis in original). In other words, 'language does things to us' (1999b: 6).

Thus, instead of conceiving of discourse as something that can be studied in its own right, within a poststructuralist framework, discourse is treated as 'something which produces something else (an utterance, a concept, an effect)' (Mills 1997: 17, cited in McIlvenny 2002a: 116–17). Discourse is invested with the power to *constitute* speakers as gendered subjects, (Hall 1995: 12), but exactly how it does this or what it looks like remains unclear. We are not offered any evidence for how these mysterious, decontextualized discourses actually work, nor how they are invested with such capabilities. Indeed, some researchers suggest that discourses are 'not even visible' (Sunderland 2004: 3).

Since poststructuralist researchers tend to focus on broad, constraining, macro-level discourses, they risk implying that they have fixed and determinate meanings. Consequently, they overlook how aspects of social structure, including gender, are constituted, reconstituted and oriented to in the detail of participants' talk. Within this framework there is no way of exploring how gender is constituted and resisted *within* discourse, nor how discourses which invoke descriptions of gender operate at the local level to maintain or undermine the gender order.

In order to counter this implicit determinism, and leave space for members' agency and creativity, Butler, along with many other proponents of a Foucauldian notion of discourse, incorporates a theory of the psyche, the internalization of norms and psychic excess. Butler is attracted to psychoanalysis and the notion of the unconscious psyche, because it allows her to account for the failure of constraining social norms. Acts of resistance, for example, are treated as the outcome or instantiation of agentic psychic and social processes, made possible through the internalization and displacement of norms. However, while the incorporation of the psyche in Butler's work prevents a thoroughgoing form of determinism, here again we have a cognitivist theory of discourse, in which resistance and resistive acts are ultimately reduced to, and explained exclusively in terms of, the world 'under the skull'. Cognitivism is a problem for Butler, not least because the idea that the psyche can be located in unitary, private individual selves, is a position that is actually profoundly antithetical to poststructuralism and Butler's own form of anti-essentialism.

Ethnomethodologists have a particularly radical way of conceiving of the relationship between macro and micro realms. They bypass the implicit determinism evident in poststructuralist-feminist and CDA approaches to discourse, and the need to resort to explanations rooted either in macro-social, extra-textual discourses or the cognitive-psychological world of the psyche. As we have seen, for Garfinkel, normative ideas about the dichotomous nature of sex, are not only created in interaction, but also structure that interaction (West and Zimmerman 1991: 18). Similarly, for Kessler and McKenna, gender is both ahistorical and historical. The idea that the practices that produce objective sex and other social structural, demographic variables or institutions, are both shaped by, and shape the context in which they are embedded, is an important one in both DP and CA, and goes to the heart of debates about the relative importance of social structure and individual agency. I will be explicating this idea further in Chapter 4. For the moment, I want to point out that within ethnomethodology we find an approach which offers feminists and others a means by which we may account for and analyse both structure and agency, and constraint and creativity, within the interactional realm of participants' practices. Structure and agency are endogenously constituted, oriented to and reproduced in members' practices, and the analyst does not necessarily need to venture outside or beneath those practices to explore their workings.

When we conceive of structure and agency in this way, then the artificial macro–micro dualism dissolves. Indeed, many ethnomethodologists assert that the macro–micro distinction is a 'non-starter', a distracting product of sociology's preoccupation with dichotomous models of society (Sharrock and Watson 1988). There is no need to build bridges between the macro and the micro, structure and agency, since the premises upon which such bridge-building exercises are based are misconceived. Ethnomethodology dissolves the structure–agency polarity completely (1988: 64). It has 'no work' for the concepts of 'social structure' and 'social actor' to do (Sharrock and Button 1991: 141).

This represents a radical departure from the sociological paradigm as it was articulated in the structural functionalist work of Talcott Parsons. Parsons (1937) argued that members internalize an institutionalized system of norms and rules and act on that basis. Ethnomethodologists suggest that this approach treats individuals as 'judgemental dopes', victims of external social forces who have no agency or ability to resist social constraints. Instead, ethnomethodologists theorize members as agents, actively participating in the construction of social order as they interact with one another and engage in ongoing, interpretative, meaning-making work.

(iii) Language as a form of social action?

As I argued earlier, Butler's theory of discourse and the constitution of gender is a rather vague and decontextualized one. In her theory of hate speech in her book *Excitable Speech* (1997a), however, she *does* talk more explicitly and concretely about language use and linguistic agency. Here Butler is influenced by Austin's (1962) argument that utterances *do* things. Thus, Butler acknowledges the context sensitivity and action orientation, of discourse. The indexicality of language, or, in Butler's terms, the 'open temporality' of the speech act, means that certain words are not intrinsically derogatory; they do not carry their meaning with them (they will not automatically carry the power to 'wound' or cause 'linguistic injury' or offence, for example). Rather, the sense of an utterance, and the precise meaning of a word, will depend on the manner in which it is deployed (the 'mode of address', for example). Its sense is inextricably tied to the interactional context within which it is embedded. In certain contexts, such as rap music, political parody and satire, for example, purportedly 'derogatory' meanings can be 'reinscribed', 'resignified' or 'reclaimed' for more positive, political purposes (Butler 1997a: 14). Indeed, one of the most interesting features of Butler, from my perspective, is her refusal to develop a legalistic yardstick against which to measure the injurious power of speech.

An approach that is sensitive to context and the 'action orientation' of meaning (i.e. with a focus on what words are used to do in specific contexts) is fully in line with the perspective adopted in this book. However, like the sex difference researchers whose work I reviewed in Chapter 2, Butler does not translate her discussions about context sensitivity and the reinscription of meaning into an analysis of actual language use.

While Butler talks about discourse, citation and iterability in a detailed and highly sophisticated fashion, her theorization of the processes underpinning the performance of gender remains an abstract one. Indeed, Butler's work is theoretically dense. For example, her notion of a politics of the performative has been criticized for remaining a purely 'abstract account of subject formation' that is 'lacking in social specificity' (McNay 1999: 176, 178). For example, her work on speech acts is, like Austin's, a decontextualized, theoretical abstraction, based on made-up, idealized typifications, that are considered outside of their use in actual interactional settings. Consequently, she does not demonstrate how the discursive constitution of subjects, or the resignification of meaning actually works. As Maloney and Fenstermaker (2002: 199) note, 'Butler's framework does not translate fully this very abstract concept of reiteration and resignification as agency into more concrete terms'. Along with other postmodern theories of language, Butler has a tendency to 'gloss over or overlook the complexities and subtleties of social practice, the crucible in which structures of language and agency are interactively performed and forged' (McIlvenny 2002c: 6). In order to understand how gender norms work in practice, an alternative approach would need to investigate how the resignification of norms is actually achieved and made 'observable-reportable' (McIlvenny 2002a: 141; for an empirical application of Butler's theory of hate speech, see Speer and Potter 2002).

So, where sex difference theorists claim to be sensitive to context, and then conduct analyses which, generally, are not, Butler claims to offer a model of discourse that is sensitive to context and its action performative nature, but she does not examine any concrete empirical materials, or offer any means by which we may analyse the context sensitivity of discourse. Indeed, there is no 'discourse' as such in Butler's approach that is accessible and amenable to an independent analysis. Her work does not provide an analytic programme for studying discourse practices.

Moreover, since Butler does not analyse 'real-life' accounts, there is no sense in her work of a peopled world in which participants interact and speak with one another (Speer and Potter 2002; McIlvenny 2002a). Consequently, her approach exists in isolation from the concrete practices of the very members whose gendered performatives she purports to illuminate. Indeed, part of the problem with Butler's theory of performativity is 'its focus on the *individual* as the agent of performance' (Cameron 1997b: 30, emphasis in original). There is, in other words, no *inter*subjectivity – no co-construction or collaborative accomplishment of meaning in Butler's work (Cameron 1997b: 30–1). Where Butler talks about discourse, she does not discuss the equally important facet of any gendered performance or act – its 'audience' and its 'reception' (McIlvenny 2002a: 140). Her approach lacks an examination of the processes through which dichotomous gender and a coercive 'heteronormativity', which so keenly binds us to restrictive notions of normative gender and sexuality, is constructed, oriented to and reproduced by people in live social situations. In sum, as McIlvenny puts it, Butler's theoretical approach 'unsettles the traditional empirical studies, but leaves little from which to proceed' (2002c: 6).

Like Butler, Garfinkel and Kessler and McKenna recognize the importance of context, and the context sensitivity of meaning. They talk about indexicality – the idea that the meaning of an expression alters with its context of use, and how 'contexts and relations in concrete interactions are of vital importance for what gender "is"' (Lundgren 2000: 59). However, unlike Butler, they demonstrate this by focusing directly on the lived experiences of people. They focus on members' activities and on observable interactions and interpretive social practices as they take place in everyday life. Thus, the Garfinkel and Kessler and McKenna studies place great emphasis on members' 'everyday interactions' (Kessler and McKenna 1978: 115); 'accounting practices' (Garfinkel 1967: 1), 'witnessed displays of common talk and conduct', 'situated indexical particulars of talk' (Garfinkel 1967: 181), and 'the ways transsexuals talk about . . . transsexualism, the language they use' (Kessler and McKenna 1978: 114).

So, where Butler had a tendency to treat the individual as an isolated unit, marginalizing the intersubjective, interactional realm, the Garfinkel and Kessler and McKenna studies show how gender is constituted in and through interaction. As Kessler and McKenna (1978: vii) show, members both *display* and *perceive* dichotomous gender as an objective fact, and this is 'a product of social interaction in everyday life'. The benefits of this ethnomethodological approach over that of Butler, then, lie in this demonstration of the interactional production of features of social structure including gender, and how sex-related norms are reproduced and sustained in the mundane practices of everyday life. As Dorothy Smith (2002: ix) notes, the ethnomethodological work on gender can be credited for 'bringing into view thinking which, unlike feminist philosophy and literary theory, is subject to the discipline of research'. In this work, 'dialogue is not only with theoretical traditions or with contemporary feminist thought, but also with a social world to be discovered as people themselves bring it into being' (Smith 2002: xi).

(iv) Analysts' claims are grounded in participants' practices?

As I noted above, Butler's approach has proven popular among a number of feminist researchers who have sought to apply her notion of gender as performance in their own studies of the discursive construction of gender and sexuality. Bucholtz et al.'s (1999) edited book, *Reinventing Identities*, contains a number of discourse analytic studies that are influenced by Butler's theory of performativity. Many of the authors in this book are critical of past research that has compared male and female linguistic behaviour, and share a commitment to a constructionist, anti-essentialist agenda. They acknowledge that gender is 'a local production rather than an enduring category' (Bucholtz 1999a: 4), that gender does not emanate from some essential or reductive category of 'woman', but is locally produced and 'shaped moment by moment through the details of discourse' (Bucholtz 1999b: viii).

However, the problem with many of these analytic applications of Butler's work is that, despite claiming a constructionist approach to gender, this constructionist emphasis is not consistently followed through. Frequently, gender identity is retained as an independent variable against which to study talk. For example, Bucholtz et al. advocate for the invigoration of the discipline an approach which is 'attentive to individual variation within, as well as across, gender categories' (Bucholtz 1999a: 21). The unit of analysis, then, is still the gendered subject, not the talk. Since many of the authors in this book *start* with gays and lesbians, teenage girls, Latinas, African Americans, Native Americans, non-western women and so on (1999a: 10) as their analytic categories, and explore how men *do* masculinity and how women *do* femininity (see particularly Coates 1999; Tannen 1999), this 'constructionist' research has a tendency to 'buy back into' the essentialist framework that it was originally designed to replace. In doing so, these studies reproduce the same dualistic assumptions about gender (the idea that 'men talk like this', and 'women talk like that') that we saw in Chapter 2. In the last analysis, one's construction of gender, or one's masculine or feminine performance, is explained, or accounted for in a circular fashion, with reference to the speaker's sex. Thus, much of the work which draws on poststructuralist ideas like Butler's adopts a model of discourse in which researchers prioritize their own analytic agenda, and impose the variables that *they* deem to be important, on their data.

As we have seen, Garfinkel and Kessler and McKenna do get closer to providing an analysis of members' perspectives. They do not impose their own 'commonsense' ideas about gender categories on their data, but are concerned to explore how gender comes to be seen commonsensically *as* a natural and dualistic analysts' category in the first place. In this sense, the ethnomethodological approach to members' methods represents a clear advancement on Butler's theory of performativity. Despite this, however, the Garfinkel and Kessler and McKenna studies appear to be rather limited in terms of precisely which members we can study. Indeed, even while they provide rich insights into the 'special' case of the construction of gender by intersexed and transsexual individuals, they do not show us situated examples of how all members – whatever their 'sex status' – construct gender.

One of the reasons for this may be traced to the ethnomethodological concern to treat members' methods and commonsense accounting practices as 'seen but unnoticed' phenomena (Hutchby and Wooffitt 1998: 31). Since Garfinkel and Kesssler and McKenna believed that for most 'ordinary' members, gender is taken-for-granted and thus *background* to interaction – as opposed to being *observable in and hence recoverable* from interaction – they chose to focus exclusively on the practices of individuals for whom the accomplishment of gender was an overt and abiding concern. As Hutchby and Wooffitt (1998) point out:

one of the problems that ethnomethodology encounters is that of how to gain analytic access to the level of commonsense knowledge which it seeks to study. Since the accounting practices Garfinkel was interested in were, on his own admission, taken for granted by members, 'seen but unnoticed', it was difficult to think of a method by which they could be revealed. The earliest research consisted of 'breaching' experiments in which the taken-for-granted routines of ordinary life were intentionally disrupted in order to observe how people dealt with their sudden lack of certainty . . . However, as Garfinkel himself realized, the possibilities of breaching experiments are essentially limited, since they necessarily only tell us about what participants do in the 'special' situation constructed by the breach: they do not show how mutual understandings are constructed and maintained in the unremarkable course of mundane interaction.

(Hutchby and Wooffitt 1998: 31–3)

When one reads the studies by Garfinkel and Kessler and McKenna, there is actually remarkably little by way of first-hand evidence of participants' accounts and interactions included in their analyses. Garfinkel's data consist of thirty-five hours of tape-recorded 'conversations' that he had with Agnes which he supplemented with unspecified 'additional' materials collected by the psychiatric team at UCLA (Garfinkel 1967: 121). Kessler and McKenna's data consist of interviews with fifteen transsexuals, letters written over a period of two years, from a male-to-female transsexual friend called Rachel, and the results of a number of games and experiments. The vast proportion of the data reported in these studies consist of short, decontextualized (i.e. typically monologic, one speaker, one line) excerpts from transcripts of interviews with intersex or transsexual individuals, and the researchers' post-hoc, recollections and reports of events. Some extended examples of 'conversations' and 'interactions' are reported by Kessler and McKenna in the letters written by their transsexual friend, Rachel (see Kessler and McKenna 1978: 192, 208, 209–10). However, here again, these are recollected self-reports rather than recorded conversations of people doing gender. What is missing from these studies is an analysis of first-hand examples of members' actual language use, their situated, conversational interactions and accounts, and their contribution to those very practices (of gender attribution and the maintenance of the natural attitude) that Kessler and McKenna and Garfinkel intended to analyse. In sum, what ethnomethodology, like Butler, lacks (indeed resists) is a systematic empirical programme for studying talk-in-interaction.

This view is echoed in Maloney and Fenstermaker's (2002) assessment of some of the divergences between Butler and the ethnomethodological work of West and Fenstermaker. Maloney and Fenstermaker argue that there needs to be 'further elaboration' and a 'more precise articulation' of the boundaries of the 'discursive' in the work of Butler, and the concept of 'interaction' in the work of West and Fenstermaker. Both need to pay more attention to the role of discourse and interaction in their accounts of the 'doing' of gender and its transgression (Maloney and Fenstermaker 2002: 203).

One reason why ethnomethodology tends not to provide the kind of empirical framework advocated here, is that it has always had an 'ambivalent' (Lynch 2000a: 521) relationship with formal analytic endeavours that aim to specify procedural regularities, and 'basic structures of interaction' (Lynch 2000b: 544). As Silverman (1998: 184) suggests, although contemporary ethnomethodology provides some extraordinarily rich analyses of members' activities, many of its proponents (e.g., Lynch and Bogen 1994; see also Lynch 1993, 2002) strongly resist turning ethnomethodology into a formal, 'scientific' approach of the kind that developed from it, in CA. For many ethnomethodologists, such a formal analytic endeavour runs counter to the ethnomethodological stress on the 'quiddity' and the 'just whatness' of the unique 'local and time-bound features of phenomena' (ten Have 2004: 26). Consequently many ethnomethodologists reject the idea that we can or should produce context free, formal descriptions of members' methods, and prefer to focus instead on the analysis of singular instances and 'the haecceities' (Garfinkel and Wieder 1992) of some local setting (Wowk forthcoming).

(v) A relativist approach?

Finally, Butler's approach is anti-foundationalist in its focus. By this I mean that Butler resists the idea that gender and gendered subjectivity are phenomena that can exist independently outside of discourse. Following Derrida and Foucault's stipulation that 'categorising creates or constitutes that which it refers to' (Livia and Hall 1997a: 8), Butler argues that there is no 'I' behind discourse (Butler 1993: 225), no referent preceding the moment of speech (Livia and Hall 1997a: 9). For Butler, the gendered subject does not precede discourse, but is brought into being in and through discourse.

As we have seen, many ethnomethodologists are anti-constructionist and so one would also expect them to be strongly opposed to versions of constructionism that are relativist in their focus. Nonetheless, in my view the Garfinkel and Kessler and McKenna studies do share many features in common with a relativist approach. For example, Heritage (1984: 196) states that Garfinkel makes some 'potentially relativizing – observations on the socially organized character of accountable sexuality' (see also Cealey Harrison and Hood-Williams 2002: 46). Similarly, Zimmerman argues that ethnomethodology's project 'is to examine how phenomena such as sex and gender are *made real*, that is, for members, made to happen as evidently natural, transcendent events through taken-for-granted cultural and localized practices' (Zimmerman 1992: 1970, emphasis added). Heritage provides a neat summary of the ethnomethodological treatment of reality. He states that the institutional realities discussed by Garfinkel

> subsisted as the robust product of an interlocking network of reflexively accountable practices. This feature of these realities reminds us that, as Garfinkel puts it, 'in doing sociology . . . every reference to the "real world", even where the reference is to physical or biological events, is a reference to the organized activities of everyday life' (Garfinkel 1967: vii). And it reminds us too that the 'real world' is not any less real for all that. At most, that reality is temporarily placed in brackets during a period in which 'the social scientist treats knowledge, and the procedures that societal members use for its assembly, test, management and transmission, as objects of theoretical sociological interest' (Garfinkel 1967: 77) . . . the specific institutionalized reality under investigation has been bracketed so that the practices underlying its maintenance *as* a reality can be more clearly delineated.
> (Heritage 1984: 229).

Unlike Butler, who argues that the reality of gender is discursively constituted, but does not provide any examples of discourse that do this 'reality constructing' work, ethnomethodologists have explored how members' methods produce a gendered reality, at the local level. Ethnomethodologists demonstrate how an 'objective reality of sex' (Crawford 2000a: 7) and a world of two genders is constructed in members' methods and situated activities, and 'how gender and sexuality are made into "natural objects"' (McIlvenny 2002b: 20). Thus, ethnomethodology is relativist to the extent that it highlights the work that gives gender dualism its *appearance as natural*.

Chapter summary

In this chapter I have provided an overview of poststructuralist and ethnomethodological approaches to gender identity, and evaluated each in relation to the five criteria for an adequate feminist discursive approach set out in Chapter 1. The studies considered in this chapter offer a theoretically sophisticated, constructionist understanding of gender, which has overcome many of the problems associated with the essentialist, sex differences research considered in Chapter 2.

While concerned more with gender *identity* than with language, both approaches have had a major impact on sociolinguistic and discursive and

CA thinking about gender, challenging us to see gender – and sex – as a performance rather than an essence. These studies have some far-reaching political implications. By challenging the naturalness of sex and gender, they upset the commonsense notion that society must inevitably and for all time be organized according to 'male–female', 'masculine–feminine' dualisms. In doing so, they open up ways for 'rethinking' and transgressing the oppressive gender norms upon which such dualisms rest. Despite the radical political potential both approaches have offered feminism, however, they too suffer a number of problems when it comes to the empirical analysis of gender and language.

Butler adopts a broadly Foucauldian understanding of discourse, which has reifying tendencies, overlooks the fine-grained, context-sensitive nature of accounts, and ultimately relies on a residual determinism which undercuts the radical political potential of her approach. In order to avoid determinism, Butler incorporates a cognitivist theory of the psyche in which agency (e.g., the ability to resist social norms) is ultimately reduced to, and explained in terms of, cognitions. This is a theory which focuses on individuals as the agents of performance – there is no notion of inter-subjectivity or the joint production of meaning in Butler's account. Consequently, where feminists have sought to apply theories of performativity to their own empirical analyses of discourse, they have frequently adopted procedures and techniques which actually serve to re-import essentialism 'by the back-door'.

Unlike Butler, Garfinkel and Kessler and McKenna focus on the lived experiences of intersexed and transsexual individuals, and view gender as a product of social interaction. They focus on the ongoing, interpretative practices and taken for granted methods that enable us to create and sustain the 'fact' of two sexes. They do not reify discourse, and offer an approach which can account for both structure and agency without resorting to determinist theories of social structure on the one hand, or cognitivist notions of the psyche on the other. Indeed, from within an ethnomethodological framework, both social structure and individual agency, macro and micro realms, are reconceptualized as endogenous productions and ultimately dissolved. In this sense, ethnomethodology offers a more viable basis than poststructuralist-feminism for the development of an analytically grounded framework for studying the discursive constitution of gender.

Despite this, the potential of ethnomethodology is undercut by its resistance to develop an analytic programme for studying general features of gendered practices across contexts. Neither Garfinkel nor Kessler and McKenna analyse 'first-hand' transcripts of conversational or linguistic data, and most of the data they use consist of recollected, post-hoc self-reports, rather than recorded conversations of people actually 'doing' gender.

In sum, even while they offer sophisticated theories of discourse on the one hand (Butler 1990a, 1993, 1997a) and in-depth descriptions of members' methods on the other (Garfinkel 1967; Kessler and McKenna 1978), neither poststructuralism nor ethnomethodology provides an adequate empirical framework for studying *talk-in-interaction*. So, is there an alternative approach which is equally radical, but which offers a more viable basis for the development of an empirical framework for studying the discursive constitution of gender – an approach which explicates and validates ethnomethodological claims using concrete, first-hand examples of transcribed recordings taken from real life? In Chapter 4 I will illustrate what just such an approach might look like.

4
A FEMINIST, CONVERSATION ANALYTIC APPROACH

In the previous two chapters I provided a focused overview and critique of sex difference perspectives (Chapter 2) and poststructuralist and ethnomethodological perspectives (Chapter 3), evaluating each in relation to the five criteria for an adequate feminist analytic approach set out in Chapter 1. I argued that although poststructuralism overcomes many of the problems associated with an essentialist 'variables and effects' model of language, the ethnomethodological focus on 'members' methods' provides a more promising framework than Butler's poststructuralist, Foucauldian notion of discourse, for the analysis of the real life 'doing' of gender. However, I suggested that ethnomethodology, like poststructuralism, lacks (indeed, resists the development of) a formal analytic programme for studying talk-in-interaction. Such an approach can be found, by contrast, in the ethnomethodologically inspired empirical framework of CA, and its close relative in psychology, DP.

As I noted in Chapter 1, CA was the first approach to translate ethnomethodological ideas into a detailed, sociological research agenda. DP developed an angle which applied ideas from CA to rethink a range of concerns around cognition in psychology. Many feminists, and others with a critical agenda, have used both approaches to set about interrogating the relevance of gender in talk, and to explore 'what counts' as gender or an 'orientation to gender' in an interaction. A related strand of work has begun to merge this focus on participants' orientations, with insights from Sacks' (1995) membership categorization analysis (or MCA), in order to examine the construction of gender as a category in discourse, and how it is used and oriented to by members. Together, this work is taking the field of language and gender research in new directions.

My aim in this chapter is to provide an overview of some of this research, noting how insights from CA and DP contribute theoretically and methodologically to the five criteria for the development of the feminist analytic approach set out in Chapter 1.

(i) A constructionist approach?

DP is constructionist in two senses: first, it studies the way discourse itself is constructed from a range of conversational resources, made up of words and categories, metaphors, descriptions and rhetorical devices. Second, it studies the way these resources are built and used in the course of performing specific social actions – for example in asking questions, providing accounts, or managing blame and responsibility. Thus, from a discursive perspective, discourse 'is both construct*ed* and construct*ive*' (Edwards and Potter 2001: 15; Potter 1996a) and it is the function of discourse just as much as its content that is of interest.

Many conversation analysts, like the ethnomethodologists discussed in Chapter 3, typically resist the suggestion that their work is constructionist (Wowk forthcoming). However, others (e.g. Buttny 1993; Potter 1996b) have argued that there is a significant constructionist undercurrent in CA. Indeed, in her CA work on male–female laughter, Jefferson (2004) notes that she tends to think of the categories of 'male' and 'female' 'as something like careers rather than conditions, i.e. *as constructed rather than biologically intrinsic*' (2004: 118, emphasis added). Since DP and CA are both fundamentally opposed to any approach in which the researcher explains what is going on in talk in terms of 'sociolinguistic variables' or the 'social identity' of the speaker (Drew and Heritage 1992b: 17), and since they treat identities as things that are interactionally invoked, oriented to, reproduced and resisted by participants in talk (Antaki and Widdicombe 1998a; Widdicombe and Wooffitt 1995), then, I am, for the purposes of this book, treating them both as *compatible* with a constructionist agenda.

An analytic example: Marsha and Tony

An analytic example which illustrates some of the differences between an essentialist, sex differences perspective, and an anti-essentialist, CA approach, is provided by Emanuel Schegloff in his well-known 1997 article 'Whose text? Whose context?' The excerpt discussed by Schegloff, which I've reproduced here, is taken from a telephone call between Marsha and Tony, who are the separated parents of their teenage son, Joey. Joey usually lives with his father in northern California, but has just spent a part of the school holiday with his mother in southern California. The call takes place on the day Joey is due to drive back up north. Tony calls Marsha to find out when Joey left, but discovers that there is a problem: Joey's car was vandalized outside Marsha's house, he has left the car at Marsha's and is flying home. Tony is concerned about how Joey will get the car back up north. The target segment for the purposes of our analysis will be lines 35 to 50.

A FEMINIST, CONVERSATION ANALYTIC APPROACH

(4.1) [Schegloff 1997: 172-3]

```
                   ((ring))
1   Marsha:   Hello:?
2   Tony:     Hi: Marsha?
3   Marsha:   Ye:ah.
4   Tony:     How are you.
5   Marsha:   Fi::ne.
6                (0.2)
7   Marsha:   Did Joey get home yet?
8   Tony:     Well I wz wondering when 'e left.
9                (0.2)
10  Marsha:   .hhh Uh:(d) did Oh: .h Yer not in on what pen'. (hh) (d)
11  Tony:     No(h)o=
12  Marsha:   =He's flying.
13               (0.2)
14  Marsha:   En Ilene is going to meet im:.Becuz the to:p wz ripped
15            off'v iz car which is tih say someb'ddy helped th'mselfs.
16  Tony:     Stolen.
17               (0.4)
18  Marsha:   Stolen. =Right out in front of my house.
19  Tony:     Oh: f'r crying out loud, =en eez not g'nna eez not
20            g'nna bring it ba:ck?
21  Marsha:   .hh No so it's parked in the g'rage cz it wz so damn
22            co:ld. An' ez a matter fact snowing on the Ridge Route.
23               (0.3)
24  Marsha:   .hhh So I took him to the airport he couldn' buy a ticket.
25               (.)
26  Marsha:   .hhhh Bee- he c'd only get on standby.
27               (0.3)
28  Tony:     Uh hu:[h,
29  Marsha:         [En I left him there at abou:t noo:n.
30               (0.3)
31  Tony:     Ah ha:h.
32               (0.2)
33  Marsha:   Ayund uh,h
34               (0.2)
35  Tony:     W't's 'e g'nna do go down en pick it up later? er
36            somethin like (     ) [well that's aw]:ful
37  Marsha:                         [H i s  friend  ]
38  Marsha:   Yeh h[is friend Stee-   ]
39  Tony:        [That really makes] me ma:d.
40               (0.2)
41  Marsha:   .hhh Oh it's disgusti[ng ez a matter a'f]a:ct.
42  Tony:                          [P o o r  J o e y.]
```

```
43   Marsha:    I- I, I told my ki:ds. who do this: down et the Drug
44              Coalition ah want th'to:p back.h .hhhhhhhhh ((1.0))
45              SEND OUT the WO:RD.hhh hnh
46                   (0.2)
47   Tony:      Yeah.
48   Marsha:    .hhh Bu:t u-hu:ghh his friend Steve en Brian er driving
49              up. Right after:: (0.2) school is out. En then hi'll
50              drive do:wn here with the:m.
51   Tony:      Oh I see.
52   Marsha:    So: in the long run, .hhh it (.) probly's gonna save a
53              liddle time 'n: energy.
54   Tony:      Okay.
55   Marsha:    But Ile:ne probably (0.8) is either at the airport er
56              waiting tuh hear fr'm in eess
57              ((conversation continues))
```

A 'variables and effects' analysis

Schegloff begins his discussion of this extract by noting how critical, politically oriented and feminist researchers might interpret the interaction within it. This, he says, is an interaction 'across gender lines' (1997: 173): the interactants are male and female, they have a 'strained relationship', and the call is one in which 'moral evaluation and censure are at issue' (1997: 172). There are two occasions during this 'interactional contest' in which Marsha is 'beaten down' or 'interrupted' by Tony, and forced to cease talking: first at line 37, 'His friend'; and then again at line 38, 'his friend Stee-' (1997: 173–4). Tony interrupts on a third occasion (lines 41–2), but this time neither Marsha nor Tony yield to the other. Schegloff notes that, from the perspective of a 'critical' analysis of this extract, the exchange needs to be understood as 'another exemplar of gendered discourse' (1997: 178) and one 'in which the asymmetries of status and power along gender lines . . . are played out in the interactional arena of interruption and overlapping talk' (1997: 173). Tony's interruptions and overlapping talk are the symbol of and vehicle for the differential, male–female 'power processes at work' (1997: 174).

Schegloff has, throughout his career (1987, 1991, 1992a, 1997, 2001), been highly critical of this kind of 'variables and effects' approach to a piece of data, in which the participants' identities *as* men and women drive the analysis. In his 1987 contribution, for example, he criticizes the early CA work on gender, dominance and interruption by Zimmerman and West (1975), because it 'aims to link an asymmetrical outcome in the talk to differential attributes of the participants of a macrorelevant type' (Schegloff 1987: 214). Schegloff suggests that the problem with this kind of approach, is that the analyst imposes their own political and analytic presuppositions and characterizations of the relevant contexts, on their data. In prioritizing their own perspective, the analyst misses what the interaction 'was demonstrably about *in the first instance – for the parties*' (1997: 178, emphasis in original). By contrast, Schegloff argues that if critical discourse analysis is to be 'compelling' (1997: 178), then it requires 'an internally analyzed rendering of the event' and an analysis 'of what was going on in it *for the participants, in its course*' (1997: 174, emphasis in original). Schegloff goes on to provide just such an analysis of this extract.

A CA analysis

Schegloff begins by noting that Tony's question turn in lines 35–6 comes to a possible completion after 'er something like ( )'. Marsha hears it this way and begins her answer, starting 'His friend' (line 37).

```
35   Tony:     W't's 'e g'nna do go down en pick it up later? er
36             somethin like (    ) [well that's aw]:ful
37   Marsha:                        [H  i  s  friend ]
38   Marsha:   Yeh h[is friend Stee-   ]
39   Tony:         [That really makes] me ma:d.
```

Although Marsha hears Tony's turn as possibly complete and begins to respond, it turns out that Tony's turn is not actually complete, and Tony goes on to produce another turn construction unit (TCU): 'well that's awful' (line 36). It's because of this that Tony and Marsha's utterances collide in overlap. This analysis, then, does not warrant the claim that Tony is deliberately interrupting or dominating Marsha. As Schegloff (1997: 176) points out, Tony's additional TCU occurs simultaneously with Marsha's, rather than 'by virtue' of it. In finding herself in overlap, Marsha 'momentarily quits' her response to Tony's question, and drops out of the overlap.

Schegloff suggests that Tony's additional TCU 'well that's awful' entails an altogether different action from the question that immediately precedes it. 'Well that's awful' is an emotional response or, in action terms, an *assessment* of what has happened to Joey. In sequential terms, and as Pomerantz (1984) has shown, when an assessment is produced, it makes relevant next an agreement or disagreement. Thus, Marsha now has to respond to the two parts of Tony's turn – the question component and the assessment. The 'canonical' (or routine) practice for dealing with a turn which makes two responses relevant is, as Schegloff points out, to deal with them in reverse order – to respond to the second part first, and the first part after that (Schegloff 1997: 177; Sacks 1987).

Once Tony has completed his assessment in the second part of his turn, Marsha says 'Yeh' (line 38) to show that she agrees with it. She then proceeds to have another go at answering Tony's question: 'his friend <u>Stee</u>-' (line 38). As Pomerantz (1984) demonstrates, in order to constitute an 'effective agreement', the recipient of a first assessment needs to demonstrate that they are *upgrading* the assessment that they are agreeing with. It follows that 'simple agreement tokens', like Marsha's 'Yeh', 'can constitute "weak agreements", and can be taken as tantamount to virtual *dis*agreement or non-agreement' (Schegloff 1997: 177). The producers of the first assessment commonly respond to such weak agreements with upgrades (1997: 177).

So, on hearing Marsha's minimal 'Yeh', Tony upgrades his first assessment to 'That really makes me ma:d.' (line 39). In doing so, Tony is working to draw Marsha's weak stance into a stronger alignment with his initial assessment (Schegloff 1997: 177). So, here again, where critically oriented researchers might interpret Tony's 'interruptive' talk as an example of male power and dominance, what this analysis shows is that what Tony does is actually a canonical feature of how members (in general and regardless of their sex) deal with weak agreements to assessments. Moreover, in making his intervention in line 39, Tony is actually aligned, in a sequential sense, with what Marsha is doing, making sure her response to the second part of his turn is 'brought to satisfactory resolution before the first part is addressed' (Schegloff 1997: 177). In finding herself in overlap for a second time, Marsha quits the production of her answer to the first part of Tony's turn, and now offers a full agreement with Tony's assessment (line 41):

```
39    Tony:         [That really makes] me ma:d.
40                         (0.2)
41    Marsha:      .hhh Oh it's disgusti[ng ez a matter a'f ]a:ct.
42    Tony:                             [P o o r   J o e y.]
43    Marsha:      I- I, I told my ki:ds. who do this: down et the Drug
44                 Coalition ah want th'to:p back.h .hhhhhhhhh ((1.0))
45                 SEND OUT the WO:RD.hhh hnh
46                         (0.2)
47    Tony:        Yeah.
48    Marsha:      .hhh Bu:t u-hu:ghh his friend Steve en Brian er driving
49                 up. Right after:: (0.2) school is out. En then hi'll
50                 drive do:wn here with the:m.
```

Marsha's turn comes to possible completion after the word 'disgusting', and Tony then 'chimes in with an expression of sympathy for their son' (Schegloff 1997: 178) – 'Poor Joey' (line 42). Note that here again, Tony's talk is not 'interruptive' of what Marsha is doing. Rather, it is highly attentive to the 'possible completion' of Marsha's assessment, and working to secure an issue on which they can both agree. Since Marsha hadn't *actually* finished her turn, her talk 'completely overrides "Poor Joey"' (1997: 178). Once the alignment on assessments has been achieved, Marsha tries again to answer the first, question part of Tony's turn, and this time, she brings her answer to completion (lines 48–50).

So, what we have here is a rather different account of what is going on in the interaction than we might expect from within an essentialist, 'sex differences' paradigm. The times when Marsha is apparently 'beaten down' by Tony and induced to terminate her talk, can be explained in this instance – not in terms of male dominance and power over women – but rather, in terms of canonical features of the way talk gets done. As Schegloff notes elsewhere:

> the rules of conversation operate in ways that are, in principle at least, independent of the extradiscursive identities of the participants . . . the turn-taking rules themselves operate in terms of locally constructed discourse statuses rather than, for example, position in a social hierarchy.
>
> (Schegloff 1992a: 480)

Thus, to the extent that identity is relevant to the analysis in the above example at all, it is in terms of the participants' 'activity-relevant identities' (1997: 180). On this occasion, it is activity, rather than power or gender, which accounts for what the participants are doing.

Nevertheless, Schegloff suggests that this analysis does not necessarily either 'undercut' or 'underwrite' critical discourse analysis. It's not that interruptions can never be explained in terms of power, dominance or gender. Rather, if they are, then some sort of linkage which explicitly grounds the relevance of characterizing the parties to the events being described as 'male' and 'female' needs to be shown (2001: 316). Without this linkage, claims about interruption, along with the results of any research which proceeds in this way, are, for Schegloff, 'profoundly equivocal' (2001: 309).

Gail Jefferson (2004) attempts to make the kind of linkage that Schegloff proposes in her analysis of asymmetry in male–female laughter. Jefferson explores Zimmerman's hypothesis that 'in male–female interaction, if the male laughed, the female would join in laughing: but if the female laughed, the male would not join in laughing' (Jefferson 2004: 117). However, the results of her analysis do not prove the hypothesis. Instead they show that where this kind of gendered asymmetry exists in a piece of data, it can often be explained with reference to other interactional business of a 'hierarchically superordinate' nature (2004: 131; see also Glenn 2003).

This does not mean that participants' gender identities will never be 'indexed' or 'made relevant' in talk. In the same 1997 article from which the Marsha and Tony extract is taken, Schegloff goes on to analyse an example of talk in which gender *is* brought to relevance by the participants. I will return to this example when I discuss 'participants' orientations' to gender later in this chapter. For the moment, I want to conclude this section by noting that unlike sex differences research, CA and DP do not assume the a priori explanatory relevance of gender or power to what gets said, or correlate the dualistic demographic variables, 'male' and 'female', with linguistic forms (such as interruption or laughter). Instead, they require us to demonstrate the relevance of invoking these categories analytically, with reference to what participants may or may not be shown to be attending to in their talk.

(ii) Discourse of mind and world as topic, not resource?

As I argued in Chapter 1, unlike most mainstream sociology and psychology, which treats language as a *resource* that can provide direct access to the world and people's perceptions of it, the approach I adopt in this book treats talk that invokes descriptions of the world and the mind, as a *topic* that is studiable in its own right. By combining insights from the sociological perspective of CA, and the social psychological perspective of DP, we can begin to rethink our traditional understanding of the relationship between, and operation of, 'macro-structural' and 'cognitive-psychological' realms. In this section, I'll describe, first, how CA builds on ethnomethodological ideas about the dissolution of macro and micro realms in sociology, second, how DP applies these ideas to reformulate traditional understandings of cognition and mind–world relations in psychology, and finally, how both perspectives can be applied to an analysis of mind–world discourse in the small scale (or 'micro') features of talk-in-interaction. I suggest that, ultimately, when we combine CA and DP, the abstract theoretical and analytic separation of macro, cognitive and micro realms may be reworked, or, in ethnomethodological terms – 'dissolved' (Wowk forthcoming).

CA's twin focus

Conversation analysts are primarily concerned to describe the methods that speakers use to coordinate their talk to produce orderly and meaningful conversational actions. In order to access these methods, they study the procedures which inform the production of both individual utterances and sequences of utterances. As I showed with the analysis of the Marsha and Tony extract, these procedures are not idiosyncratic, but display relatively stable patterns and organized regularities that are oriented to by participants, and which are evident in all of our talk. The goal of CA is to establish the structural frameworks that underpin and organize such regularities in interaction – or 'the structures of social action' (Atkinson and Heritage 1984).

Heritage (2004: 223) states that there are at least two kinds of conversation analytic work in existence today. The first explores 'the social institution *of* interaction as an entity in its own right', or how talk-in-interaction is organized at the local, sequential level of turns and sequences (what is traditionally understood as the 'micro' level), and the second studies 'the management of social institutions *in* interaction' and how that talk is implicated in the broader forms of social organization (e.g., social structures and institutions) in which it is situated (what is traditionally understood as the 'macro-structural' level) (Boden and Zimmerman 1991; Drew and Heritage 1992a; McHoul and Rapley 2001). Although, as Heritage (2004: 223) notes, both approaches overlap in certain respects, they are nonetheless distinct enough in their focus to merit my dealing with each in turn.

The social institution of interaction

Some of the earliest CA papers were focused on identifying normative structures and regularities in talk. Some examples of aspects of talk that have regular predictable patterns include the turn-taking system, overlap onset, the organization of repair, openings and closings, and preference organization (see, for example, Jefferson 1986; Pomerantz 1984; Sacks 1987; Sacks et al. 1974; Schegloff 1968, 1979; Schegloff and Sacks 1973; Schegloff et al. 1977).

The turn-taking system describes how, when talking to others, we literally 'take turns' at speaking. The turn-taking system means that we avoid talking at the same time, or interrupting each other too frequently (Sacks et al. 1974). One of the most basic sequences in which turn-taking occurs is the adjacency pair (Schegloff 1968; Schegloff and Sacks 1973). These 'paired action sequences' are pairs of utterances which are ordered, and in which the first-pair-part makes relevant, and requires the production of a particular second-pair-part. Examples of adjacency pairs include question – answer, greeting – return greeting, invitation – acceptance/declination, assessment – agreement/disagreement, and so on.

These regular, sequentially organized features of talk can be thought of as *normative* frameworks: they provide *to be expected* grounds for action, and speakers can be held accountable for their implementation. So, if you greet me as we walk past one another in the corridor, and I ignore you, then you will usually have the right to repeat your greeting, sanction me for my failure to respond with a return greeting, or 'draw sanctionable inferences' from my lack of response (Heritage 1988: 129). I may be being rude, or I may not have heard you, for example.

One way in which the analyst can access participants' orientations to conversational norms is to explore how first-pair-parts are responded to by participants – or what kind of action respondents' uptakes (their reactions, responses or 'next turns') implicate them as. Consider the following examples from Heritage (1988):

(4.2) [Heritage 1988: 129]
A: Why don't you come and see me some[times.
B: [I would like to.

(4.3) [Heritage 1988: 130 (Invented variation on (1))]
A: Why don't you come and *see* me sometimes.
B: I'm sorry. I've been terribly tied up lately.

In the first example, speaker B treats speaker A's question as a future-oriented invitation, and speaker B accepts that invitation. In the second example, by contrast, speaker B treats speaker A's turn as a past-oriented complaint directed at B, and responds with an apology and an account. Importantly, these understandings are shown to be correct or incorrect in any third turn in a sequence, where speaker B's displayed understanding of what speaker A meant can become the object of repair (Schegloff 1992b). Through this process participants construct and display their 'mutual understandings' in a sequential 'architecture of intersubjectivity' (Heritage 2004: 224).

According to Heritage, the normative rules that tie the first and second actions of adjacency pairs together are 'important resources by which interactants can shape the trajectory of sequences of action' (1988: 129). As we saw in the analysis of the Tony and Marsha extract, for example, in producing an assessment, Tony (interactionally) encourages Marsha to produce an agreement or a disagreement with it. Although these resources can 'influence' the conduct of one's co-participants (1988: 129), these norms are not mechanical templates which *determine* our actions. Showing that a practice or activity appears regularly, or even routinely in talk, does not provide evidence of a 'pre-discursive' rule that operates 'out there in the world' or 'inside the heads' of participants, governing the way we speak and behave (cf. both Foucauldian notions of 'discourse' and Parson's 'judgemental dope' discussed in Chapter 3). Even while the production of a first assessment, such as Tony's 'well that's awful', sets up the normative relevance of, and generally occasions, its appropriate second-pair-part – in this case Marsha's agreement token 'Yeh' – it does not mean that Marsha is somehow pre-programmed to respond in this way. Rather, in order to say that some rule or norm is operative in talk, one must be able to demonstrate that participants treat these rules and norms as recognizable and relevant when they interact with one another. In Marsha and Tony's case, Marsha's failure to provide a (normatively, expectable) 'full' or 'strong' agreement is oriented to by Tony, who produces a further, upgraded assessment, which encourages Marsha to 'have another go' at responding to this aspect of Tony's turn. Thus, the 'locus' or 'site' of normativity – the place where it is found, if you like – is in participants' turn-by-turn orientation to it.

The idea that participants can treat each successive turn as a resource through which to establish how others understand their actions (Heritage 1988: 129) ties in with the ethnomethodological concept of indexicality. As we saw in Chapters 1 and 3, the notion of indexicality describes how we settle or 'fill in' the meaning of an utterance on any given occasion, by noting information about the context in which the words are uttered. 'Context' here refers to the sequential environment of the talk itself, in which events unfold turn-by-turn (the 'proximate' context), as well as the interactional setting in which an activity takes place (or the 'distal' context). It is with this latter notion of context that we can begin to see how CA analyses of the institution *of* interaction can be used to inform analyses of broader features of social organization at the social structural and institutional level.

The management of social institutions in interaction

Research on 'the management of social institutions *in* interaction' (Heritage 2004: 223) has been conducted using data from a variety of institutional settings, including courtroom trials (Atkinson and Drew 1979), public speaking (Atkinson 1984), doctor–patient interaction (Heritage and Maynard 2005) and broadcast talk (Clayman and Heritage 2002). The key feature which differentiates the CA approach from most social scientific accounts of the relationship between talk and social structure is that within CA, institutional talk is deemed to be observable *as* institutional talk, by virtue of features that are internal or 'endogenous' to it. Heritage puts it thus:

> Rather than starting with a 'bucket' theory of context (Heritage, 1987) in which pre-existing institutional circumstances are seen as enclosing interaction, CA starts with the view that 'context' is both a project and a product of the participants' actions . . . it is fundamentally through interaction that context is built, invoked, and managed, and that it is through interaction that institutional imperatives originating from outside the interaction are evidenced and made real and enforceable for the participants.
> (Heritage 2004: 224)

Thus, within CA, just as the local, sequential rules and norms linking first and second actions do not determine what people say or do in a mechanical way, so too, this broader notion of context is not meant to imply a form of contextual determinism. Neither demographic variables nor social-structural contexts contain or determine participants' actions. Rather, utterances are 'doubly contextual' (Drew and Heritage 1992b: 18): they are *context shaped* in the sense that they 'cannot be adequately understood except by reference to the context in which they participate' (1992b: 18), and they are also '*context renewing*' in that 'every current utterance will itself form the immediate context for some next action in a sequence'. It follows that the interactional context is not exogenously (i.e. from outside) predetermined, but is 'continually being developed with each successive action' (1992b: 18), and contexts are 'inherently locally produced and transformable at any moment' (1992b: 19). The process of analysis does not require us to look *beyond* the talk to establish the context and understand what the talk is orienting to. Instead, participants' talk constructs and orients toward the relevant context, and does so on a turn-by-turn basis. Heritage draws attention to this point when he states 'it is thus through the specific, detailed and local design of turns and sequences that "institutional" contexts are observably and reportably – i.e., accountably – brought into being' (1984: 290), and this applies equally to other (purportedly) 'macro' contexts typically assumed to exert their influence from outside of talk – such as gender norms and power, for example (Schegloff 1997). Thus, the question the analyst must ask when they encounter situations that are routine and familiar (e.g., 'gendered' discourse) is not 'what, from outside those situations, ensures their routine, familiar, standard character?', but rather, 'how are recognizable routineness, typicality and standardization built into the situation?' (Sharrock and Watson 1988: 74).

The idea that social contexts do not 'contain' or 'determine' our actions represents a significant departure from most mainstream sociology which conceives of the social world in terms of two contexts or realms – the 'macro' context of social structures and institutions, and the 'micro' realm of local social processes and actions. This approach is evident within the sex differences research discussed in Chapter 2, for example, where demographic, 'macro-structural' features of social context, such as the speaker's sex, are treated as independent variables which condition or contain our actions. It is also evident in much poststructuralist and critical discourse analysis, where researchers tend to adopt a reified, Foucauldian understanding of discourse, in which talk is conceived as constrained, influenced or otherwise determined by pre-existing discourses or forces of power 'from above' or 'beyond' the talk. Indeed, as we saw in Chapter 3, many discourse researchers influenced by poststructuralism divide their version of society (if only implicitly) into macro–micro and structure–agency parts, and import macro-level notions of context into their analyses. What both sex differences and poststructuralist approaches share, then, is a reliance on the analyst's *assumptions* about the purported existence, operation, and relationship between essentially abstract macro and micro contexts. These contexts seem to float free outside talk, and as such, they remain mysterious and elusive.

One of the distinctive features of CA, by contrast, is that it does not conceive of the macro-structural and micro-interactional relationship in such strict dualistic terms. In an extension of the ethnomethodological reworking of structural functionalism that I discussed in Chapter 3, CA rejects the abstract theoretical separation of macro and micro contexts, and fundamentally reconceptualizes 'how social action is related to social structures' (Hutchby and Wooffitt 1998: 4) and 'contextual and sociological variables' (1998: 5). From a CA perspective, macro-social structures, like institutions, are endogenously constituted within talk, and one does not necessarily need to venture beyond or behind the talk to demonstrate this. Indeed, as we saw in Chapter 3, when we conceive of social structure as an endogenous production, then the artificial line separating structure from agency, and macro from micro contexts, breaks down. Unlike ethnomethodology, however, CA has developed a detailed empirical programme which *demonstrates* what the endogenous constitution of these contexts, and their dissolution, looks like in practice.

Power and asymmetry in talk

Ian Hutchby (1996a, 1996b 1999) provides a compelling illustration of this approach. Rather than treating power as something that is predetermined by 'external', macro-demographic features of social context, Hutchby shows how we might begin to use CA to understand the *in situ* construction and operation of power asymmetries in discourse (see also Markova and Foppa 1991; Sacks 1972; Thornborrow 2002). The institutional setting for Hutchby's analysis is a British talk radio show. Hutchby argues that in talk radio, while callers typically proffer an opinion, the hosts debate such opinions and often take up opposing stances. Thus, the principal activity within this setting is that of *argument*.

Drawing on the work of Harvey Sacks (1992, vol. 2: 348–53), Hutchby suggests that those who 'go first' in an argument, and set their opinion on the line, are in a weaker position than those who 'go second' (the host), 'since the latter can argue with the former's position simply by taking it apart' (1996b: 487). Hutchby suggests that this asymmetry is built into the very structure of talk radio and the management of calls. The host, by virtue of going second, has at his disposal 'a collection of argumentative resources which are not available in the same way to callers' (1996b: 488). These argumentative resources allow the host to point to weaknesses in the caller's stance, and the caller is required to build a defence, expand upon or account for their claims. One upshot of this asymmetry is that the host 'is often in a more powerful position discursively to constrain the actions of his or her co-participant' (Hutchby and Wooffitt 1998: 170).

One way in which hosts take issue with the caller's argument is by using a class of utterances including 'So?' and 'What's that got to do with it?' These utterances challenge the validity or relevance of the caller's opinion to the issue being discussed (Hutchby 1996b: 489). A second way in which the host may seek to establish control of the agenda is by 'selectively formulating the gist or upshot of the caller's remarks' (1996b: 490):

(4.4) [Hutchby 1996b: 491]
```
1   Caller:  ...but e:r, I- I think that we should be working at
2            breaking down that separateness I [think] these
3   Host:                                      [Ho:w?]
4            (.)
5   Caller:  these telethons actually increase it.
6   Host:    Well, what you're saying is that charity does.
7   Caller:  .h Charity do::es. ye[::s I mean-        ]
8   Host:                         [Okay we- so you]'re (.) so
9            you're going back to that original argument we
10           shouldn't have charity.
11  Caller:  Well, no I um: I wouldn't go that fa:r, what I
12           would like to [see is-
13  Host:                  [Well how far are you going then.
14  Caller:  Well I: would- What I would like to see is...
```

In this extract, the caller has been criticizing telethons for exacerbating the distinction between the 'donors' and the 'recipients' of charity. He argues that this 'separateness' needs to be broken down (lines 1–2). The host responds by proposing two formulations or 'upshots' of the caller's argument. On the first occasion he says 'Well, what you're saying is that charity does' (line 6), and on the second occasion 'so you're going back to that original argument we shouldn't have charity' (lines 8–10).

The host's first formulation 'proposes that the caller's argument in fact embraces charities in general and not just telethons as one sort of charitable endeavour' (Hutchby 1996b: 491). Interestingly, even while the caller has not in fact made such a generalization in his prior talk, he nonetheless agrees with this in his next turn (line 7) By agreeing, the caller thereby equips the host with a resource for reformulating the agenda (Hutchby and Wooffitt 1998: 169). The host's second formulation suggests that the caller is returning to an argument that a prior caller has already made – that 'we shouldn't have charity' (lines 9–10) (1998: 169). Thus, both of the host's upshots serve 'to contentiously reconstruct the position being advanced by the caller' (Hutchby 1996b: 491).

Hutchby's analyses demonstrate clearly how power emerges in talk as a consequence of the of the way calls are structured. However, Hutchby and Wooffitt stress that this asymmetry is not a mechanical, one-way process that is 'caused' by the institution of talk radio, or by participants' roles within it. Instead, power is produced sequentially, as talk unfolds, 'rather than being predetermined by theoretical features of the context' (Hutchby and Wooffitt 1998: 166). Indeed, callers can resist hosts' challenges by moving into second position themselves if the host expresses an opinion (1998: 171).

These analyses may be especially pertinent to feminist work, since they demonstrate how we might begin to study social-structural features of context, without resorting to 'interaction-external' explanations. Indeed, Hutchby sets his work apart from the well-known feminist approach of Davis (1988), for example, who believes that a CA analysis of power in doctor–patient encounters must be subsidized with a broader theoretical apparatus deriving from the work of Giddens (1984). Hutchby (1996b: 483) notes: 'I do not believe that we need to bring in theories of power external to CA. I show how conversation analysis can be used to address the question in its own terms and without incorporating external theories of social action'. Feminists have begun to use the kind of approach advocated by Hutchby to provide a fine-grained examination of *resistance* in talk (see Kitzinger 2000a: 174–6; 2000b; Speer 2002d; Widdicombe 1998a). A future challenge for feminist researchers is to explore further how power and resistance get played out in a range of settings, and in a way that reproduces or transcends gender norms.

DP's anti-cognitivism

While ethnomethodology and CA have done much to transcend the macro–micro dualism in sociology, DP adds a further level of detail to our reformulation of context, in that it applies ideas from CA to rethink traditional understandings of cognition and mind–world relations in psychology (Edwards 1997; Edwards and Potter 1992; Potter 1999; Te Molder and Potter 2005). Drawing on the philosophical ideas of Wittgenstein (1953) and the ethnomethodological sociology of Coulter (1979, 1989), DP advocates an explicitly *non-cognitivist* research agenda. By this I mean that it recasts traditional, cognitive theories of mind based on technical inner entities and processes, including feelings and emotions (Edwards 1999; Frith and Kitzinger 1998; Locke and Edwards 2003; Potter and Hepburn 2003), attitudes and evaluations (Potter 1998a; Puchta and Potter 2002; Wiggins and Potter 2003) and violence and aggression (Clarke et al. 2004; Lea and Auburn 2001) in practical, discursive terms (Edwards and Potter 2001).

This does not mean that cognitions do not exist – that there is nothing going on inside people's heads, or that we can never explain people's actions in terms of the world 'under the skull'. Instead, it means that explanations for what people say and do cannot be *reduced* to cognitive processes (Middleton and Edwards 1990: 41–2). Our talk consistently describes cognitive processes as part of *doing* things (Edwards 1997). Thus, as we saw in Chapter 1, within DP, the proper focus for analysis is not 'the world out there' or 'the world in here', but how descriptions of mind (e.g., claims which evoke an inner life of mental states and cognitive processes, perceptions and experiences) and descriptions of the world (e.g., claims which evoke an external, objective realm of events and social processes, as well as broader social and historical structures, and relations) are formulated and used to do things in interaction. The focus is on how mind–world descriptions are built in discourse in order to construct plausible versions or accounts, and how people attend or 'orient to' the interactional implications of those descriptions (Edwards and Potter 2001). Thus, in contrast to mainstream psychology, DP researchers, move '*both* the *analytic* and *explanatory* focus from cognitive processes and entities, to discursive practices and the resources they draw on' (Potter 1998a: 235–6, emphasis in original).

While DP has always been explicitly anti-cognitivist in its approach, CA's stance in relation to cognition is rather more ambiguous. As Potter (1998c) points out, while some conversation analysts have made arguments against the cognitivist interpretation of conversational phenomena (e.g. Heritage 1990–1) and have conceived of cognitivist notions, such as evaluations and assessments in interactional terms (e.g. Pomerantz 1984), they 'have often been agnostic with respect to cognitive issues or even willing to consider some integration of cognitive and conversational approaches (Mandelbaum and Pomerantz 1990; Pomerantz 1990–91; Drew 1995a, 1995b)' (Potter 1998c: 34). Nonetheless, an increasing number of studies use CA to provide a non-cognitivist account of a range of utterances that index mental process, such as 'I think' and 'I don't know' (see Hutchby 2002; Jefferson 1984; Potter 2004a; Te Molder and Potter 2005). In this sense I regard both DP and CA as compatible with an anti-cognitivist agenda.

A non-cognitivist analysis of the gender attribution process

So what does a non-cognitivist approach to interaction look like? And how does this approach help us to illuminate how gender (and gendered behaviour) 'gets done' in talk? By way of an illustration, consider Extract 4.5, which is taken from an informal dinner discussion where I showed friends and relatives a range of visual prompts of men and women engaged in a range of non-traditionally gendered activities (men's ballet and women's rugby, for example). The data that these pictures generated allowed me to explore the interactional organization of the 'gender attribution process' (see Speer 2005).

As we saw in Chapter 3, the gender attribution process is a term coined initially by Kessler and McKenna (1978) to describe the methodical procedures through which members come to identify others as male or female. Unlike Kessler and McKenna, however, whose analyses were based on the retrospective accounts of transgendered individuals, or on their own recollections and reports of events, what I wanted to do in my study was to provide a detailed, turn-by-turn analysis of transcripts of real life, interactional examples of members *doing* gender attributions. What I found was that members often had trouble identifying the gender of the person in the image. I analysed the procedures through which they managed that trouble, and collectively assigned a coherent gender identity to the person in the picture – thus re-establishing what Garfinkel (1967) has termed the 'natural attitude' toward 'normally sexed persons'.

Just prior to the interaction at the start of Extract 4.5, I showed the participants a picture of a female rower. I pick up on Keith's negative evaluation of a prior prompt (in which he noted that the woman in the image was 'butch') and invite him to produce a negative evaluation in this case: 'do you think that's butch then that coz that looks quite aggressive an?' (lines 1–3).

(4.5) [Speer 2005: 80–1]

```
1     Sue:      I mean do you think that's (0.4) that's (.)
2               butch then that (.) coz that looks quite
3               aggressive an'
4               (1.0)
5  → Keith:     Now ↑wha'- is that a male or a female I don't
6               [know? Sorry]
7     Pamela:   [°That's a female] I would think°
8               (0.8)
9     Donald:   (That was) Billy Beaumont he never knew which
10              was the difference
11              (0.6)
12    Keith:    >Really?<
13              (.)
14    Donald:   on Question Of Sport=
15    Keith:    =Yeah [that's true that's true]
16    Sue:            [hahh. .hh]
17    Donald:   He [got Princess A - ] er- Princess erm (0.8)=
18    Alice:       [(Yeah I like that)]
19    Donald:   =Anne wrong didn't he
20              (0.4)
21    Keith:    [Ye:ah]
```

```
22    Donald:    [He(h)] thought she was a male
23               (.)
24    Keith:     No that (.) tha- that's a female (.) I would say
25               isn't it yeah
26    Sue:       Do you think that's butch?
27               (0.2)
28    Keith:     .hh No (.) not particularly (.) ↓no no [no]
29    Pamela:                                           [(Mm)]
30               (0.8)
31    Alice:     Oh is it erm a female [mm]
32    Pamela:                          [It's] a rower isn't it=
33    Alice:     =Ye:s [°it] could be a male°
34    Pamela:          [Mm] (she's got )
35    Alice:     Oh: that's okay=
```

What is interesting here is that Keith does not even attempt to produce a gender attribution. Instead, he responds by making explicit his cognitive inability to identify the gender of the person in the image, and apologizes for his failure to attribute gender in this case: 'Now what is that a male or a female, I don't know, sorry' (lines 5–6).

There are two main ways in which we might interpret this utterance. First, if we wanted to approach it from within a cognitive psychological framework, we might treat it as a factual reporting by Keith of his uncertainty about the gender of the person in the image. He is simply offloading his thoughts as they happen. A second possibility, however – and one that I want to explore here – is that topicalized uncertainties which invoke cognitive doubt, also do interactional work

Notice, for example, that Sue's opening question may pose an interactional 'dilemma' for Keith. If he takes up her invitation and responds that this image does indeed look just as 'butch' as the previous one, then such a response may provide the basis for negative judgements about his identity – that he is prejudiced, for example. It may be no coincidence, then, that Keith's claim to uncertainty is placed just at the point where he becomes accountable for having prejudiced motives. Keith may be attending to an issue of stake here (see Potter 1996b: 131–2). He uses his displayed doubt in order to avoid a direct 'yes' or 'no' response to Sue's identity implicative question, thereby inoculating himself against accusations of prejudice.

One consequence of this turn is that it allows Keith to exploit the temporary disruption to the natural attitude engendered by his attributional 'problems', in order to implicitly problematize the image in front of him – and without saying so directly (and what better way to problematize a person or image than by indicating that one simply does not have the capacity to identify them/it). Thus, in this context, Keith's topicalized inability to attribute may itself become an interactional resource, used as a relatively 'safe' form of negative identity attribution.

There are a number of features of this extract which support this interpretation. Sue asks Keith whether the person in this image could be described as 'butch' (line 2). Although 'butch' is a term that can be used with reference to women or men, in the context of Keith's immediately prior use of the term to evaluate an image of a woman, it is likely that Sue is using it to refer to a woman in this case. However, Keith does not appear to pick up on this in his identification turn. If Keith were working to assign gender here, it is perhaps expectable, given members' adeptness at 'noticing' implicitly gendered cues in the other extracts I analysed (Speer 2005), that he would be alert to any such clues, and to the strong possibility that 'butch' may denote 'female' on this occasion.

The variability evident in this extract also provides evidence for the interactional (as opposed to the factual-cognitive) import of Keith's uncertainty. So, despite first claiming that he 'doesn't know' whether the image in front of him is that of a man or a woman, Keith subsequently does go on to produce a definite gender attribution (lines 24–5). Of course, it's possible that he has simply picked up on, and is merely aligning with, Pamela's attempted female attribution (line 7). However, Keith's moment of clarity comes at precisely the point at which Donald has teased him by comparing him to Bill Beaumont – a well-known sports personality on the BBC television programme, *A Question of Sport* – who, like Keith, was incapable of identifying the gender of persons in images. In making the comparison, Donald implies that Keith's failure to attribute, like Beaumont's, reveals some failing about him as a person, and he could thus be heard to be indirectly teasing or 'poking fun' at Keith (Drew 1987). Keith moves from displayed uncertainty to displayed certainty precisely in order to manage these local interactional circumstances. He demonstrates, at the moment where doubts about his attributional abilities are most acute, that he is a competent person in full grasp of his perceptual powers.

Finally, when Sue repeats her opening utterance 'do you think it's butch?' (line 26), Keith again works to avoid a definite 'yes' or 'no' response. He is somewhat equivocal, noting simply that it is 'not particularly' butch (line 28). This equivocation is perhaps surprising, given the apparent ease with which members in the rest of my data indexed non-normativity precisely in order to account for why they had trouble assigning gender in the first place (Speer 2005). What's different in this case, however, is that here again, Keith's equivocation, like his initial 'uncertainty', comes at the exact point at which he may be held accountable (by Sue) for having prejudiced motives. Keith thereby engages in identity work to prevent and deflect just such inferences.

So, while in most of the instances I analysed, an 'uncertain' or 'incorrect' gender attribution was treated as an accountable phenomenon which requires identity work on the part of the speaker, Extract 4.5 shows that members may topicalize cognitive doubt and their inability to attribute, specifically in order to avoid responses which may provide the basis for negative judgements about their character (that they are prejudiced for example). Moreover, even while such responses may appear neutral, and not directly evaluative, such topicalized attributional failures themselves perform moral, evaluative work on the picture or person described (showing, for example, that persons who transcend gender norms are non-identifiable), thereby reinforcing the natural attitude.

When analysis proceeds in this way, it becomes apparent, as Potter (1998c) points out, that the social and the psychological are not as neatly separable realms as the 'abstract analytic language' of researchers implies. In this case, Keith's claim to lack of knowledge, in which he invokes a mental world, is used to build a particular gendered *reality*, in which gendered ambiguity is morally accountable. As Potter notes, in participants' discourse, 'constructions of the world and cognition are often mutually implicative' (1998c: 35): 'cognition and reality blur as talk unfolds; neither stands as a separable contextual frame against which to explain talk' (1998c: 40). Much of what we are doing when we describe 'inner states' is to construct versions of gendered reality that are factual, plausible and objective. Similarly, much of the work we are doing when we describe the world or invoke 'facts' about gender, is to present ourselves as having a particular kind of (non-prejudiced) identity.

In Chapters 5 and 6 I will extend this discussion, to show how insights from CA and DP can be applied to, and used to rework our understanding of, the relationship between the purportedly 'external' macro-social structural context of gender norms, and ideology, on the one hand (Chapter 5), and the purportedly 'internal', cognitive-psychological context of prejudicial attitudes and beliefs on the other (Chapter 6).

(iii) Language as a form of social action?

The idea that discourse *does* things, that it is a form of social action, can be demonstrated with the notions of 'variability' and 'ideological dilemmas'. We have already begun to explore what variability and ideological dilemmas look like in Keith's interaction in Extract 4.5. In this section, I will focus in more detail on what these features can tell us about the action-performative, context-sensitive nature of discourse, and members' construction of and orientation toward 'normative' gender and sexuality.

Discourse is variable

Participants will often say variable or contradictory things – even in the course of the same interview, or across one spate of talk. Many non-CA and non-DP researchers treat this variability as a problem and as something that might be overcome by using better measurement techniques. However, for discursive psychologists and conversation analysts, this variation is not a problem but is central to discourse (Potter and Wetherell 1987). We contradict ourselves frequently, precisely because talk is action-oriented, and we construct what we say in order to fit the local interpretative context in which we find ourselves. An analysis of variability helps us to understand what participants are doing with their talk (Potter et al. 1990: 208). Extract 4.6, which is taken from a mealtime discussion as part of my research exploring the way participants justify women's non-participation in 'male-identified' leisure activities (Speer 2002b), provides a neat example of variability in action.

(4.6) [Adapted from Speer 2002b: 363]
```
1   Matt:   Why would you choose rugby (.) being a very
2           rough sport, (.) you're liable to get in- (.)
3           horrible injuries, (.) it's twenty-four
4           blokes this year in this country alone (.)
5           rugby players who've broken their necks
6           (0.4)
7   Keith:  Yeah
8   Chris:  Yeah-[well]=
9   Sue:         [Really?]
10  Chris:  =a girl[I know that lives underneath me she]
11  Matt:          [I mean would you (0.4) would you]
12          rather do that than per'aps play tennis or
13          something which is less likely to be?
14          (0.9)
15  Sue:    But if I was- if I was male now would you be
16          saying the same things to me?
17          (0.3)
18  Matt:   Well no because I think a bloke c'n: (0.8)
19          look after himself more
```

Matt makes two apparently contradictory claims about the 'injury prone' status of male rugby players in the course of this sequence. On the first occasion he claims that 'it's twenty-four blokes this year in this country alone rugby players who've broken their necks' (lines 3–5), while on the second occasion he states that 'I think a bloke c'n look after himself more' (lines 18–19). This apparent contradiction or 'variability' is not a sign that there is something wrong with the method that was used to collect the data, or that Matt is experiencing some kind of mental confusion or 'cognitive dissonance'. Rather, just as in Extract 4.6, where Keith's variable ability to attribute gender to the person in the image can be explained with reference to identity implicative, interactionally consequential features of the surrounding talk, the variation in this extract provides a clue to, and can be explained in terms of, the interactional work that Matt is engaged in at different moments in the interaction.

Matt uses the first description in which he invokes horrific injuries in the men's game, in order to highlight how dangerous it is, and to justify why Sue – and perhaps *anybody* – shouldn't play rugby. He uses the second utterance about men's ability to 'look after themselves more', to justify why *women* in particular shouldn't play rugby. The variability in this extract highlights the context-sensitive, action-oriented nature of descriptions, and the variable local uses to which 'injury arguments' can be put (for more on this see Speer 2002b). This does not mean that there is no regularity in discourse. Rather, as Wetherell and Potter (1988: 172) put it, 'regularity cannot be pinned at the level of the individual speaker. There is regularity in the variation'.

Ideological dilemmas

The variability evident in some discourse may provide evidence for the existence of an 'ideological dilemma' (Billig et al. 1988). The concept of ideological dilemma was developed in DP by Billig and colleagues as a counter to traditional cognitive and sociological theories of ideology which treat individuals as automatons, or 'the blinded bearers of a received ideological tradition' (Billig et al. 1988: 2). In contrast to this unilinear, non-social model of ideology, Billig and colleagues stress 'the dilemmatic aspects of ideology ... Ideology is not seen as a complete, unified system of beliefs which tells the individual how to react, feel and think. Instead ideology, and indeed common sense, are seen to comprise contrary themes' (1988: 2). For example, commonsense tells us both that 'absence makes the heart grow fonder' and 'out of sight, out of mind', that 'nothing ventured, nothing gained' and 'look before you leap', and that 'many hands make light work' and 'too many cooks spoil the broth' (1988: 16). According to Billig et al. (1988) these contrary themes of commonsense are what give rise to dilemmas, and encourage debate and argument.

Just as with the concept of variability, many social psychologists treat such dilemmas from within a cognitivist framework and 'as evidence for the hopeless confusion of common sense' (Billig et al. 1988: 16). However, within a DP framework, dilemmas are rich resources because they can be studied for what they show us about members' *orientations to* ideology and normativity in culture. Ideological dilemmas are evident in the way participants attempt to manage dual concerns, or 'conflicting demands for accountability'. Although the concept is DP rather than CA, and CA researchers do not talk about dilemmas in these terms, as I will show later, Schegloff (1997: 182) does refer in his analyses to the 'competing proprieties of action' that a first pair part (e.g., a request) can generate, and this captures something of what the concept is meant to grasp here.

We have already seen in the analysis of Extract 4.5 how Sue's question 'do you think that's butch?' (lines 1–2) posed a dilemma for Keith, in that an agreement or a disagreement potentially makes relevant his identity as a prejudiced or a non-prejudiced person. An example of another interactional dilemma in action is included in Excerpt 4.7, below, which is taken from an interview with Ben, who is in his mid-twenties. In the moments preceding this sequence, Sue asks Ben if he has ever been to a gay club, and he describes a time that he went to a gay bar with his girlfriend and some of her friends 'coz she was intrigued'. We join the interaction approximately halfway through the interview, at a point where Sue asks Ben if the man that he says 'chatted him up' in the bar was 'attractive'. As we shall see, Ben's dilemma centres around the issue of how, as a heterosexual man, he might go about describing his experience, without seeming gay *or* homophobic.

(4.7) [Adapted from Speer and Potter 2002: 168]
```
 1   Sue:    Was he attractive?
 2           (0.6)
 3   Ben:    Phh. (1.8) I s'pose he was reasonably well looking, ↑Yeah.
 4           (1.6)
 5           But you know it doesn't interest me,
 6           (.)
 7           I'm definitely (0.8) not interest(h)ed(h) in(h) men(h).
 8   Sue:    hhh.
 9           (0.8)
10   Ben:    You know I think, yeah some men as- as, I'm sure it's the same for
11           women (0.6) find (.) other men– think that other men – 'he looks really
12           good'.
13           (0.4)
14           That's definite. You know, some men will deny that
15   Sue:    Mm
16   Ben:    but I know people who I think 'bloody-hell he's absolutely awesome (.)
17           figure, awesome'. You know.
18           (.)
19           Looks cool. Totally and utterly. Because I know I don't.
20           You know the- the- the Adonis type=
21   Sue:    =Mm=
22   Ben:    =physique and (.) whatever, you know
23   Sue:    Mm
```

Sue's question about the man in the gay bar, 'was he attractive?' (line 1), sets up a possible dilemma for Ben, or conflicting demands for accountability, which have implications for his sexual identity. Indeed, it could be said to trigger his sexual orientation into becoming relevant or at risk in the interview situation. On the one hand, if Ben answers 'yes, he was attractive', then he may be held accountable for being gay himself. On the other hand, if he responds 'no, he was not attractive', he may be interpreted as anti-gay, or perhaps as someone who is in denial about his own sexuality. Either action, said immediately and without qualification, may indicate that Ben has already considered the attractiveness of this man, prior to being asked, with the associated, potentially problematic implications for his identity this may bring. It is important to note that these possibilities are not simply the analyst's speculation, but are oriented to by Ben, and are therefore tractable within the data (and in this case, within Ben's carefully crafted response). Ben manages this dilemma, and the conflicting proprieties of action it entails, by constructing an identity as somebody who, at this moment, is neither gay, nor homophobic, *nor* someone who ponders the issue of men's attractiveness on a routine basis. In other words, Ben positions himself as a liberal rather than anti-gay.

Lines 2 onwards are particularly interesting for what they tell us about what Ben treats as accountable, and relevant to his identity. First, Ben constructs his response in such a way that indicates he has not thought about whether the man in the gay bar was attractive or not until now. He pauses, demonstrates some difficulty with Sue's question (Phh.), pauses again, and goes on 'I s'pose he was reasonably well looking, yeah' (line 3). This construction works to present Ben's views as not previously having been thought through or articulated. Since he has to construct an answer 'on the spot', Ben demonstrates that this is not something he has a readymade attitude or opinion about. The description 'reasonably well looking' is interesting for its (productive) vagueness. While the word 'attractive' may indicate sexual interest or desire, 'reasonably well looking', as a rather minimal, non-committal response, does not. The move from such vagueness to the upgraded specificity of 'but you know it doesn't interest me' (with the 'it' presumably meaning 'gay behaviour') (line 5), 'I'm definitely' not interested in men' (line 7), may be motivated sequentially by the long 1.6 second pause (line 4). Indeed, the pause comes at a transition relevance place (Sacks et al. 1974), but Sue does not come in. Ben treats Sue's non-response as evidence that his prior turn was insufficient, and as requiring an extended account. His response is interpolated with laughter, which diffuses the delicacy of the situation at the same time as orienting to it *as* delicate.

Having established that he is not gay, Ben works to deflect the possibility that his remarks may be interpreted as prejudiced (that he says he is not interested in men because he is homophobic, for example) *or* be taken by Sue as a sign that he is in denial about his own sexual identity. First, he shifts his footing (Clayman 1992), conceding that 'some men' (and women) 'think that other men – 'he looks really good'' (lines 10–12). This footing shift, along with the active voicing of what others might say (Wooffitt 1992), allows Ben to defer accountability for his views about attractive men onto non-present others. These views are not peculiar to him, nor are they exclusively related to his gender. The phrase 'some men will deny that' (line 14) is marvellously robust, able to account for all possible circumstances: individuals who say other men are not good looking are in denial, while those who do think other men are good looking render Ben 'normal'.

Ben upgrades the voicing of 'he looks really good' to 'bloody-hell he's absolutely awesome figure, awesome' (line 16–17). The contrast in this upgrade, between what Ben voices 'some men' as saying, and what he himself 'thinks', presents Ben as even more liberal than these others. Moreover, while this provides evidence that Ben is not averse to commenting on, and appreciating the looks of other men, it is, again, a carefully constructed description of the stature and physique of certain men, not a description of their intrinsic sex appeal. Ben, therefore, positions himself as someone who is able to admire what other men look like, without finding them attractive in a homoerotic sense.

It is through this carefully managed accounting and identity work that Ben constructs sexuality *as* dilemmatic, and orients to the non-normative nature of the phenomena that he purports to be liberal about. In other words, his delicacy, and the necessity for management of issues around same-sex attraction, is evidence for the way homosexuality is treated as accountable and problematic in culture. What this shows is that for Ben – and possibly in 'straight' culture generally – it is problematic being prejudiced *and* being gay.

As we have seen in previous chapters, many feminists believe that an analysis of talk alone cannot tell us much about the existence and workings of constraining social norms, and that we need to venture *outside* talk, to the extra-discursive realm of macro-social contexts, or *beneath* talk to some internalized (homophobic) attitude inside the head of the speaker, to access ideologies around gender and sexuality in culture What the analysis of Extract 4.7 demonstrates, however, is that members' dilemmas can offer immensely rich and productive insights into how cultural understandings and norms about gender and sexuality are constructed and oriented to in people's discourse. I will expand on the ways in which gender normativity and prejudice get played out and oriented to in participants' talk in Chapters 5 and 6.

(iv) Analysts' claims are grounded in participants' practices?

As I have shown, CA is critical of any approach which prioritizes the analyst's agenda over and above an analysis of what the participants can be shown to be attending to in their talk. So what does a participants' orientations approach to gender identity entail? Conversation analysts typically answer this question by noting that there are an indefinitely large number of ways in which context – and identity – can be formulated. Recall the description I opened with in the Preface: I am a white woman, a brunette, a daughter, a sister, an aunt, a 32 year old, a driver, a feminist academic, and so on. As Schegloff (1987, 1991, 1992a) contends, just because all of these descriptions of identity are *potentially* available, it does not mean that they are actually consequential for any piece of interaction. For the conversation analyst, there is no automatic *causal* relationship between language and demographic variables. What is crucial is being able to show participants orienting to the relevant contexts in their talk.

This means that a whole range of purportedly 'extra-discursive' features of context, such as participants' age, class, gender, sexual orientation, participants' goals and so on, should not be assumed to be relevant to the interaction, or be imposed on the analysis by the researcher. Rather, 'one should take for analysis only those categories that people make relevant (or orient to) and which are procedurally consequential in their interactions' (Antaki and Widdicombe 1998b: 4). Within this framework the analyst does not conceive of gender as a pre-given variable or trait that determines the linguistic resources men and women use to speak (cf. the sex difference perspective discussed in Chapter 2), but instead treats it as something that is constructed and *oriented to* in talk. As we saw in the analysis of Marsha and Tony's talk in Extract 4.1, this approach shows how 'even though a woman may be speaking, that does not mean that she is always speaking "as a woman"' (McElhinny 2003: 33).

Orienting to gender

Participants can be said to 'orient to' something when they treat it is as significant for, or pertinent to the interaction at hand (Antaki and Widdicombe 1998b: 4–5). Thus, I can 'orient to' what you have said as if it were an invitation, an accusation, or as a joke. I can 'orient to' you as my sister, a teacher, or as a feminist, and so on (1998b: 5). The following videotaped exchange from Schegloff (1997) offers an example of talk in which gender is oriented to as relevant by the participants. Michael and Nancy are having dinner with Shane and Vivian.

(4.8) [Schegloff 1997: 181]
```
1  Shane:        [.hehh huh .hhhh Most wishful thinkin
2         →      hey hand me some a dat fuckin budder willyou?
3                (0.8)
4  ?Shane:       °°Oh::yeah°°
```

```
 5                    (1.1)
 6  Nancy:    →       C'n I have some t[oo
 7  Michael:                       [mm-hm [hm:
 8  Nancy:                                [hm-hm-^hh[m      [^he-ha-] ha .hehh]
 9  Vivian:   →                                     [Ye[h [I wa]nt] sometoo.]
10  Shane:                                             [N[o:. ]    [( )-
11  Shane:            No.
12                   (0.2)
13  Shane:    →      Ladies la:st.
```

At line 2 Shane asks Michael for the butter, who responds compliantly. Shane takes the butter and just as soon as he does so, Nancy and Vivian ask Shane for it (lines 6 and 9 respectively). As Schegloff (1997: 181) notes, Nancy and Vivian's requests potentially compete with Shane taking the butter for himself. Shane responds with 'the ironic or mock rejection' of their requests (lines 10 and 11). But shortly after, he produces an account for that rejection – 'Ladies last' (line 13). Schegloff notes that this utterance makes the gender of Shane's co-participants relevant when the current activity (rejecting Nancy and Vivian's request for the butter) does not necessarily warrant it (1997: 182). Schegloff seeks to explain *why* Shane invokes gender as a relevant context at this moment, and he does so in terms of how 'the activities just preceding' may have 'prompted' it (1997: 182).

Schegloff suggests that Nancy and Vivian's requests for the butter pose a dilemma for Shane. They 'confront Shane with competing proprieties of action, ones embodied in various adages concerning orders of service: on the one hand "first come, first served", on the other hand "ladies last"' (1997: 182). While 'first come, first served' would 'yield as the proper next action that Shane continue to help himself to the butter', 'ladies first' 'yields as the proper next action that Shane defer continuing to serve himself and pass the butter' (1997: 182). What's interesting here, then, is how 'ladies last' serves as an account which reformulates in an ironic manner the gendered rule that Shane is *not* observing (1997: 182). Shane thereby deals with and orients towards socially normative 'matters of etiquette' by reversing them (1997: 186, note 5.). Thus, here again, we see a fine example of how gender normativity can be invoked and oriented to endogenously in talk, rather than as something that is necessarily external to, and constraining of it.

How gender creeps into talk

In their article 'How gender creeps into talk', Hopper and LeBaron (1998) sought to develop our understanding of how gender becomes a relevant feature of the context, and describe how participants advance gender from a peripheral, to a focal status in their talk (1998: 60). Drawing on Sacks' (1992) work on 'noticings', Hopper and LeBaron (1998) argue that gender creeps gradually into talk as a relevant part of the context through a 'noticing series' of three phases: 'peripheral gendered activity', a 'gendered noticing' and finally, the 'extending of gender's relevance' (1998: 72). This turn-by-turn 'increasing salience of gender' (1998: 68–9) is evident in Extract 4.9.

(4.9) [Hopper and LeBaron 1998: 69]
```
1    Jill:  I've signed up for one of those informal classes about
2           car maintenance and repair.
3    Pip:   That's a good idea. A lot of women can really learn a
4           lot from these classes
5           ((short pause))
6    Pip:   Well, I guess there's a lot of guys who can learn from
7           'em too.
```

Jill announces that she has enrolled in a car mechanics class (lines 1–2). Hopper and LeBaron suggest that this announcement contains a possible 'implicit indexing of gender' which is contained in the cultural stereotype that women do not know much about cars (1998: 69). Pip invokes gender as an explicitly relevant feature of context in her response (lines 3–4), which 'pragmatically presupposes the particular relevance to women of this kind of class' (1998: 69). She then corrects this presupposition (lines 6–7), which indicates a sensitivity to the possible offense she may cause by indexing a gender stereotype. In doing so, she increases the salience of gender as a relevant part of the context that she had already indexed in her immediately prior utterance. Hopper and LeBaron (1998: 59) suggest that it is in this way that 'speakers interact to gender context in the scenes of everyday life'.

Membership categorization analysis

Where Schegloff and Hopper and LeBaron have explored the interactional environment in which 'gender noticings' occur, a number of CA and DP researchers have drawn on Sacks' (1979, 1995) work on membership categorization analysis (MCA) to provide a detailed exploration of the work of *gender categories in use* (for descriptions of MCA, see Hester and Eglin 1997; Järviluoma and Roivainen 2003; Lepper 2000; Silverman 1998). Derek Edwards (1998, see also 1995) uses MCA to show how participants use membership categories such as 'girl' and 'woman' interactively. Although such categories are 'inference rich' and carry subtle nuances of meaning (young and available, mature and part of a couple, and so on), they are also indexical, context sensitive resources, that can be deployed variably in talk to do interactional work. As Edwards (1998) notes:

> Categorization is approachable discursively as something we actively do, and do things with (Edwards, 1991), rather than some piece of perceptual machinery that gets switched on by 'stimulus' events. Social categorizations are interaction's business, its matters in hand, not its causal effects or conditions.
> (Edwards 1998: 33)

We categorize ourselves and others differently, across different situations and contexts, precisely because our selections are 'not driven by objective category membership, nor a slavish adherence to semantics' (Edwards 1998: 26). Thus, we can correctly categorize someone as a woman, girl, lady, mother, wife or daughter, but the precise category that we use on any particular occasion will depend on the interactional business that our talk is designed to achieve.

One route we have into understanding the rhetorical work that gender categories can do, is to explore what happens when such categories are used contrastively, or when one category is used, and then repaired. A number of researchers have pursued these kinds of analyses (see, for example, Baker 2000; Beach 2000; Kitzinger and Wilkinson 2003; Nilan 1995; Speer 2002b; Stringer and Hopper 1998; Weatherall 2002b; West and Fenstermaker 2002a, 2002b; Wowk 1984). Consider the example from Edwards' analysis in Extract 4.10, below. Here a married couple are talking to a counsellor about their troubles. Connie has argued that she believes Jimmy's affair was the reason he left her. Prior to the interaction in this extract she says 'I just believe that this girl was here all along, and that's why' (Edwards 1998: 25). Some lines later Jimmy responds:

(4.10) [Edwards 1998: 26]

```
98   Jimmy:        (...) U::m (0.8) it's >not right, to sa:y that (0.5)
99                 >I didn't leave Connie for another woman.<
100                (0.6)
101                But (0.4) I was liv- sleepin' away for (0.5) 'bout
102                three- three weeks (.) ↓four weeks three weeks (0.4)
103        →       whatever, (0.6) when I moved in: (.) with a wo- girl,
104                which I did have (1.0) uh: a bit of a fling with (.)
105                when Connie went on holiday last year.
106                (1.2)
107                U::m
108                (2.0)
109                a:nd moved in with her, (0.6) (uh, what, three weeks?)
```

110	(2.8)
111	uhh (0.8) then moved back ↑out.
112	(2.0)

Jimmy denies that he left Connie for another woman (line 99). At line 103 Jimmy appears to start to say 'woman' and repairs it to 'girl'. Edwards' analysis points to how this repair is not inconsequential, but can be explained with reference to features in the prior talk. By aligning himself with Connie's description, 'girl', Jimmy is able to 'make his own use of any downgrading of her status that the switch allows'. This shift also fits with other features of the talk. So where Connie had talked about Jimmy's 'affair', Jimmy downgrades it to 'a bit of a fling' (line 104). Likewise, where Connie had referred to how Jimmy was 'living with' this woman, Jimmy notes simply that he 'moved in with' her (line 103), which is 'a more locative rather than sexual kind of expression, reinforced by how he shortly "then moved back out" (line 111)' (Edwards 1998: 26). It is in this way that Jimmy counters Connie's argument that something more serious and 'marriage-threatening' had been going on (1998: 26). Crucially, Jimmy uses the term 'girl', not because *that is what she was or how he thinks of her*, but because it does 'rhetorically potent business' in the talk (1998: 30).

So, how might a participants' orientations approach, and the close analysis of membership categories, be of use to feminists? In a series of articles Elizabeth Stokoe (2003, 2004, in press; Stokoe and Edwards 2005; Stokoe and Smithson 2001, 2002) argues that MCA provides feminist language researchers with the tools and framework for understanding how 'taken-for-granted "facts" about gender-appropriate behaviour . . . are worked out routinely' (Stokoe in press) and 'locked into place (see Baker 2000)' in talk (Stokoe in press). As I will show in my analysis of Extracts 4.14 and 4.15 later in this chapter, when a speaker juxtaposes a category such as 'girl' with *activities* that are not normatively associated with that category, such as 'rugby' (that is, when there is a disjuncture between the use of a particular category and the 'category bound activities' to which it refers), such contrasts can be used to make non-normative or 'transgressive' behaviours *morally accountable* (Heritage 1984: 197). By exploring the moral work that such categories and contrasts achieve, we can gain a better understanding of the mundane 'gendering of everyday life' and how categories 'function in maintaining the everyday social world as gendered' (Stokoe 2003: 332).

This approach also demonstrates how we might begin to access and study *social change*. According to Stokoe (in press), for example, just as categories can lock gendered meanings into place, the corresponding flexibility of categories means that 'category labels and their associated predicates and activities can be "revolutionized"' – something that lesbians and gay men have relied on in their reclaiming of words that were traditionally used as terms of abuse – such as 'queen' and 'dyke', for example. Likewise, there is no reason why our conventional rules for applying the categories 'secretary' or 'mother' cannot be transformed, and MCA can be a useful method for tracking such transformations (Stokoe in press).

(v) A relativist approach?

While DP has always been explicitly relativist in its focus, some conversation analysts argue that there is a 'strong realist orientation in CA's epistemology' (Hutchby 2001a: 76), and that there are certain 'intransitive' phenomena whose 'affordances' place oriented-to constraints on interactional practices (see, for example, Hutchby 2001a, 2001b, 2003). Nonetheless, since CA and DP both treat 'reality as a members' phenomenon' (Widdicombe 1998b: 195) and focus on how members build a shared sense of a concrete, objective reality as they interact with one another and engage in ongoing, interpretative, meaning-making work, then I am, in this book, treating them both as compatible with a relativist agenda.

DP has a particularly well-thought-out approach to the relation between talk and reality. Instead of engaging in ontological discussions about what is real and what is not real (a fundamentally realist enterprise), DP *brackets* issues of ontology, and focuses instead on the rhetorical and discursive resources that members use to construct phenomena (things, events and processes) as real, timeless and objective (i.e. beyond construction) in the first place. In other words, DP does not comment on the existence of gendered selves, or psyches, but treats what is real and not real, and matters of truth and falsity (including the reality and truth of gender), as themselves discursively constituted, action-oriented accomplishments (Edwards et al. 1995; Potter 1996b).

From this perspective, realism is just one rhetorical device among many others 'with no special or absolute basis' (Hepburn 2003: 9), and in much discourse work, 'realism', or what counts as real and factual, is treated as a research topic (Potter 1996b). The truth and reality of gender is treated as a matter for members, rather than analysts, to deal with (Stokoe 2005) and the focus is on understanding how members, through their 'reality analysis', 'constitute the world, themselves, and other people, as recognizably, take-for-grantedly, gendered' (Stokoe 2004). One way in which we can access members' reality constructing work is through an examination of the *rhetorical* organization of discourse (Billig 1991, 1996).

Discourse is rhetorically organized

Rhetorical analysis is concerned with two related features of discourse. First, it is concerned with how realism is achieved in talk and texts, that is, how discourse is organized to establish a particular version of the world as unproblematic, uncontestable and as 'solid, real and independent of the speaker' (Potter and Wetherell 1995: 81). We use a range of rhetorical forms and mechanisms in order to make our descriptions persuasive (Potter 1996a: 133), to establish something as factual (Potter 1996b), and to legitimize courses of action that might otherwise be seen as problematic, such as racism and sexism, for example (Wetherell and Potter 1992; Wetherell et al. 1987). DP studies how these rhetorical resources are mobilized to warrant speakers' accounts.

Second, rhetorical analysis is concerned with the argumentative organization of discourse. Accounts are typically designed to counter actual or potential alternatives, and in turn, to resist being countered (Potter 1996b: 108). Such possible or actual counter-arguments might present our accounts as false, or partial, or as a product of our own stake and interests (Potter 1996b). Thus, we can use rhetoric to respond offensively: directly against an attack, or defensively, in anticipation of possible uptakes (Edwards and Potter 2001; Hutchby and Wooffitt 1998: 196; Potter 1996b). Many of the resources that people use to establish the plausibility and facticity of an account gain their rhetorical power by virtue of their *sequential* position in relation to other statements or utterances.

Take Dorothy Smith's (1978) classic study 'K is mentally ill'. Smith analysed how K's descent into mental illness was constructed so as to make the illness appear a neutral fact. The account she examined was written up by one of her students as part of a class exercise. Smith argued that in order to work as an account of mental illness, the teller had to demonstrate that K's behaviour was not simply in breach of a norm or a rule, but was also anomalous. This was achieved rhetorically through the use of a number of contrast structures:

(4.11) [Smith 1978: 39]
When asked casually to help in a friend's garden,
she went at it for hours, never stopping, barely looking up.

(4.12) [Smith 1978: 42]
(i) she would bath religiously every night and pin up her hair,
(ii) but she would leave the bath dirty.

(4.13) [Smith 1978: 43]
(i) We would go to the beach or pool on a hot day,
(ii) I would sort of dip in and just lie in the sun
(iii) while K insisted that she had to swim 30 lengths

Smith argues that contrast structures typically include two parts (Extracts 4.11 and 4.12). The first part contains the context, and the instructions for the reader to ascertain what might be deemed 'fitting behaviour', and the second part contains the description of K's behaviour which does not appear to 'fit' with those instructions. It is through this juxtaposition of the two parts of the contrast structure that we come to see K's behaviour as anomalous (1978: 39). Indeed, Smith (1978: 45) argues that if the first part of the structure were missing, then the description of K's behaviour on its own would not produce the same rhetorical effect.

Extract 4.13 is slightly more complicated in that it contains three parts. Here, parts one and three of the sequence would not work on their own to establish that K's behaviour is anomolous. The second part provides an example of behaviour that fits the occasion and in this sense it provides a 'precedent' which strengthens the overall structure. It allows us to interpret the teller's behaviour as normal and K's as abnormal (1978: 43). Smith argues that the overall construction of these sequences plays a 'crucial part' in the reader coming to see 'the fact' that K is mentally ill (1978: 52).

Although Smith's analysis is based on a written account – or a 'monologue' rather than a conversation – similar contrast structures are used in multi-party conversations in order to justify sexism. In Extracts 4.14 and 4.15 the participants contrast images of normative femininity with detailed references to horrific injuries in order to justify why women should not play rugby.

(4.14) [Speer 2002b: 357]

```
 1 A  →  Matt:    If you were interested in a girl (1.0) you
 2                know and she was nice looking and everything
 3 B  →           you wouldn't want her to go out and get all
 4                smashed up
 5                (0.2)
 6        Keith:  Right. (1.0) There is a [propri-]
 7        Matt:                           [with] broken
 8                nose, (0.8) missing teeth, (0.6) cuts and
 9                (0.4) grazes, and cauliflower ears
```

(4.15) [Speer 2002b: 358]

```
 1        Keith:   No: as we were saying, [who- >I mean<]=
 2        Donald:                         ['nd I think]
 3 A  →   Keith:   =w- w- a young girl of (.)
 4                 y- your (.) fiancée,
 5                 she's twenty years of age,
 6                 she's going out playing rugby.(.)
 7 B  →            That night, she comes in,
 8                 she's got half her teeth missing.
 9                 .Hhh you know, wouldj-
10                 [would you] like that?
11        Pamela:  [(Exactly)]
```

These extracts are strikingly similar in terms of both their content and their structure. Keith and Matt's choice of words and their sequential placement is important and consequential for the overall rhetorical organization of their account. They both begin, in part A of the sequence, by producing a hypothetical image of normative femininity and heterosexuality, and position the recipients as the partner or potential partner of a female rugby player. In Extract 4.14, for example, Matt describes someone who may be 'interested' in a 'nice looking girl' (lines 1–2). He uses the generalized list completer 'and everything' (Jefferson 1990), which encourages recipients to invoke images of normative (i.e. heterosexual) femininity. Similarly, in Extract 4.15, Keith describes a 'young girl' of 'twenty years of age' (lines 3 and 5), who is situated in a loving relationship with 'you': she's 'your fiancée' (line 4).

These images of normative femininity and heterosexuality are then contrasted, in part B of the sequence, with scenarios in which those same women suffer horrific injuries. So, in Extract 4.14, Matt notes that she might 'go out and get all smashed up . . . with broken nose, missing teeth, cuts and grazes, and cauliflower ears' (lines 3–9). Similarly in Extract 4.15, Keith notes that she might have 'half her teeth missing' (line 8). This generates an image which contrasts rather strongly with the 'nice looking' 'girl' (Extract 4.14) and 'young girl' (Extract 4.15) that Matt and Keith's hypothetical man might be interested in. Indeed, these particular injuries do not appear to be randomly chosen. These 'girls' could equally have had broken arms, cracked ribs or concussion. The distinctiveness of these injuries is that they affect the face in some way. Thus, Matt and Keith rely on and work to invoke the recipients' commonsense knowledge about femininity in order to build a rhetorically powerful position through which claims about the appropriateness of women's non-participation can be made.

Note that both Keith and Matt talk about the hypothetical wants and likes of their co-participants (Extract 4.14, line 3; Extract 4.15, line 10). The discourse of likes and wants is particularly robust when deployed in this manner. For example, in Extract 4.14, one may need to do quite a lot of interactional work to deny that the injuries Matt describes are problematic. To undermine his claims, one would have to construct a potentially sadistic counterclaim, such as 'actually you would *want* to see them all smashed up'. Similarly, it may be hard for anyone to come back to Keith (Extract 4.15) with the potentially dubious counterclaim that they do indeed '*like* that' (line 10) or else assert that 'actually, girls without teeth are rather appealing'. By phrasing their utterances in this way, Keith and Matt neutralize any stake that would be associated with presenting or putting forward their own views, thereby working to bolster their (arguably gendered) arguments against possible counters. Indeed, these contrast structures are organized such that the speaker's justifications for why women should not play rugby are presented as rationally arrived at – as what any reasonable person would agree with in the circumstances. Overall, the rhetorical contrasts enable the speaker to deal with the asymmetry and prejudice of their arguments in a way that makes them appear less asymmetrical and susceptible to possible counters.

Chapter summary

In this chapter I have provided an overview of some key features of a CA and DP approach, noting how insights from both perspectives contribute theoretically and methodologically to the five criteria for the development of a feminist analytic approach as set out in Chapter 1.

This approach challenges both the essentialist gender-typing story associated with the vast bulk of variationist and sociolinguistic research conducted to date, as well as the 'broader' forms of analysis associated with poststructuralist, 'top-down' approaches to discourse. It offers feminists new ways of exploring the relationship between gender and language, and 'allows questions to be asked that are not steeped in gender difference or underpinned by essentialism' (Stokoe 2000: 558). By insisting that gender becomes a feature of analysis only where it is made relevant and oriented to by members, this approach demonstrates precisely how a social constructionist understanding of 'doing gender' might be grasped analytically.

The CA reformulation of the macro–micro debate in sociology offers feminists a method for accessing and exposing demographic and ideological features of social context without resorting to 'interaction external' explanations, or by relying on abstract, Foucauldian notions of broad, constraining 'discourses'. Rather than treating members as determined by gendered discourses from outside talk, this approach demonstrates how members *construct, orient toward, resist and subvert* gender normativity in their talk, and in ways that are observable and amenable to analysis.

Likewise, the DP, anti-cognitivist reformulation of mind–world relations in psychology, challenges the idea that talk reflects gender identity or subjectivity in a causal way. It shows how phenomena that are typically understood as 'internal to the subject' (e.g., thoughts, feelings and 'attitudes' about gender) can be redefined in discursive, interactional terms. Indeed, when we combine the sociological perspective of CA, and the psychological perspective of DP, the abstract theoretical and analytic separation of macro-structural, cognitive-psychological and micro-interactional realms may be reworked, and ultimately dissolved. This allows us, as feminists, to radically rethink our traditional understandings of the relationship between, operation of, and methods for accessing, gender ideology, identity, and talk, and, in turn, to create new possibilities for feminist politics and action.

A FEMINIST, CONVERSATION ANALYTIC APPROACH

As a method, this approach is rhetorically powerful. Indeed, unlike the studies considered in Chapter 3, which either fail to provide a formal analytic programme for studying discourse practices (as with Butler's poststructuralist, Foucauldian notion of discourse) or else resist providing such a framework (as with Garfinkel and Kessler and McKenna's ethnomethodological approach), what we have here are the tools to develop a systematic, empirically grounded form of feminism which *validates* (Peräkylä 2004) our politics and theories of the workings of powerful, patriarchal structures and the constitution of gender identity in an analytically tractable fashion, in the turn-by-turn, line-by-line analysis of live interactional materials. This analytic grounding is not some form of mindless empiricism for empiricism's sake. The technical discipline it demands requires commitment and hard work, but it pays dividends in providing deeper insights into the very phenomena that we often (prematurely) think we already know, but yet which we seek to explain and remedy.

In my view, an analytic approach that works at this fine-grained level of detail is perhaps the most likely method to remain true to constructionist principles. It is the most theoretically and methodologically fruitful form of DA for feminism, and has the greatest potential for reinvigorating and reinventing the field of language and gender research. I will provide a more detailed analysis of what this 'participants' orientations' approach to discourse looks like, and how it can be used to challenge the anti-CA critics, in Chapters 5 and 6.

5
RECONCEPTUALIZING GENDER IDENTITY
'HEGEMONIC MASCULINITY' AND 'THE WORLD OUT THERE'

In Chapter 4 I introduced some key features of the analytic approach that I argue for in this book, and some illustrative examples of how feminists and others have used this approach in their own work. I showed how an approach which draws on insights from CA and DP overcomes many of the problems associated with a 'variables and effects', sex differences perspective, and with the broad and largely abstract approach to discourse associated with poststructuralism. At the same time, by translating ethnomethodological ideas into an empirically grounded framework for studying discourse practices, I showed how CA and DP provide an analytically tractable method for exploring the construction of gender in talk. My aim in this chapter and the next is to deal 'head on' with what has become a hotly debated issue among gender and language researchers, and which is at the heart of debates about the relative utility of approaches informed by 'critical' forms of discourse analysis on the one hand, and CA on the other. The issue at stake here is the amount of 'mileage' that one can 'get out of' a technical, participants' orientations approach. Precisely how much of a piece of interaction can it explain? Is it sufficient (for feminists) on its own, or do we need to supplement it with 'interaction-extrinsic' analyses?

The Wetherell–Schegloff debate

The political and analytic utility of critical discourse analysis and CA has been the topic of a well-known debate between Wetherell (1998) and Schegloff (1997, 1998). This debate is the exemplar *par excellence* of the tensions and disagreements that currently exist within the field. As such, it has generated a number of further debates and commentaries; see especially the debate between Billig (1999a, 1999b) and Schegloff (1999a, 1999b), between Speer (2001a, 2001b) and Edley (2001b) and contributions from Lakoff (2003), Stokoe and Smithson (2001) and Weatherall (2000).

In the 1997 article that started the debate, Schegloff argues that critical discourse analysts should bracket their politics in favour of conducting, first and foremost, a fine-grained 'technical' analysis. He suggests that it is only once we have conducted a formal analysis and understood 'the object – the conversational episode – in its endogenous constitution' (1997: 168) (that is, the interaction on its own terms, as it is for the participants) that we can begin to know what kind of political issues our data will allow us to address (1997: 168). In doing so, we may find that the social and political is already 'a constitutive element of the object in the first instance' (1997: 170) and that we do not, therefore, need to import or 'add-in' a sociopolitical analysis at all.

Wetherell's (1998) response to Schegloff addresses the issue of whether this CA approach to participants' orientations and the technical analytic grounding of claims can offer an adequate answer to its own classic question about any piece of discourse – 'why this utterance now?' Using data from her project on masculinity in which a group of young men discuss a promiscuous night out, Wetherell proposes that, while a focus on participants' orientations (as outlined in Schegloff 1997) may be 'extremely revealing' (Wetherell 1998: 404), 'a complete or scholarly analysis . . . must range further than the limits Schegloff proposes' (1998: 388). Wetherell's own, more 'eclectic', critical discursive approach would, she says, be able to answer questions about her data, such as 'why in this community does it seem to trouble identity to "be on the pull" but multiple sexual encounters can be also successfully framed as "good"?' (1998: 404). Wetherell's approach can, in other words, explain the 'whys' of talk-in-interaction, when CA seems only relevant to the 'hows' (for a useful reanalysis of Wetherell's data from a CA perspective, see Wooffitt 2005).

In his response to Wetherell, Schegloff (1998: 416) argues that such questions are *not* beyond the scope of CA, and one does not need to turn to 'concerns extrinsic to the interaction' to find answers to them. Indeed, the 'why that now?' question is, for Schegloff, a pervasive one for the *participants* to a piece of interaction, and they do indeed 'seem oriented to [these questions] as relevant' (1998: 415). Therefore, Schegloff warns 'it would be useful not to underestimate what the reach of CA's questions is' (1998: 416) and that 'rather than beginning with gender ideologies . . . the analysis might begin by addressing what the parties to the interaction understand themselves to be doing in it' (1998: 415). Here, Schegloff appears to be 'throwing down the gauntlet' of this challenge to researchers interested in gender issues.

Although Schegloff's argument is, in my view, an extremely powerful one, the majority of feminists who adopt a broadly critical discursive approach share Wetherell's concerns, and have chosen not to take up Schegloff's challenge. Like Wetherell, they believe that we need to venture further than the limits of the text and an analysis of participants' orientations to be able to say anything politically effective. In particular, as I have noted in previous chapters, many feminists are concerned that CA-inspired forms of analysis fail to provide an adequate account of the constraining influence of the macro-social structural context of gender norms, ideology and 'the world out there', and the cognitive-psychological context of gender identity, subjectivity, prejudicial attitudes and beliefs and 'the world in here'.

New analytic topics: from femininity and homosexuality, to masculinity and heterosexism

In this chapter and the next, I take up Schegloff's challenge, and explore the utility of a participants' orientations approach in relation to two substantive topics: hegemonic masculinity (this chapter) and heterosexism (Chapter 6). Since the late 1990s, there has been a growing interest in theorizing masculinity (Gough 2001; Gough and Edwards 1998; Korobov and Bamberg 2004; Sidnell 2003) and heterosexism (Clarke et al. 2004; Gough 1998b; Kitzinger and Peel 2005; Korobov 2004) from a discursive perspective. This represents, in part, an attempt to redress the balance evident in much early work on gender and language, where it was the experiences and language of women, and lesbians and gay men, that researchers thought needed to be explained. By scrutinizing masculinity and heterosexism, we shift the analytic lens from the oppressed to the oppressor (Coates 2003; Johnson 1997; McIlvenny 2002b). Moreover, if one of the aims of a radical feminist psychology is to challenge patriarchy, and set about 'ending the social and political oppression of women' (Wilkinson 1997: 189), then it makes sense to try to capture the *object* of our critique in as much detail as possible, and to understand what talk about, or displays of masculinity and heterosexism do for members. If we can increase our understanding of how masculinity and heterosexism get done in talk, then we may find ourselves in a stronger position from which to expose the weapons of a patriarchal rhetoric and our 'straight imaginary' (McIlvenny 2002b: 13), and undermine or 'disarm' them.

I will demonstrate how an approach which sticks closely to an analysis of participants' orientations can be used to trace the constitution of masculinity and heterosexism discursively, without venturing beyond the talk to the purportedly 'external' macro-social structural context, or 'the world out there', on the one hand (this chapter), or beneath the talk to the purportedly 'internal', cognitive-psychological context, or 'the world in here', on the other (Chapter 6). In the course of doing so, these chapters show both how and why the anti-CA arguments may be unfounded.

I begin, in this chapter, by providing a review of Wetherell and Edley's (1999) critical discursive reformulation of the concept of 'hegemonic masculinity'. Wetherell and Edley's research on masculinity (1998, 1999; Edley and Wetherell 1995, 1997, 1999, 2001; Wetherell 1998, 1999a) provides a significant contribution to debates at the heart of the feminism,

DP and CA interface. Wetherell's early work in particular was central in developing the field of DP (Potter and Wetherell 1987) and in applying discursive psychological ideas to gender and other forms of inequality (Marshall and Wetherell 1989; Wetherell and Potter 1992; Wetherell et al. 1987). Although some of Wetherell's recent work draws on CA (see, for example, Antaki and Wetherell 1999), her work on masculinity with Nigel Edley is located more firmly in the critical discursive, poststructuralist tradition. It is this critical and poststructuralist strand of her work that I am concerned with here.

Using the analytic approach set out in Chapter 4, I explore how participants construct masculinity and situate themselves and others in relation to those constructions. I explore whether participants themselves orient toward something that analysts have glossed, in more abstract, theoretical contexts, as hegemonic masculinity, and consider what such orientations may be doing interactionally. Specifically, I look to see just how far an approach which does *not* go beyond participant orientations can take us in our understanding of the discursive constitution of gender identity.

The concept of hegemonic masculinity

The notion of 'hegemony' developed initially in the work of Gramsci (1971) and is used to define the maintenance of social power by certain groups, through persuasion and other means. Hegemony is thought to invoke power by consent rather than coercion. The ruling classes, for example, maintain their domination by defining and legitimizing a certain definition of the situation, framing the way events are understood and morality is defined. Consequently, the organization of society appears natural, inevitable and ordinary (Donaldson 1993: 645).

The concept has been developed and applied to masculinity by Connell (1987, 1995) and colleagues (Carrigan et al. 1985) and subject to various refinements and applications. Although the term is commonly used, it is rarely explicated in a way that can be easily applied to data. Thus, it has been described as a notion 'as slippery and difficult as the idea of masculinity itself' (Donaldson 1993: 644). This difficulty and slipperiness is demonstrated perfectly in Connell's (1995) own, somewhat convoluted definition. For him, hegemonic masculinity is 'the configuration of gender practice which embodies the currently accepted answer to the problem of the legitimacy of patriarchy, which guarantees (or is taken to guarantee) the dominant position of men and the subordination of women' (1995: 77). However, such impenetrable definitions give little sense of how we might be able to find such a thing, or identify it in our data.

Some consensus does appear to exist around the defining characteristics of the hegemonic ideal, which are 'naturalized' in the form of the hero in films (such as *Rambo*), books and sporting events (Donaldson 1993: 646). Therefore, in this society, and at this moment in history, dominant or 'hegemonic' masculinity equals white, heterosexual, successful masculinity. Indeed, Donaldson argues that heterosexuality and homophobia are its 'bedrock' (1993: 645). While it is argued that many men do not live up to the culturally hegemonic type, they do, nonetheless, benefit from its existence, and are 'complicit' in sustaining it (Edley and Wetherell 1995: 129). In this respect, it is not *determinate* of identity, but there is space for resistance, with subordinate forms constantly striving for ascendancy (1995: 165).

Since the late 1990s, researchers have begun to express 'worry about how scholars are using Connell's hegemonic masculinity concept' (Martin 1998: 473). As Edley and Wetherell argue, 'there are some areas of ambiguity . . . and it is not quite clear . . . just what counts as hegemonic masculinity' (1995: 129). Indeed, it has been described as a 'hybrid term', which, under the guise of explaining everything, actually explains nothing (Miller 1998: 194–5). Given such conceptual confusion, and despite – or perhaps – *because* the concept has become so influential since the mid-1990s, it is hardly surprising that hegemonic masculinity, along with the concept of 'hegemony' itself, has been the subject of a wide-ranging theoretical and methodological critique (see Wood 1998).

Wetherell and Edley's approach to hegemonic masculinity

In their 1999 article, 'Negotiating hegemonic masculinity: Imaginary positions and psycho-discursive practices', Wetherell and Edley offer one of the most comprehensive critiques of hegemonic masculinity to date. They point to a number of problems with the concept. For example, it cannot account for how male identities are 'reproduced', whether more than one hegemonic strategy can exist at any one time, and whether men can experience conflict or tensions as they move from one version of masculinity to another. They highlight its nebulous, 'impossible' nature, arguing, 'as social psychologists . . . we wonder about the appropriateness of a definition of dominant masculinity which no man may actually ever embody' (Wetherell and Edley 1999: 337).

In particular, Wetherell and Edley argue that Connell's formulation of hegemonic masculinity, while having a number of advantages, does not help us to understand 'the nitty gritty of negotiating masculine identities' and how such forms actually 'regulate men's lives' (1999: 336). Their critique, then, points toward some methodological recommendations. They suggest 'most emphasis needs to be placed on the exact mobilisation of accounts within a discursive field rather than on semantic content defined a priori' (1999: 352). This is translated into a form of critical discursive psychology which analyses the ways in which men themselves 'negotiate regulative conceptions of masculinity in their everyday interactions as they account for their actions and produce or manage their own (and others') identities' (1999: 337).

Wetherell and Edley's analyses

Wetherell and Edley set about demonstrating the utility of this approach using data from interviews and responses to picture prompts. These data are analysed by examining the way 'men position themselves in relation to conventional notions of the masculine' (1999: 335), and the implications of these positionings. As they explicitly state (and in contrast to the approach I develop here), 'we will not be concerned with the fine detail of the discursive and rhetorical work evident in the specimen extracts' (1999: 339). Drawing on the notion of 'imaginary positions' (1999: 335), they outline three 'distinct and highly regular' (1999: 350), 'global strategies of self-positioning' (1999: 338), 'typical discursive paths', 'discursive strategies' or 'psycho-discursive practices', through which members construct themselves as masculine and negotiate membership of this category.

The first pattern identified – 'heroic positions' – is the one which, they argue, 'could be read as an attempt to actually *instantiate* hegemonic masculinity' (1999: 340, emphasis in original) and represents the alignment of self with a 'conventional masculine ideal' (1999: 341) or 'man as courageous, physically tough and yet able to keep his cool' (1999: 342). The three men whom Wetherell and Edley suggest exemplify this position, align with such characteristics as the pleasure of being in control, meeting challenges in risky situations (Michael), showing southerners how to drink (Simon) and accounting for enjoying a violent sport such as rugby in terms of an 'unreflexive and conventionally masculine self' (Graham) (Wetherell and Edley 1999: 340–1).

One of the extracts Wetherell and Edley use to illustrate this form of discursive positioning is reproduced as Extract 5.1, which is taken from an interview with Simon, who is a 30-year-old white electrician. He is responding to the interviewer's question about whether the north of Britain is more macho than the south:

(5.1) [Wetherell and Edley 1999: 341]
Nigel: So (.) I mean (.) are the Northern regions (.) well Scotland and the northern regions more macho then?
[. . .]
Simon: I know that in my job (.) because we travel around the country a fair bit working and you sort of (.) there is a thing of looking down on southerners as

being wimps (*James*: Oh yeah) yeah (.) yeah the thing is SSB (.) soft southern bastards and that's (.) you know (.) when you go down there (.) you know how we were saying that in the army you're sort of (.) everybody's in there and in isolation (.) you're self contained whereas sometimes if we're working in London or in Kent or somewhere like that you would go out and you almost feel like (.) you know (.) right we're an invading army like (.) a load of contractors going out for a few bevies and you know (.) showing these southerners how to drink (.) so I think *in reality* the southerners are no more wimps than we are (.) but there is a bit of a (*Paul*: north-south rivalry) yeah (.) we like to think that we're more manly possibly than them.

(OU2: 9–10)

Wetherell and Edley (1999: 341) argue that Simon aligns himself, 'initially at least, with a conventional masculine ideal and in those terms produces an exalted or heroic self'. However, they suggest that this is not the most common form of positioning. In fact they say 'heroic masculine imaginary positioning was quite a rare event in our data' (1999: 343). In a second form of discursive positioning – 'ordinary positions' – men separate 'self from certain conventional or ideal notions of the masculine which . . . get reconstructed as social stereotypes' (1999: 343).

The following example of this form of positioning is taken from an interview with Raj and John. Raj is a 37-year-old Jordanian man who works as a contract engineer, and John is a 37-year-old white British man, employed as a mechanical maintenance engineer. The interviewer has spread out some magazine images of men representing different styles of masculinity and asks the interviewees if they can identify with any of them.

(5.2) [Wetherell and Edley 1999: 344]
Nigel: Okay (.) now is there any one of those six images who you would *most* erm identify with? (.) is there anyone there that you would say (.) you know (.) *that's* most like me?
John: Out of those I'd probably go for 4 [Image of Tony Parsons]
Nigel: Number 4 (.) Raj (.) what do you think?
Raj: *Yes* number 4 it seems to be (.)
Nigel: Okay why him?
John: He looks the most normal (laughs)
Raj: Sorry?
John: He looks the most normal I suppose
Raj: Yes that's right.
John: In the dress and (.)
Raj: Yeah half way (.) he's middle of the road.

John: I suppose Mr Average you might say (.) (*Raj*: Mm)
Nigel: Okay (.) right so (.) is it true to say then that erm (.) you two both feel (.) or don't have a very strong sense of yourself as being masculine? (.) you know (.) it's not a erm (.) a very prominent part of your identity?
Raj: I would say yeah (.) that's my understanding (.) yes (.) I'm not a masculine man
Nigel: Hm m (.) John (.) what do you think?
John: Yeah probably the same (.) yeah.
Nigel: Yeah?
John: I would (.) I would have said averagely so
Nigel: Hm m (.) okay yeah (.) I wasn't saying that you feel that you're un-masculine (*John*: Yeah) but that it's not a very (.)
John: What I'm saying is (.) it's not (.) if you took your (.) like your archetypal macho man (.) I'm not there (.) I'm just middle of the road (.) just er (.) average again I suppose.

(OU17: 4–5)

Rather than align with macho ideals, Wetherell and Edley argue that John and Raj emphasize their normality and ordinariness. In presenting themselves as 'normal and ordinary kinds of men' (1999: 343), they dissociate themselves from 'an exalted masculinity' which becomes repackaged as 'alien, over the top or extreme' (1999: 344).

In the third and final form of positioning that Wetherell and Edley identify – 'rebellious positions' – men also reject 'macho' ideals but 'define themselves in terms of their unconventionality' (1999: 347). They flout social expectations and take pride in non-conformity (1999: 349). In Extract 5.3, Dave, 'a 39-year-old, white manager of a timber company', talks about whether it is masculine to wear jewellery.

(5.3) [Wetherell and Edley 1999: 348]
Dave: The only reason I don't wear jewellery is purely and simply I'm a wimp and I don't want the pain of having my ears pierced (Laughter) I used to wear a ring when I was married and no doubt would wear one again if my partner wanted me to wear one (.) um I do quite often wear sort of coloured string bracelets (*Nigel*: Uh Uh) and in the summer especially I wear a lot of very loose (.) um flowering bright clothes probably going back to my old hippie background if you like (.) so I've got no taboos there really.

(OU1: 3)

Wetherell and Edley (1999: 349) note that Dave positions himself as a 'gender-rebel'. He celebrates his unconventionality, and is not afraid to stand out as different from other men. In sum, 'what is being celebrated in this discourse is . . . the courage, strength and determination of these men *as men* to engage in these potentially demeaning activities' (1999: 350).

Wetherell and Edley's conclusions

Wetherell and Edley conclude that both positive and negative implications may derive from their analyses. On the one hand, 'some men do appear to be abandoning macho masculinity' (1999: 350). On the other hand, however, this does not mean that men are 'beyond gender power' (1999: 351), or that the 'alternative identities' of 'ordinary' and 'rebellious' positions do not work in 'gender oppressive ways' (1999: 350). Sometimes, they argue, 'one of the most effective ways of being hegemonic, or being a 'man', may be to demonstrate one's distance from hegemonic masculinity' (1999: 351).

Wetherell and Edley challenge the assumption that hegemonic masculinity is an invariant style or label for a type of man. Instead, they say, men can position themselves in multiple ways, depending on the context (1999: 352). Indeed, they can appear 'both hegemonic and non-hegemonic . . . at the same time' (1999: 353). In short, Wetherell and Edley suggest that we need to give greater emphasis to the numerous and contradictory discursive resources through which hegemonic gender identities are constructed (1999: 352). This type of approach will, in turn, eventually help us to understand 'the reproduction of the social in the psychological' (1999: 354).

A participants' orientations approach to hegemonic masculinity

Wetherell and Edley's research goes some way towards reformulating the way masculinities may be understood discursively (and they go much further than others in this respect). Indeed, there are several points of overlap between their approach, and the more fine-grained analytic approach that I develop here. Both are committed to exploring 'the constitutive role of discourse' (Wetherell 1995: 136; Wetherell and Potter 1992: 62) and the variability and action orientation of talk (Potter and Wetherell 1987; Wetherell and Edley 1999: 338). Both approaches treat identities as 'actively accomplished' (Edley and Wetherell 1999: 182; Wetherell and Potter 1992: 78) and gender is conceived as 'a discursive practice', 'a method of description, not a psychological attribute' (Wetherell and Edley 1998: 165; Wetherell 1995: 141). There are, however, some important points of difference in both theory and analysis, which, I argue, relate to Wetherell and Edley's combination of elements from what they describe as 'two competing theoretical "camps"' (1999: 338): the conversation analytic, ethnomethodological camp (Widdicombe and Wooffitt

1995) and the more Foucauldian-inspired, poststructuralist camp (Parker and Shotter 1990; see also Wetherell and Edley 1999: 338).

Wetherell and Edley's 'synthetic approach' enables them to join the 'macro' (top-down) with the 'micro' (bottom-up) emphasis on context (see also Willott and Griffin 1997: 111), and, in terms reminiscent of Marx's famous dictum, 'to embrace the fact that people are, at the same time, both the products and the producers of language' (1999: 338) or 'the master, and the slave, of discourse' (Edley and Wetherell 1997: 206; 1999: 182). As Edley (2001a: 196) puts it, 'men are not free to construct themselves as they wish. To some extent, it is their cultural history which determines the kinds of identities they can assume'. The impetus behind this style of research, as we saw with Judith Butler's work in Chapter 3, is the desire to account for *both* constraint and creativity, determinism and agency in women's and men's lives. In this way, Wetherell and Edley hope to demonstrate how participants are neither totally determined by macro-social structures or discourses, nor totally free.

Wetherell and Edley argue that this approach can account for discursive regularities across time and space, such as 'much broader or more global patterns in collective sense-making' (1999: 338), 'interpretative repertoires' (Edley 2001a), 'ready-made resources' (Edley and Wetherell 1999: 182), the 'inter-textual social context' (Wetherell 1995: 140) and the 'broader social/discursive practices imbued with power' (Edley and Wetherell 1999: 191).

From this perspective, then, identities are not fluid resources, but are 'a sedimentation of past discursive practices', which can subject and regulate individuals (Wetherell and Potter 1992: 78–9), or be 'close(d) off' (Wetherell 1995: 136). Again, echoing Marx, men are both 'positioned by a ready-made or historically given set of discourses' (Edley and Wetherell 1997: 206) and 'active creator[s]', both 'practitioner[s]' and 'practised upon' (Wetherell and Edley 1998: 168).

In the analysis that follows, and in line with the analytic perspective set out in Chapter 4, I retain some familiar elements from Wetherell and Edley's discursive approach. For example, I explore the way masculinity(ies) are rhetorically constructed and deployed by participants in the management of certain interactional dilemmas (Billig et al. 1988), paying close attention to the variability (Potter and Wetherell 1987) and indexicality (Garfinkel 1967) of resources. Unlike Wetherell and Edley, however, and in line with Schegloff's emphasis on the endogenous production of macro contexts, I do not assume in advance of the analysis that we need to venture further than the limits of the text to explain *why* participants say what they do, or that we must always go *beyond* participant orientations to be able to say anything politically effective. Instead, I adopt a more technical, CA sensitivity to my data, and an analysis which is more attentive to participant orientations (Schegloff 1997) and gendered category membership (Edwards 1998; Hopper and LeBaron 1998; Stokoe 2004, in press) than that used in the analysis of masculinity thus far.

Differentiation

Masculinity as 'extreme'

Consider Extract 5.4. We join the interaction at a point where Sue has just queried how she can ask her participant, David, a question designed for female participants ('do you think you ever behave in a way that's not traditionally feminine?'). He responds with a suggested version of just such a question.

(5.4) [Speer 2001b: 115–16]
```
 1   D:   [Well you could] say (.) do you ever (.) °think you behave in a
 2        way that's not traditionally [masculine?]°
 3   S:                                [Masculine.] Okay then. (.)
 4        [Do you?]
 5   D:   [You know] the whole masculine (0.8) image of (.) what you
 6        should be. ↑Er:m (.)°yeah. Well I don't think (0.8) I (.) comply
 7        to the real° (2.4) well there's differen- you know the extreme
 8        (1.0) form of (0.4) the laddish image I don't (  ) [live up to.]
 9   S:                                                     [Yeah.]
10        Yeah. [But]
11   D:         [But] (.) even at the best of times now I don't think I do.
12        (0.8) Because I don't (.) I don't try and pull all the time, I don't
13        (0.6) feel obliged to drink lots. (1.0) I d- I'm not very (0.8) I'm
14        not o:verly competitive in sport.
```

In this extract, David identifies something that one might gloss – from a superficial reading – as hegemonic (or 'heroic') masculinity. He refers to the 'laddish image' and outlines its apparently limited category boundedness ('pulling', 'drinking' and being 'competitive in sport': lines 12–14). This three-part list (Jefferson 1990), which refers to different features of the same 'masculine' phenomenon, and David's reference to 'what you should be' (line 6), constructs masculinity as having a normative nature, and as something prescriptive rather than reflective of the 'type' of man David is.

However, it does not automatically follow that we should interpret this as meaning hegemonic masculinity actually exists as an identity (and conclude that, since David constructs, and then seems keen to differentiate himself from such a form of masculinity, he is not a hegemonic person). Instead, the interaction provides clues as to why – on this occasion – David constructs masculinity in such a way (or – as it is framed in the Wetherell and Schegloff debate – 'why this utterance now?'). In fact, this construction helps him to manage an interactional dilemma, that alternative, less technical analyses may miss.

For example, David to some extent 'lands himself in it' in the opening sequence by helpfully reformulating Sue's question. Being asked if you ever behave in a way that is not 'traditional' is something which can be risky to respond to, and David's speech is hearably quieter at the moment of asking the question (which may signal his orientation to some problem with its contents: line 1). If he responds 'yes, I do cooking, sewing and flower arranging', then he may risk appearing effeminate, and thus not in a position to talk about (his own) masculinity at all. However, if he replies, 'no, I always act in such a traditional fashion', thus identifying fully with the category, he may risk appearing conformist or stereotypical, a dope who lacks authenticity. Therefore, David is faced with a dilemma, or conflicting demands for accountability. On the one hand he is a man, with the category entitlement that brings – who better to comment on what it's like to be a man than a man? (Potter 1996b) – *and* he is someone who (for the purposes of a social science investigation) is asked to hold masculinity accountable. How does he do this without undermining his position as a 'proper', normal man (maintaining his entitlement to speak as such) and retain some sense of being authentically individual or unique (see Widdicombe 1998a; Widdecombe and Wooffitt 1995). David's orientation to, and attempt to manage this dilemma, is evident in the data. For example, he makes a distinction between the type of man he himself is, and the type of man (or 'image') he wishes to hold accountable. It is in the service of this distinction (and the dilemma it is designed to manage), that David's particular version of 'extreme' machismo is deployed.

For example, when David is talking about the type of man he is *not*, he repairs 'real' to 'extreme' (line 7). While 'real' would implicate David as somehow 'unreal', and less authentically a man (the long 2.4 second pause may signal some interactional trouble with this construction, and David's orientation to the dilemmatic nature of these issues: line 7), the 'extreme form of the laddish image' (lines 7–8) allows David to construct traditional masculinity as somehow unreasonable and 'other' by virtue of its extremity. It is then perfectly reasonable for David to differentiate himself from it and assert that he is not such a man.

David subtly *constructs* the meaning of masculinity in such a way that makes the business of differentiation less problematic and more rhetorically persuasive. Since all words and categories contain rhetorical affordances, they can be used contrastively to bolster an argument (Edwards 1999). In this extract, for example, David not only constructs the version of masculinity that he chooses to hold accountable *as* extreme, but also uses a number of extreme case formulations ('at the best of times' (line 11), and 'pull all the time' (line 12), for example), which work contrastively with other alternative interpretations, rhetorically warding them off (Pomerantz 1986).

There is, then, a *dual* sense in which masculinity is worked up as extreme, and this dual sense of extremity works as an interactional resource, helping David to manage the conflicting demands of the interview situation. He draws attention to masculinity as a category, an extreme image or ideal type, which he is then able to distance himself from and contrast with his authentically real, less extreme, and more reasonable version (Day 1998).

A participant's construction of masculinity and the way they situate themselves in relation to it is never final. Indeed, there is a different set of concerns attended to in Extract 5.5, which comes several turns later.

Masculinity as 'self-confidence'

(5.5) [Speer 2001b: 117–18]
```
1   D:   Well I d-hhh. I wouldn't do it but I'd like to be able to. I'd like
2        to (1.0) have the self-confidence and the (0.8) the (0.8)
3        approach that would get (me there.) -I wouldn't=
4   S:   =Yeah.
5   D:   I don't think I would do it if I could but.
6   S:   What do you think women think of these blokes that do that?
7        (1.0)
8   D:   I don't ↑know. C'z (1.8) you would have thought that they'd
9        (0.4) be wary of them.
10  S:   [Yeah.]
11  D:   [And.] of their reputation, and er (0.4) avoid them, but then
12       (0.6) they're always still the ones that seem to pull, and
13       they're always the ones that attract the women. (0.6) The re-
14       the really self-confident ones that are out-going an -and -and
15       do pull all the time and ar -are known to've snogged everybody
16       in sight.
```

We join this extract at a point where Sue has just asked David if he 'admires' the men who – in his words – 'cop off two or three times a night' and 'always end up going back for a shag'. Again, David orients toward a version of masculinity that an analyst concerned with abstract generalizations might gloss as 'hegemonic'. These 'blokes' are 'confident' and 'out-going', have 'snogged everybody in sight', and 'pull' women easily (lines 14–16). Although this construction is very similar to the one we saw in Extract 5.4 (again, extreme case formulations are used on lines 12 onwards for their contrastive effect), notice that masculinity is given its precise meaning on this occasion with the repetition of the notion of 'self-confidence' (lines 2 and 14). This is significant for the identity it helps David portray, and the interactional contingencies it is deployed to manage.

For example, David is asked a question about whether he 'admires' the men who engage in behaviours that he has previously differentiated himself from (Extract 5.4). In answering this question, David has to negotiate a path through two, possibly negative (for his identity) alternatives. He could, for example, say that he does *not* admire these men, but might risk distancing himself from an identity which is (commonly thought to be) culturally exalted (to be sexually successful is to be a 'proper' man). Alternatively, he might say that he *does* admire them, but might then appear hypocritical, buying back into the extreme machismo that he has just been working to hold accountable. Again, we do not need to go beyond the data to find evidence of this dilemma. We can see David attending to the question as troublesome in the hearably exasperated 'Well I d-hhh.' (line 1) and the three, noticeably considered pauses in 'I'd like to (1.0) have the self-confidence and the (0.8) the (0.8) approach' (lines 1–3). This particular construction enables David to manage these implications in a way that does not undermine his own identity.

For example, 'self-confidence', like other categories, is inferentially rich (Sacks 1995). It is a fairly safe, non-gendered notion, a domain of one's personality that it is legitimate to want more of, and yet also something one might not be held accountable for lacking. However, it is also a flexible, indexical *resource*, which is used, on this occasion, for some interactionally sensitive business. In this case, David's lack of success with women is not because he's not handsome or sexually attractive enough. It is simply that he lacks confidence. The ultimate reason why David is unsuccessful with women, however, is constructed as a result of *choice* rather than *incapacity*. For example, the 'I wouldn't do it but I'd like to be able to' and 'I don't think I would do it if I could' constructions (lines 1 and 5), suggest that David would like to have the *ability* to attract women, but would not choose to exhibit the *behaviour*, even if he were able.

Moreover, when David is asked 'what do you think women think of these blokes that do that?' (line 6), he works to avoid the implication that his own behaviour is somehow questionable, by distinguishing between what one would ordinarily *think* to be the case, and what is *actually* the case: 'you would have thought that they'd be wary of them ... but then they're always still the ones that seem to pull' (lines 8ff). David constructs this as a weird, perhaps illogical *phenomenon* (which women irrationally collude in – despite all the negative evidence about these men's reputations: lines 11 and 15–16), rather than something peculiar or intrinsic to himself. Indeed, it is the simultaneously negative slant given to women, and the masculine activity of 'pulling', which helps David manage his own identity, and present himself as a reasonable person.

The extracts considered so far have come from the same interview. It could, then, be argued that David is somehow unique in his construction of and degree of alignment with masculinity. However, in the next extract, a second interviewee – also a man in his early twenties – orients toward a strikingly similar construction of masculinity, and again, differentiates himself from it, though this time via a more direct denial of possessing criterial features (Widdicombe 1998a: 58).

Masculinity as inauthentic

(5.6) [Speer 2001b: 119]
```
1   S:   >what would you say to people< who think say (0.4) that what you do
2        is geeky? If anyone said 'you're an anorak'. You like Star Trek. ↑You
3        haven't talked about ↑Star Trek.
4   B:   Yeah. (0.6) ↑Erm. (1.8) what would I say?=
5   S:   =Or you're a typical BL:oke.
6   B:   I'm not a typical bloke, I think I'm very different.
7   S:   °In what ways? °
8   B:   Well I'm (.) I'm not one of these (0.4) lads, I s'pose if you can label it
9        as a ↑lad=
10  S:   =Wha's a lad then? (.) leisure-wise?
11       (1.0)
12  B:   Goes out on the ↑pull. (0.6) Goes out jus- (.) on a weekend just to get
13       totally stoned or to pull a woman. (0.8) I'm not that kind of ↑person.
14       (0.4) I'm more a (0.4) sort of (0.8) e-erm (1.8) well, like l-looking in
15       on the world from outside (.) sort of person (.) er, a window on the
16       world person.
```

The first thing to note about this extract is the way Sue's opening question links Ben's leisure pastimes with potentially negative identity characteristics: 'geek', 'anorak' (a slang term like the word 'nerd') and later, 'typical bloke'. Ben delays his response until line 6, where he asserts categorically that he is not such a man: 'I'm not a typical bloke, I think I'm very different'. Again, like David in the previous two extracts, Ben uses extreme case formulations to construct the typicality of 'bloke' or 'lad' behaviour: 'Goes out jus- on a weekend just to get totally stoned or to pull a woman' (lines 12–13). This extremity helps him to build a rhetorical contrast case, an alternative identity, that vividly differentiates him from the traits that Sue accuses him of possessing earlier in line 1 (albeit in a thinly disguised hypothetical form: 'what would you say to people who think . . .'). Unlike these 'typical blokes', Ben is contemplative, thoughtful and distant: a 'looking in on the world from outside sort of person, a window on the world person' (lines 14 to 16). In the space created by rejecting the 'typical bloke' or 'lad' identity, Ben forges a special and unique alternative.

We might infer, on the basis of a purely cursory analysis of the data so far, that, since both David and Ben describe masculinity in similar ways across extracts, that they are attending to the objective existence of what analysts have termed 'hegemonic' or 'dominant' masculinity. However, this inference would miss the subtle and context-sensitive nature of their descriptions. It is in the particularities of these descriptions, for example, where most of the interactional work gets done. The participants construct masculinity differently on each occasion (as 'extreme', 'traditional', about 'self-confidence', or whatever), depending on the particular identity/ies that are at stake and the work that needs to be done to manage them. They choose from among the words and inferences available to them in culture, using them contrastively to build a rhetorically effective position from which to differentiate themselves, and develop an alternative, more authentic identity.

These types of descriptions are common to accounts where one's genuineness or authenticity may be questionable (Sacks 1984; Wooffitt 1992). Indeed, Wetherell and Edley discuss this in their analysis of 'ordinary positions' (1999: 343), identifying a contrast (for their participants) between 'ordinary' masculinity and 'some version of the macho man as an archetype, simplification, or extreme caricature' (1999: 345).

An alternative way to construct masculinity and avoid resisting membership of a category outright, is to identify with, or embrace elements commonly associated with the category, while portraying that embracing as a lack of *choice*. In other words, the speaker uses choice as a *resource* to manage both alignment (with the category of masculinity), and differentiation (in terms of their own accountability), at the same time. Consider the use of this strategy in the next extract, which is taken from the same interview as Extracts 5.4 and 5.5.

(Partial) alignment

Masculinity as a determined 'mind-set'

(5.7) [Speer 2001b: 121]
```
1   S:    Right. Do you think the fact you're male affects your
2         leisure in an[y way?]
3   D:               [Yes] Yeah.
4   S:    How?
5         (1.0)
6   D:    hh. Well it's just a mind-set isn't it –it's –it's what you're
7         indoctrinated with when you grow up. (1.0) Sport for blokes is a
```

8   <u>must</u> win, <u>must</u> beat the opposition, <u>grind</u> them into the dust
9   sort of thing, (.) and going out is a <u>must</u> drink fifteen pints,
10   throw up, have a fight, and pull.

In direct contrast to David's portrayal of extreme machismo in Extracts 5.4 and 5.5, here we have one of the most graphically deterministic constructions of masculinity one would think possible. Indeed, we now get some idea of the level of variation in both the construction of, and degree of alignment with masculinity *within the same interview*. Here maleness is a 'mind-set', it is 'indoctrinated', and is representative of things one 'must' do. It is normative, and prescribed, ingrained from 'when you grow up' (lines 6 to 10), and very much something David is subjected to (as opposed to responsible for).

We begin to understand why David should so patently contradict himself (or 'why this utterance now?'), if we look in closer detail at the opening sequence. First of all, David does not answer the question about leisure and his maleness ('Do you think the fact you're male affects your leisure in any way?': lines 1–2), in quite the way one would expect, given that he is asked a probing 'how?' question (rather than an account seeking 'why?' question: line 4).

Rather than provide a description of *how* his maleness affects his leisure – such as 'I do all those traditionally masculine pursuits like rock-climbing, cricket etc', which he has mentioned elsewhere in the interview are pursuits he enjoys – David instead provides an account of *why* maleness affects his leisure: 'Well it's just a mind-set isn't it – it's what you're indoctrinated with' (lines 6–7), thus treating the question about gender as a possibly problematic, instantly accountable issue. A clue to this response may lie in the fact that the categories 'man' and 'woman' are inferentially associated with different sports and activities and were David *not* to engage in 'manly' pursuits (being quite obviously a man), he might be seen as accountably strange, 'other' or different. David can not (easily) deny his maleness, but in responding 'yes' to the question, and then explaining *how* it affects his leisure, he opens himself up to being just like any 'typical' man and, again, not an authentic individual. His spontaneous accounting here, therefore, along with the portrayal of men's leisure as socially determined rather than freely chosen, may stem from his attending to the possibility that he might somehow be to blame for being 'typical' – or worse – stereotypical, by virtue of his maleness, and all in front of a female – perhaps feminist – social science interviewer.

David denies responsibility for the link between his maleness and his behaviour, and cannot be held accountable for it. This is a negative construction of his *own* masculinity, very unlike the identity of choice David portrays in other extracts.

Masculinity as a 'mask'

(5.8) [Speer 2001b: 122]
```
1   S:   But what are the characteristics of laddishness then? I mean
2        do you try and emulate these characteris[tics?]
3   D:                                           °[No] no° but it's=
4   S:   =Na(h)tura(h)l (hh)
5   D:   ((laughs)) it's a very -it's a peer pressure thing, it's -
6        laddishness is all a peer pressure thing . Everybody -it's the
7        mask thing you know? A group of lads, (.) just first arrived at
8        university, (.) some rugby players amongst them, some big
9        drinkers amongst them,
10  S:   Mm
11  D:   some people that like to try and pull all the time, (.) and (.)
12       everybody's (.) – everybody wears the mask the 'hey (no)' you
13       know, tough macho 'I can pull all the time, I (.) can drink lots, I
14       can fight' and all this
15  S:   Mm=
16  D:   =and anybody that doesn't try and live up to that is -is sco:rned
17       by the group
```

Masculinity is given a slightly different meaning in this extract. The image of social determinism continues with the use of lay social scientific examples. 'Laddishness' is a result of 'peer pressure' (lines 5 and 6) and is subject to social sanction: 'anybody that doesn't try and live up to that is scorned by the group' (lines 16–17). Moreover, this is not an authentic and 'real' self, but is a 'mask' that you 'wear' (lines 7 and 12) (David's lay version of 'gender as performance': see Marshall and Wetherell 1989). Indeed, the reason for this particular construction may be prompted by Sue's question about whether David tries to 'emulate' masculinity (lines 1–2), which makes the issue of authenticity and choice directly relevant.

For example, to suggest that someone might *emulate* a characteristic is to imply that they are not *authentically* that person at all – a point Sue attends to in her tease (line 4) suggesting it is 'natural' (see Drew 1987). One way to avoid the negative implications of responding 'yes, I try to emulate masculinity', then, is to suggest that one is laddish simply because one has no choice in the matter, thus further distancing one's accountability or responsibility for being just such a person.

Having provided numerous examples to demonstrate this lack of choice, however, a few turns later (and in response to the local interactional circumstances), David's tack changes slightly. Having deferred accountability to such a great extent, he now reclaims some agency and responsibility.

Masculinity as a 'hive mind'

(5.9) [Speer 2001b: 123]
```
1   S:                    [So] were
2        you put in that situation then?
3   D:   No coz I -I -I picked who I hung a -hung about with very
4        carefully, but -well not carefully but I just happened- you know
5        like attracts like and you hang about with people who are like
6        yourself [(       )]
7   S:            [Who are] not 'laddish' then?
8   D:   Yeah I was lucky to- >but there was still the laddish< (1.0) er
9        only -only as far as -as drinking went definitely coz I -I was in
10       (.)-I was on like 2 or 3 of my group were big drinkers and it was
11       'you've got to match pint for pint at the same rate of drinking
12       as I do or else you're queer, or else you're weak, or else you're a
13       Southerner' you know and that's [(all this)]
14  S:                                   [Did they] actually say that?
15  D:   Oh yeah! all the time mm [(     )]
16  S:                            [Yet you] hung around with
17       these people?
18  D:   No well I was doing it to others as well you know [it's all]=
19  S:                                                    [really?]
20  D:   =it's a -it's a -it's a: -a hive mind (.) you know=
((lines omitted))
28  D:   and it's -it's like a group mind and everybody (.) thinks the
29       same and talks the same and you have the same phrases and
30       you have the same likes and dislikes.
```

In this extract, which follows almost immediately from the preceding one, the issue is no longer about whether David *tries* to emulate masculinity (cf. line 2, Extract 5.8), but is instead about his own relationship to this peer pressure: 'So were you put in that situation then?' (lines 1–2). In other words, the questioning instigates a move from David as accountable for the behaviour, to David as accountable for having agency or not, and there is selective variation between the two. The interactional benefits of asserting lack of choice are all but gone, and what's at stake has changed. To respond 'yes' to this question would paint a tragic picture of David's inability to resist membership if he so chooses. Thus he responds 'No coz I picked who I hung about with very carefully' (lines 3–4). However, when his responsibility for 'hanging around' with people who call others derogatory names is at issue (lines 16–17), David reverts again to constructing masculinity as a lack of choice, deferring his accountability, and thus blame-worthiness for Sue's implied criticism. Indeed, he finishes several lines later, with wonderful images of social contagion, of 'hive minds' (line 20), where 'everybody thinks the same and talks the same' (lines 28–9).

The extracts in this section, like Extracts 5.4–5.6, have tended to portray masculinity as a negative phenomenon. However, while its meaning may *often* be constructed (and oriented towards) as negative, it may also, on certain interactional occasions, be given a more positive gloss. In the account that follows, for example, the speaker relies on the characteristics typically associated with the category of masculinity, to divert attention from another – possibly even more accountable or (constructed as) problematic aspect of their identity – their sexuality.

The display of masculinity in the management of a problematic identity

We join this extract at a point where the discussion turns to marihuana-smoking, and Ben, in relaying his repertoire of drug experiences, has announced that he has done a 'blow back' – 'where you take a drag, (.) and breathe into the other person' with a 'lad at college', and that he 'used to do it all the time'.

(5.10) [Speer 2001b: 124–5]
```
 1   S:   =>°That's a bit (.) risque< isn't it? °
 2   B:   No::
 3        (.)
 4   S:   It's like ↑kiss[ing someone]
 5   B:                  [Actually]      yeah it is like kissing- it's like-
 6        almost like French kissing but without tongues.
 7        (1.0)
 8   S:   And that's okay?
 9   B:   >Yeah it didn't bother me. He was a good mate<
10   S:   hhh. ((laughs))
11   B:   Yeah he- he- when he first said he said 'have you ever
12        done a blow-back?' We were totally and utterly (.) ss – pissed
13        out of our heads. And we were laffing our 'eads off coz
14        we'd already had a couple of (0.6) joints, (0.6) and we were
15        actually in a- in a hall that wasn't ours, and there was a
16        telly in there and he said 'that window's open do you fancy
17        ha(h)ving the te(h)lly(h).'
((9 lines omitted))
27                   He said 'have you ever done a blow-back?' I
28        said 'what the hell's a blow-back?', he says 'it's where I
29        take a drag and then pass it onto you (0.8) by like kissing
30        you', he says 'it's a bit queer but you know it doesn't bother
```

```
31            me if you want.' [I said 'go on then']=
32    S:                       [((laughs))]=
33    B:    ='let's have a go. >Because it doesn't bother me<.' (0.8) He said
34          'sure?' I said 'yeah no worries'. (1.0) Steve °w's° a bloody
35          great laugh he was. (0.6) You'd have liked him coz he was a right (.)
36          lad from Brighton and he was a right down to earth guy.
```

In stark contrast to Ben's account in Extract 5.6, where he *distances* himself from the 'typical blokes' who go out 'jus- on a weekend just to get *totally stoned*' (lines 12–13, emphasis added), in this extract, by contrast, he tells a story about just such drug-taking behaviour. Unlike previous extracts, however, here Ben invokes characteristics commonly associated with masculinity, so as to manage what Sue constructs as a potentially problematic *sexual* identity: 'That's a bit risque isn't it? . . . It's like kissing someone' (lines 1 and 4).

For example, in recalling the 'blow-back' incident, Ben does some accountability-reducing scene setting: they were 'totally and utterly pissed out of our heads', 'laffing our 'eads off', and had 'already had a couple of joints' (lines 12–14). These activities are what one might regard as 'laddish' behaviour, all of which point to the alcohol and drug enhanced – 'not to be taken seriously' nature of the occasion. The daredevil antics of Ben's reported suggestion 'that window's open do you fancy having the telly' (lines 16–17), contribute to the impression of wild schoolboy pranks (rather than rampant homo-eroticism). The whole incident is given innocent immediacy and an unplanned 'spur of the moment' feel, by the use of active voicing (Wooffitt 1992), which again, forecloses any suggestion that this activity might represent the expression of some innate desire. This is reinforced further by Ben's display of ignorance: 'what the hell's a blow-back?' (line 28). Thus, the level of detail in this short narrative may provide a warrant, an experiential document of 'being there' (Geertz 1988, cited in Edwards 1999: 281) that works to bolster the validity of arguments that may be in danger of being contested (see also Edwards and Potter 1992). In this case, the danger may be that Ben's behaviour is somehow pre-planned, calculated or inherently meaningful.

Interestingly, while Ben initially *counters* Sue's construction of the 'blow-back' as 'a bit risque' – and thus problematic in terms of the sexual identity it indexes (line 1) – here Ben constructs Steve as already having mentioned, at the time of the incident, the homosexual connotations implicit in the 'blow-back' manoeuvre: He says 'it's a bit queer but you know it doesn't bother me if you want' (lines 30–1). This is, then, a clever *display* of recognition, that retrospectively constructs *and counters* just such connotations, inoculating the speaker from their effects.

Ben's story works to convince us of Steve's (the proposer of the 'blow-back') credentials as a proper 'laddish' 'bloke' in the closing sequence, where Ben says he's a 'great laugh', and argues that Sue would have liked him 'coz he was a right lad from Brighton and he was a right down to earth guy' (lines 35–6). Being 'right' of any characteristic leaves one in little doubt that it is a quality in plentiful supply, and Ben can bask in the glory of his friend's macho credentials. In sum, Ben retains the identity of a 'proper' man by replacing one commonly 'othered', yet stereotyped category ('queerness') with another – perhaps more acceptable one (masculine activities and 'laddishness'). In doing so, he relies on traits that are normatively associated with (and culturally recognizable as) masculinity.

Chapter summary and discussion

In this chapter I have provided a review of several features of Wetherell and Edley's (1999) critical discursive approach to masculinity, and demonstrated what an alternative, participants' orientations perspective might look like. I want to use the remainder of this chapter to summarize my findings and their implications for research which adopts a broadly poststructuralist or top-down approach to gender norms and other 'ideological' or 'social-structural' phenomena.

As we have seen, Wetherell and Edley claim that hegemonic masculinity is not an 'invariant style' or 'label' for a type of man, and that men can position themselves in multiple ways, depending on the context. However, when it comes to their analyses, Wetherell and Edley link the three different types of discursive positioning they identify with *different* men. As such, they imply that 'heroic', 'ordinary' and 'rebellious' positions are indeed invariant labels for types of men. Likewise, they treat 'heroic' masculinity as a somewhat decontextualized, mapping notion, such that, even if men distance themselves from it (as in 'ordinary' and 'rebellious' positions), it will have the same meaning for their participants, across contexts.

This approach is consistent with Wetherell and Edley's overall analytic framework (and with poststructuralist approaches to discourse more broadly), in which gendered subjects are 'positioned' or partially 'constituted' by an 'external public dialogue' (Wetherell and Edley 1999: 7), established 'global patterns' (1999: 8) or 'repertoires' (Edley 2001a), and in which there is some abstract, discursive 'constraint' on people's lives. Indeed, Edley explicitly *reifies* hegemonic masculinity 'as something that exists outside of and prior to particular conversations' (2001b: 137).

Thus, even while Wetherell has elsewhere argued against the reifying tendencies of some styles of discourse work (Potter et al. 1990) and refused an 'ontological distinction between the discursive and the extra-discursive' (Wetherell 1995: 140) in their analysis of masculinity, Wetherell and Edley nonetheless advocate some form of discursive determinism, treating language and discourse as itself an extra-discursive, constraining influence on talk.

In my own analyses, by contrast, I have not reified masculinity, or linked discursive positions with personality types. Rather, I have demonstrated a number of context-sensitive ways in which the *same* men may construct masculinity and align with or differentiate themselves from those constructions, in the course of one stretch of talk. In doing so, I have shown how it is not simply the degree of alignment with (what is constructed as) masculinity which changes, but it is also participants' *definitions* of masculinity which change. These different descriptions and uses of masculinity give it a different meaning across contexts.

Although, on the basis of a less technical analysis, the analyst might conclude that these participants *seem* to be attending to the existence of something that non-CA researchers have glossed as 'hegemonic' masculinity – for example, Ben and David alternate between alignment with and differentiation from a version of masculinity which they define in remarkably similar ways across the extracts ('drinking', 'pulling' and 'sport', for example), 'hegemony' and 'hegemonic masculinity' are *not* participants' categories. Moreover, in its particularities, these participants define masculinity in different ways (as 'extreme', 'typical', about 'self-confidence', an 'image', 'hive mind', a 'mask' and so on), appropriate for the local interactional context, and the work that needs to be done to invoke or manage a particular identity.

Thus, masculinity is not a mapping notion, and members' discursive 'positioning' does not take place in an interactional vacuum (Kitzinger and Wilkinson 2003). Instead, there are a range of rhetorically effective constructions and reconstructions of masculinity which can be applied and reworked to include or exclude the self, and which are tailored to the local business at hand. As I argued in Chapter 4, the precise meaning of gender categories is context sensitive (or indexical) *and* context free (or 'inference rich': Sacks 1995), and participants make use, in action, of both these elements of the category of masculinity. Indeed, it is this feature of all words and categories which helps explain both the similarities (in terms of similar descriptions) and differences (in terms of the precise definition and interactional usage of these descriptions) across the extracts.

It is important to note that I am not 'rejecting' or 'discarding' the concept of hegemonic masculinity (cf. Edley 2001b: 136) or suggesting that ideology and oppressive gender norms do not exist. Nor am I suggesting that what hegemonic masculinity describes 'is entirely absent from everyday talk' (Edley 2001a: 3). Instead, I wish to problematize analytic approaches which reify such concepts, and which treat them as determining members' talk or the discourses that are 'available' to them in a top-down fashion. In my view, such an approach does not do justice to the flexibility of people's discourse, and to the fluidity of identity work. The concept of hegemonic masculinity is, by its very nature, an abstract 'uncapturable' yardstick, used to describe something which extends beyond members' local practices and actions.

Of course, ways of talking about gender, and the meaning of gender categories, are not variable without limit. Each set of conversationalists is not, on each occasion, spontaneously generating the dilemmas to which we see them orienting, as if 'from nowhere', and people do not live in hermetically sealed, discrete interactional packages, where gender norms and social structures have no effects, or do not exist. As I showed in Chapter 4, the reason why we find people repeatedly orienting in their talk to certain concerns and dilemmas (like dispelling any suspicion that they might be gay), and not others, is because, as CA has convincingly demonstrated, certain normative patterns recur across contexts and participants. Indeed, without such patterns, social order would not be possible, and our lives would descend into chaos.

The crucial difference between my approach, and critical or poststructuralist approaches like Wetherell and Edley's, is that where they ask 'what constraining structures, and normative features *from outside discourse* account for or cause these patterns to occur?', CA asks, 'how do members build, orient to, and reproduce these recognizable patterns, structures and norms *within their talk*?' This is not a deliberate, cavalier denial of the 'extra-discursive'. Rather it is a way of evidencing and validating claims about norms and social structures on the page.

In his response to the article where I initially reported some of these findings (Speer 2001b), Edley argues that 'in attempting to maintain a "participants' orientation", conversation analysis (CA) renders itself particularly unsuited to researching questions of hegemony and ideology' (2001b: 137). However, I believe my analyses provide answers to CA's own classic question about 'why this utterance now?', and indeed, to the more pressing question for feminists – 'why this ever?' (Deborah Cameron, personal communication). As I have shown, we do not necessarily need to use Foucauldian poststructuralism or make references to features *extrinsic* to the interaction, to render answers to 'why?' questions, 'macro contexts', 'ideology', 'gender norms' and all things typically conceived as beyond CA's scope 'in the world out there' explicit. Rather, they are observable and oriented to by members in their talk. It is precisely because social structures *are* analytically tractable (Drew and Heritage 1992a; Hutchby 1996a, 1996b; Markova and Foppa 1991; Speer 1999), that an approach which does *not* go beyond participants' orientations is so important and radical for feminism.

Some readers might retort 'but masculinity exists – indeed you pre-classify your speakers as men and women in the interactions you analyse, and thereby impose your own essentialist, reified reality on your data from the start'. To this I would respond that I am not denying that masculinity or gender 'exists'. The approach I advocate, as we saw in Chapter 4, brackets issues of ontology in favour of exploring how members construct gender *as* real. Thus, while the characteristics of masculinity each participant identifies may well exist 'out there in the world' for them, this does not mean that we (as analysts) should interpret this as justifying its overt reification (cf. Edley), or as meaning that we might be able to identify a hegemonic or heroic *person* or personality type, or make judgements about the 'abandonment' of hegemonic or heroic positions. No matter how many times I say 'I am a man' or orient to *you* as a man, it does not prove that either of us *is* one. It is one thing to talk about regularities in discourse, but quite another to comment on what is 'real'. The reason why I classify speakers by using their personal gendered names, 'Sue', 'David' and 'Ben', is not because I am somehow buying the idea of essentialized gendered selves, but because, as Schegloff (1999a: 566) notes, 'this is the form the participants appear to use if they can . . . This is how they address one another'.

Finally, I would suggest that a participants' orientations approach does not *exclude* politics as some feminist critics are wont to argue. Instead, it can help us to discover something fruitful about the political *uses* to which identity categories can be put, and to reach politically efficacious conclusions. Thus, if we take a broad view of politics as *rhetoric*, as taking up a position for strategic ends, then participants, like analysts, are also engaged in a political project, albeit with (often – though not always) different goals. From this perspective, 'why that now?' is a *political* question, for participants as well as analysts, that we can answer by focusing on participants' practices. David and Ben *do* identity politics with their talk, and political implications can be built from our analyses of it.

In Chapter 6, I will show how this participants' orientations approach can be extended to an analysis and reconceptualization of what we mean by heterosexist talk, prejudice, and 'the world in here'.

6
RECONCEPTUALIZING PREJUDICE
'HETEROSEXIST TALK' AND 'THE WORLD IN HERE'

In Chapter 5 I demonstrated how the analytic approach that I adopt in this book may be applied to an analysis of gender identity, 'hegemonic masculinity' and 'the world out there'. In this chapter I will extend my empirical demonstration of a participants' orientations approach, by providing a non-cognitivist analysis of 'heterosexism' and 'the world in here'.

As we have seen in previous chapters, many feminists are sceptical of using an approach which relies almost exclusively on participants' orientations, because they believe that we must venture outside discourse, to the extra-discursive, macro-social context, in order to provide an adequate explanation for what is going on within it. A related layer of debate concerns the analytic tractability of *prejudice*. Key to this debate is the commonly held idea that when people produce prejudiced statements and descriptions, they are often 'unaware' that they are doing so. Consequently, if the speaker and his or her co-participants 'do not know' that they are being rude or offensive, then they will not explicitly attend or 'orient to' their talk *as* problematic – by reflexively passing comment on, or repairing it, for example. It follows that if the participants do not provide such 'oriented to' evidence for trouble, then on what grounds can we, as analysts, say that an act of sexism, heterosexism, or some other form of prejudice has occurred? For many gender and language researchers, a participants' orientations approach risks leading us into a political and analytic black hole.

For example, in her feminist conversation analytic work, Kitzinger (2000a: 171) argues that 'it would be unbearably limiting to use CA if it meant that I could only describe as "sexist" or "heterosexist" or "racist" those forms of talk to which actors orient as such'. Kitzinger's solution is to explore how it is that members routinely incorporate heterosexist and sexist assumptions into their talk without anyone commenting on, or noticing them. In other words, she explores what members' *failure to orient* to their talk as troublesome can tell us about the constitution and reconstitution of a heterosexist reality (2000a: 171–2; see also Kitzinger 2005).

Stokoe and Smithson (2002: 104) are also sceptical about the utility of 'a strict sequential implementation of conversation analysis' which, they say, 'may be inadequate to address feminist concerns, especially when dealing with interactions in which gender and sexuality (and particularly sexist and heterosexist assumptions) are "unnoticed" by participants' (2002: 104). Stokoe and Smithson suggest that an alternative, Sacksian, MCA approach is a more viable framework than sequential CA 'for studying the links between gender, sexuality and discourse' (2002: 105). Unlike sequential CA, this approach 'can work well to inform us about the social and political relevance of micro-level interaction' (2002: 104).

The approach I adopt in this chapter offers an alternative way of proceeding. I am of the view that, even while there may indeed be instances where prejudice goes unnoticed by participants, and where members fail to orient to their talk *as* troublesome, that rather than assuming we can know in advance of an analysis that members will not orient to their talk as problematic or troublesome, that what interactants take to be a prejudiced statement or act is – from a CA and DP perspective – a matter for analysis. Again, this chapter is intended to show how arguments against a participants' orientations approach may be premature. In conversation analytic terms, just as I did in Chapter 5, I am concerned to take the challenge offered by Schegloff (1997), to ground critical arguments in the orientations of participants.

I will begin by providing an overview and critique of existing psychological and feminist discursive work on heterosexism, highlighting the way its operationalization tends to obscure flexible discursive practices and settle them into stable, causal attitudes within individuals. Then, drawing on my work on the discursive constitution of heterosexism with Jonathan Potter (Speer and Potter 2000), I will interrogate what counts as an instance of heterosexism from the interactants' perspective. More broadly put, my analytic task is to show how descriptions of cognition and context, mind and world, are used to orient to, justify and manage (potentially) heterosexist claims.

Psychology and heterosexism

The notion of 'heterosexism' was developed in psychology to improve on the notion of 'homophobia', which was criticized for suggesting anti-gay and lesbian actions are a result of an individual pathology, discrete from broader sociological considerations (Kitzinger 1996a, 1996b; Kitzinger and Perkins 1993). Ken Plummer has described heterosexism as 'a *diverse set of social practices – from the linguistic to the physical . . . covert and overt . . . in which the homo/hetero binary distinction is at work whereby heterosexuality is privileged*' (Plummer 1992: 19, emphasis in original). Heterosexism is not simply about discrete acts, but describes 'the bias of a whole culture' (Kitzinger 1994a: 126) that 'denies, derogates, or penalises any nonheterosexual form of behavior, identity, relationship, or community' (Kitzinger

2000c; Herek 1995: 321). It is an 'offensive milieu' (Kitzinger 1994a: 126), where human experience is conceptualized 'in strictly heterosexual terms' (Herek et al. 1991: 957).

Despite the definitional shift of emphasis from the individual to the social, it is still common to divide heterosexism into *cultural* heterosexism, on the one hand (its institutional, religious and legal manifestations) and *psychological* heterosexism, on the other (its attitudinal and behavioural manifestations (Herek 1995; Hunter et al. 1998)). There have been numerous attempts by psychologists to measure and operationalize psychological heterosexism, and to identify heterosexist individuals. One of the most well-respected methods used in this endeavour has been the Attitudes Toward Lesbians and Gay Men (ATLG) scale, developed by Herek (1994; the scale is reproduced in the box on the next page).

Positive scored items on the scale consist of statements such as 'female homosexuality is a sin', 'homosexual behaviour between two men is just plain wrong' and 'female homosexuality is a threat to many of our basic social institutions'. Individuals who agree with these statements may be given a psychological diagnosis as heterosexist, and be considered in need of treatment and correction. Although this type of research is widespread, the notion of 'psychological heterosexism' has been criticized by some feminist and lesbian researchers.

Celia Kitzinger (1996b), for example, has argued that the notion of psychological heterosexism has the consequence of silencing political issues by redefining them in psychological terms: 'Psychology has systematically replaced *political* explanations (in terms of structural, economic and institutional oppression) with personal explanations (in terms of the dark workings of the psyche, the mysterious functioning of the subconscious)' (1996b: 36–7). Turning 'psychological heterosexism' into a psychopathology reinforces the very assumptions that the notion of 'heterosexism' was originally designed to replace. For Kitzinger, the attitude scales based on such concepts depoliticize lesbian and gay identities by individualizing the problem, portraying the 'homophobe' as someone with a selective, prejudiced and stereotyped belief system that masks or distorts some objective reality (Kitzinger 1996a, 1996b; Kitzinger and Perkins 1993). In this chapter, I will develop some of these lines of criticism drawing on current thinking in DP and CA.

Reconceptualizing attitudes and prejudice

As we saw in Chapter 4, DP builds on work on the interactional organization of evaluations in CA (e.g. Pomerantz 1978, 1984) to provide a non-cognitivist approach that specifies what attitudinal or evaluative practices do in particular settings (Billig 1989, 1991; Burningham 1995; Myers 1998; Potter 1998a; Potter and Wetherell 1988; Puchta and Potter 2002;

> The ATLG consists of two 10-item subscales, one of attitudes toward gay men (ATG) and the other for attitudes toward lesbians (ATL) . . . The 20 statements were presented to respondents in Likert format, usually with a 9-point scale ranging from 'strongly disagree' to 'strongly agree' . . . total scale scores can range from 20 (extremely positive attitudes) to 180 (extremely negative attitudes).
>
> (Herek 1994: 209)

The Attitudes Toward Lesbians and Gay Men (ATLG) Scale

Attitudes Toward Lesbians (ATL) Subscale
1. Lesbians just can't fit into our society. (S)
2. A woman's homosexuality should *not* be a cause of job discrimination in any situation. (R)
3. Female homosexuality is detrimental to society because it breaks down the natural division between the sexes.
4. State laws regulating private, consenting lesbian behavior should be loosened. (R; S)
5. Female homosexuality is a sin. (S)
6. The growing number of lesbians indicates a decline in American morals.
7. Female homosexuality in itself is no problem, but what society makes of it can be a problem. (R; S)
8. Female homosexuality is a threat to many of our basic social institutions.
9. Female homosexuality is an inferior form of sexuality.
10. Lesbians are sick. (S)

Attitudes Toward Gay Men (ATG) Subscale
11. Male homosexual couples should be allowed to adopt children the same as heterosexual couples. (R)
12. I think male homosexuals are disgusting. (S)
13. Male homosexuals should *not* be allowed to teach school.
14. Male homosexuality is a perversion. (S)
15. Just as in other species, male homosexuality is a natural expression of sexuality in human men. (S)
16. If a man has homosexual feelings, he should do everything he can to overcome them.
17. I would *not* be too upset if I learned that my son were a homosexual. (R)
18. Homosexual behavior between two men is just plain wrong. (S)
19. The idea of male homosexual marriages seems ridiculous to me.
20. Male homosexuality is merely a different kind of lifestyle that should *not* be condemned. (R; S)

Note: R means the item was reverse scored and S means that the item appears on the short form.

(From Herek 1994: 210)

Verkuyten 1998; Wiggins and Potter 2003). Rather than conceiving of attitudes as inner mental constructs 'that drive behaviour' (Edwards and Potter 2001: 14), things that can be used to distinguish between individuals, or predictors of future behaviour, DP treats attitudes and evaluations, like all talk, as performing actions.

The discursive psychological move, then, is from considering underlying, stable, cognitively represented attitudes, to evaluative practices that are flexibly produced for particular occasions. Psychologists from more experimental or cognitive approaches might argue that this move flies against the great body of research that highlights attitude stability. However, discursive psychologists suggest that this apparent stability may be a methodological artifact produced by the way traditional attitude measures are insensitive to evaluative variability (Billig et al. 1988; Potter 1998a; Potter and Wetherell 1987) and by interactional processes in more qualitative measures that obscure variability and rhetorical design (Puchta and Potter 2002). It is important to stress that the DP argument is not primarily that attitudes are not stable; it is that moving to considering evaluations in interactional settings is itself an analytically productive exercise.

From a DP perspective, the invented statements contained in attitude scales miss these interactional subtleties. Take the example of the ATLG scale. It could be argued that, like all attitude scales, it has a tendency to reify the object it attempts to measure (heterosexism), by presenting its contours as relatively self-evident and objectively measurable prior to – and not as a result of – an analysis of actual instances. Moreover, it assumes that the object of people's attitudes remains stable, while individuals' attitudes to that object differ (Potter and Wetherell 1988). When one analyses actual evaluative practices in discourse, this distinction between attitude and object becomes hard to sustain. From a discursive perspective, one cannot separate out the attitude or evaluation (e.g., 'homosexuality is a sin') from the attitudinal object (homosexuality), as the former is bound up in the *construction* of the latter; people do description and evaluation simultaneously (Potter and Wetherell 1988; Potter 1996b).

Many studies influenced by CA and DP have focused on how negative, prejudicial attitudes are constructed and managed in participants' talk. Indeed, this approach has proven particularly useful in feminist research exploring how members' justify and reproduce sexism, racism, and other forms of inequality (Billig et al. 1988; Edwards 2003; Gill 1993; Gough 1998a; Potter and Wetherell 1988, 1989; Speer 2002b; Van Dijk 1987; Wetherell and Potter 1992; Wetherell et al. 1987). A number of discursive psychological studies have highlighted how attitudes are rhetorically organized, and the way in which concerns about being heard as speaking from a prejudiced position are managed by constructing evaluations as mere factual descriptions, unmotivated by an inner psychology of threat or hatred (Edwards 2003; Potter 1996b; Wetherell and Potter 1992). As we saw in Chapter 4, participants may inoculate themselves from the potential for their remarks to be interpreted as prejudicial or biased, by constructing that view as rationally arrived at (Edwards 2003). In 'sexist' and 'racist' talk, for example, denials of prejudice often coexist with practical 'factual' reasons which force constraints on the speaker's espoused desire for egalitarianism, and which ultimately justify the status quo (Wetherell et al. 1987). This work shows speakers orienting to a dual concern: to not only express a view but also to manage it in a way that portrays the speaker as caring and egalitarian. Thus, often members' views display an orientation to – and work to pre-empt and deflect – potential counter-arguments and challenges.

One of the simplest examples of this kind of rhetorically organized evaluation is the disclaimer (Burridge 2004; Hewitt and Stokes 1975; Van Dijk 1992). With disclaimers, speakers will essentially preface or suffix their (arguably prejudiced) talk with pronouncements that they are not prejudiced, (e.g., 'I'm not racist but . . .', or 'I'm not sexist but . . .'). By framing their views in this way, they display that their upcoming talk may be problematic, and that it requires 'some careful . . . accountability work' (Stokoe and Smithson 2001: 235). Consider Extract 6.1 below:

(6.1) [Adapted from Stokoe and Smithson 2001: 235–6]
```
1   H:    To be honest I really (.) I don't want to be sexist but I really
2         can't see myself (0.2) ironing and stuff like that I don't know
3         if I could (.) I mean I'm =
4   ?:    = mm =
5   H:    =washing and stuff (0.2) I don't I don't I wouldn't expect
6         my wife just (.) Go wash! go iron!
```

Stokoe and Smithson (2001: 236) note that the disclaimer at line 1 displays the speaker's orientation to the possibility that his talk will be heard by the other participants as sexist. By acknowledging 'I don't want to be sexist but', H works to pre-empt and deflect accusations of prejudice.

Alternatively, participants may 'own' their prejudice in some way, by chastising themselves for their upcoming or preceding remarks:

(6.2) [Adapted from Stokoe and Smithson 2002: 90]
```
15  H:    I hate myself for sa↑ying this (.) but I don't think that even
16        though it's far more open (.) I don't think that having gay
17        couples is right for bringing up the child (.) I don't think
18        it's normal in society it won't be accepted and it might be
19        different (.) I shouldn't really be saying that but I do still
20        believe that (.) I don't think it's right
```

In this extract, H is responding to the moderator's question (lines 10–14) 'does anyone here have a strong opinion on whether gay parents should be allowed to have children?' Here again, the utterances 'I hate myself for saying this' and 'I shouldn't really be saying that' (lines 15 and 19) display the speaker's reflexive 'awareness' that his remarks are problematic, which in turn, deflects the accusation that he is being unreflexively or 'unknowingly' prejudiced.

Other examples of these kinds of disclaimers include 'I'm not a gay basher, but I think this is an issue that since he [Clinton] brought it up, we have to deal with it' (from Meyers 1994: 328) and 'I'm not bothered – as long as they don't come on to me' (from Gough 1998b: 34). Disclaimers are particularly problematic for the attitude theorist as they raise the issue of precisely which part of the disclaimer the analyst should treat as evidence for an individual's views. In the above two instances for example, is it the first (positive) part of the evaluation, which is a claim that one is not prejudiced toward the object ('not a gay basher', 'not bothered') or the second (contrastively more negative) part ('since he [Clinton] brought it up, we have to deal with it', 'as long as they don't come on to me'), which seems to display the very prejudice that has just been denied. Forms such as disclaimers present particular difficulties for the attitude researcher who is using a decontextualized scale that presupposes that speakers are doing their best to accurately represent a relatively static internal position. And to use attitude measures to distinguish between individuals becomes a circular exercise, as attitude displays are often (among other things) precisely part of local identity management (see Antaki and Widdicombe 1998a; Antaki et al. 1996; Widdicombe and Wooffitt 1995).

A number of studies have adopted a broadly discursive approach to explore heterosexism in talk and texts (Armstrong 1997; Baker 2004; Gough 1998b; McCreanor 1996; Meyers 1994; Morrish 1997; Praat and Tuffin 1996). These studies highlight the situated production of prejudice that is often lost in research using traditional attitude scales. Each conceptualizes heterosexist talk in a slightly different way. Meyers (1994), for example, provides a critical discourse analysis of newspaper coverage of Clinton's attempt to repeal the ban on lesbians and gays in the military. She argues that 'coverage presented a male, heterosexist discourse which reinforced homophobic myths and stereotypes' (Meyers 1994: 322). A variety of statements are interpreted as heterosexist, including references to gay men and lesbians as 'special interest groups' (1994: 329), and the use of the word 'gay' to describe both gay men and lesbians (1994: 333). Similarly, Armstrong (1997: 328) describes 'homophobic slang' as 'any adaptation and extension of terms referring to homosexuals that can be interpreted as derogatory in the sense that the quality, action, attribute, or individual to which the term refers is being devalued'. Usage of the term 'homo' is described as 'almost inevitably derogatory' (1997: 328) and accordingly, Armstrong argues, there is 'hostility and . . . devaluation *implicit* in the usage of homophobic terms' (1997: 328, emphasis added).

Heterosexist talk and participants' orientations

Although I support the critical stance of these studies, and take them to be an improvement on cognitivist attitude studies, I suggest that their notion of heterosexist talk tends to be rather static and insensitive to occasions of use. One of the main problems with these studies is that they assume that they know 'what counts' as an example of heterosexist talk, prior to an analysis of interaction. In a similar manner to many of the linguistic studies on sexist talk referred to in Chapters 1 and 2, they treat heterosexist words and utterances as having relatively fixed, 'non-indexical' meanings (cf. Butler's notion of 'hate speech', Chapter 3).

More recently, some researchers have begun to move away from this 'broad-brush' approach to discourse, with its associated use of decontextualized statements and a priori definitions, toward a more nuanced, participants' orientations approach to heterosexism. Although not explicitly concerned with the question of 'what counts' as heterosexist talk, these studies provide rich and empirically grounded insights into issues around homophobic bullying (see Clarke et al. 2004), and the 'de-gaying' and 're-gaying' of AIDS in lesbian and gay awareness training (Kitzinger and Peel 2005). In the analysis that follows, I will build on this body of research by showing what participants themselves treat as problematic or troublesome in their talk.

The analysis has a dual focus. First, I will ask whether the interactants attend to something that might be glossed in a more theoretical context as 'heterosexism'. Can we find participants orienting to their own talk, or that of others, as potentially heterosexist, prejudiced or problematic in some way? Is there something in the way the utterances are rhetorically designed which attends to possible counters or alternative claims? Second, I will consider what such 'attending to heterosexism' is doing interactionally. What is the significance of such orientations? How can potentially, hearably derogatory remarks get said? How might such saying be related to issues of managing displays of identity? How do conversationalists deal with, pre-empt and foreclose counter-arguments and challenges? More generally, I hope to improve our understanding of the construction and precise nature of the 'myths', 'stereotypes', 'discourses' and 'practices' discussed in the critical discursive literature on heterosexism, and how they are constituted in talk and action.

In a search of the corpus I picked out sixty-four candidate instances where sexuality was made relevant, either directly by the interviewer or documentary host, or spontaneously by the other speakers. I focus on nine of these instances that have been chosen to illustrate the wide *range* of members' practices.

Discounting heterosexism

Let us start by considering some of the dilemmas that may confront conversationalists when talking about gay and lesbian concerns and topics. The issue at interest is the way heterosexism may be oriented to in the course of the interaction and the way the dilemma is managed through constructing descriptions of events and mental states. The following sequence is taken from an interview with Ben, a man in his mid-twenties, who has described himself earlier in the interview as heterosexual. We enter the sequence at the point where Sue asks Ben about his perceptions of a gay club:

```
(6.3) [Speer and Potter 2000: 549-50]
  1   S:   Did you enjoy going to the gay club?
  2   B:   Yeah I ↑did. I had a bloody good ↑time.
  3   S:   Was it a different kind of experience from a:
  4        (.) ( ) the pubs you're used to?
  5   B:   ↑Erm (2.0) yeah it was a different experience
  6        but (1.0) it didn't bother me (0.4) you know.
  7        The difference was (.) er:, (1.0) knowing the
  8        fact that the: (.) No, it wasn't knowing the
  9        fact. (0.4) >You know< it wouldn't have
 10        bothered me if I didn't know. (0.4) The
 11        difference was they're very (0.4) °↑erm°
 12        (2.0) well, the fact that you get men (.)
 13        going past you and saying "excuse me darling"
 14        (.) instead of (.) "excuse me mate" or (0.6)
 15        "coming through" or what- you know, they're
 16        (0.8) ob(h)viously more feminine a lot of
 17        them. (1.0) Or er (.) you know, you get men
 18        coming onto you sometimes. (0.8) But it
 19        doesn't bother me. (.) You know, I'll be
 20        straight and honest with anyone °and say°
 21        "I'm sorry I'm not interested".
```

Let us start by considering how Sue's question in line 1 might be a tricky one for Ben to respond to. For simplicity, I will first consider how this question might offer two potential sources of trouble for Ben. On the one hand, if he avows a lack of enjoyment this might be an indication of psychological trouble with gay people, it might be a sign of heterosexism.

On the other hand, enjoyment might be an indication that Ben himself is gay or harbours homosexual desires.

Note the emphatic way Ben responds to the question in line 1. He agrees that he 'enjoyed' going to the club, and then upgrades this to a 'bloody good time'. This upgraded assessment could certainly counteract the idea that Ben might harbour negative feelings toward gay people. That is, it could address the first of these potential sources of trouble. There is evidence that Ben is orienting to these concerns from the way the interaction continues. Note in particular the way he responds to the interviewer's follow up question about whether he enjoyed the experience. Despite having given the upgraded description of the good time he had, he almost immediately claims that the experience 'didn't bother' him (line 6), and this formulation appears two further times (lines 10 and 19) in this extended answer. In rhetorical terms (Billig 1996), these denials orient to the potential counter-claim that he is, in fact, bothered by this experience of a homosexual club.

Ben's enjoyment and reiterated lack of bother with the club could be grounds for the other source of potential trouble. Is the pleasure here because of Ben's own sexual orientation, explicit or otherwise? Again there is evidence of Ben's orientation to this trouble in the way he fashions the end of his turn. His actively voiced 'I'm sorry I'm not interested' is glossed as 'straight and honest' (line 20). This attention to his heterosexual status in the described event also attends to that status for the current interaction. Note also that the voiced interaction displays politeness with no suggestion of trouble or hostility in the reported speech. Further indication that Ben is caught in an interactional dilemma here comes from the mis-starts, frequent pauses at non-transition-relevant places, hesitation and explicit self-repair throughout his answer.

There is a lot going on in this extract. However, the point that I wish to emphasize is that we can consider the way heterosexism is oriented to in the interaction, both directly and indirectly. Put another way, we can see that what counts as heterosexism or prejudice, might not only be an analyst's concern, but is also a concern for the participants – and particularly for Sue, the interviewer. This extract also raises problems with the distinction between 'cultural' and 'psychological heterosexism' that I referred to above. For the participants, at least, there is no easy separation of the two realms. For Ben, as he denies psychological bother at his exposure to homosexual people, he at the same time reflexively implicates the existence of norms or expectations in which sexual identity is a notable particular (cf. Chapter 4, Extract 4.7).

Displaying a lack of understanding

In Extract 6.3, Ben works to avoid the implications of the interviewer's potentially heterosexist question. However, in other extracts, where the social science agenda appears background to the current interaction, and where the talk is arguably more extreme, orientations to heterosexism are less explicit. Nonetheless, we can still find evidence of speakers working to bolster their claims against (potential or actual) counter-arguments and challenges. As I showed in my discussion of gender attribution in Chapter 4 (Extract 4.5), sometimes, a speaker might display ownership of, or investment in a view, such as 'I have a problem with' or 'don't understand' a, b or c, in order to make the 'a, b, or c' seem problematic. In this sense, then, the expression of a *personal* difficulty can be used as a resource, to construct something or *someone else* as problematic. This style of accounting is not peculiar to 'prejudice talk', but is pervasive in interaction and the management of stake and interest (Edwards and Potter 1992; Potter 1996b). Consider the way knowledge claims work in Extract 6.4 below:

(6.4) [Speer and Potter 2000: 551]
```
1   D:   well I must say [in the pantomime]=
2   A:                   [No::          ]
3   D:   =last Sunday there were the girls doing the
4        dancing and there was one ↑man doing it-
5        dancing as ↑well, and he looked com↑plete
6        poof doing it.
7   A:   [yeah]
8   K:   [yeah] (.) yeah
9   A:        [Mm]
10  D:        [and] how he could
11       do it ↓there, I just don't know, the
12       one man on his own.
13  A:   Was it what he was wearing
14       [and the form you saw or?]
15  D:   [NO:: the way, -no]        the way he was
16       (0.8)
17  P:   Moving
18  D:   moving rea:l↓ly.
```

Donald begins by telling a story about his visit to the pantomime where there was 'one man' dancing who 'looked complete poof' (lines 5–6). Despite getting alignment from A and K in the turns that follow, Donald provides an *account* for his view: 'And how he could do it there I just don't know, the one man on his own' (lines 10–12).

As I showed in Chapter 4, the words 'I don't know' are not necessarily a straightforward factual reporting of the speaker's lack of psychological knowledge (Hutchby 2002; Potter 2004a). Rather, they can also work interactionally to *display* a lack of knowledge. Here, Donald's 'I don't know' works rhetorically to bolster his argument about what a 'complete poof' this 'one' person dancing is. His claim is reinforced with the exasperated 'how he could do it there' and the word 'just', which reflects the extent or degree of Donald's despair and frustration at having tried and failed to comprehend how this male dancer could do such a thing. Donald constructs his account in a way that makes ballet dancers appear odd, in contrast to Donald himself, who has simply tried and failed to grasp the reasons behind this dancer's peculiar behaviour. Donald's difficulty, then, is *caused* by this dancer's incomprehensible behaviour, and Donald cannot be held accountable for *that*. As Drew remarks in his analysis of complaints about transgressions, reporting a 'sense of grievance', 'enables complainants to characterize how far the other's behaviour has caused offense' (Drew 1998: 311). Donald's description of his own lack of understanding works as a kind of complaint, to exhibit the other's (and logically, not his own) behaviour as 'reprehensible' (Drew 1998: 312).

While not *explicitly* attending to his remarks as heterosexist in the way that Ben does in Extract 6.3, then, Donald still conveys his 'strong views' (Billig 1989) in a way that attends to or orients towards possible rhetorical counters, signaling perhaps the necessity for him to do so in the first place. Indeed, it is significant that Donald does *not* provide the kind of straightforward, decontextualized statement that one might expect to find in an attitude scale, such as 'male ballet dancers are poofs'. Rather, he is sensitive to the ways in which potentially negative comments can reflect poorly on the identity of the speaker, and he works to pre-empt and deflect such inferences. It could be argued that Donald 'talks with an expectation of the listener preparing a response' (Bakhtin 1986: 69, cited in Shotter 1993: 121) and with 'the possibility that the account might receive an unsympathetic or sceptical hearing' (Hutchby and Wooffitt 1998: 196). It is this anticipation of a possibly negative uptake which accounts for the rhetorical design of Donald's claims.

Softening the blow

A further way in which speakers manage their potentially prejudiced claims is to portray other people as prejudiced, which works contrastively to imply that they themselves are not. Here claims that invoke 'facts' are used to undermine other people's 'views' or 'presumptions' about women's rugby. Consider Extract 6.5 below:

(6.5) [Speer and Potter 2000: 552–3]
1   R: I think that's becoming erm, (.) more common
2   now (   ) °female rugby players°.
3   (.) And there's sort of the erm (0.6)
4   presumption that they're **all gonna be**

```
5          butch and (0.4) stuff, but they're not, a
6          lot of them (      ) (0.8)
7    J:    (°          °)
8    ():   °hmm°
9    R:    especially in Birmingham.
```

In this extract, Rachel makes sexuality relevant by referring to the 'presumption', by (unspecified) others, that female rugby players are 'all gonna be butch' (lines 4–5). Unlike Donald in Extract 6.4, in this extract Rachel is concerned to undermine such 'presumptions'. Indeed, an ideal way to portray oneself as non-prejudiced (and knowledgeable about other people's prejudice) is to refer to the prejudicial assumptions of others, and then undermine the factual basis of those assumptions. Rachel does this by constructing the 'presumption' in a way that makes it rhetorically easy to falsify with counter-evidence. The extreme case formulation (from here on, 'ECF') 'all gonna be butch' does not simply work up the prejudice as normative in the context of possible doubt (see Pomerantz 1986), but is also *hearably* extreme, in the sense that it is more than would be factually necessary to say to convey the prejudiced views of others (it would be enough to suggest simply that 'others presume rugby players are butch', for example, and without making a reference to the numbers involved). As Derek Edwards claims, 'the sheer extremity of ECFs makes them available for a range of "as if", "essentially so", nonliteral or metaphoric uses and uptakes' (Edwards 2000: 365).

Rachel's claim is not a *literal* description of the presuming person's or people's views, but is constructed and deployed to show the strength (and ultimately, the unreasonableness) of others' prejudice.

Edwards suggests that the extremity and non-literalness of such claims means that ECFs can be 'rhetorically brittle, occasioning the use of softeners as responses to, or forestallings of, actual or potential challenges' (Edwards 2000: 369). Rachel cleverly uses this requirement for softening hearably non-literal descriptions as a *resource*. She is able to undermine the extreme claim 'all gonna be butch' (lines 4–5) with a (constructed as factual) contrastive counterclaim: 'but they're not, a lot of them' (lines 5–6). The interesting thing about this extreme case softener is how – even when the view expressed is (constructed as) a rather liberal 'to be heard as non-prejudiced' one – the talk is still managed in such a way that leaves many of the prejudiced assumptions of the original (constructed as disputable) presumption intact. For example, Rachel does not say 'but *none* of them are butch' (which would be equally extreme), or 'but what's the problem with butchness anyway?' and 'butch lesbians do disproportionately like rough sports' or even 'some butch women like rugby just as some non-butch women like rugby'. Instead, Rachel offers only a partial counter to the extreme generalization (marked with the 'but' on line 5).

This portrays her as reasonable and knowledgeable about all the cases of women who play rugby (and see line 9). At the same time, however, it leaves open the possibility that a team with a high proportion of butch players might be a problematic, to-be-accounted-for phenomenon (rather than a perfectly acceptable, non-comment-worthy one).

Rachel's remarks are particularly resistant to the imputation of prejudice, precisely because of the softened format, which shows her to be or *displays* that she is undermining a prejudicial claim. This makes it hard to come back to her and assert that she is producing just such a claim herself. As Derek Edwards says, 'although a non-extreme generalization is logically and semantically weaker than an ECF, it can be rhetorically and interactionally stronger' (2000: 354).

In this extract, then, Rachel uses factual descriptions to convey the existence of, and her orientation towards, what counts as a prejudicial assumption. In doing so, she inoculates herself from the possibility that her own claims might be criticized for being motivated by similar assumptions, and thus orientates to the rhetorical possibility of negative uptakes.

In the extracts considered so far, I have been dealing with *potential* counters to participants' remarks, and with the internal rhetorical design of their utterances. While working to pre-empt or inoculate their remarks from attack, the speakers display their orientation to the potentially troublesome nature of their comments. Extracts 6.6 and 6.7 demonstrate an alternative way in which such talk is managed, where the problematic nature of a potentially troublesome claim is oriented to by another speaker, or the recipient of that remark (in this case, Sue – the discussion leader), in the form of a 'next turn repair initiator' (marked in the transcript with →). The NTRI repeats a problematic part of the prior utterance, thus encouraging the original speaker to repair it (Schegloff et al. 1977):

(6.6) [Speer and Potter 2000: 554]
```
1      K:    =it's a little bit like getting the ladies
2            [in the services]=
3      M:    [they (.) they]=
4      K:    =[actually]
5      M:    =[always] make you think they-
6            [they all- all look like]=
7      K:    [I don't mind ladies in the]=
8      M:    =[dykes don't they?]
9      K:    =[services driving] vehicles [(           )]
10  →  S:                                 [All look like]
11           dy(h)kes? °hh hh hh°
12     K:    [I don't]
```

RECONCEPTUALIZING PREJUDICE

```
13    S:    [that is,] - that's what a lot of people say
14          but like at Birmingham [we've got lots of]
15    M:                            [they prob]'ly are
16          ↑not, actually (.) [but] I mean=
17    S:                       [yeah]
18    M:    =they- it's just that they don't look
19          feminine
```

(6.7) [Speer and Potter 2000: 555]

```
1     M:    what, -what would you s-consider female-like
2           sports?
3     S:    ( hh  )↑just the job.(.) I've got a male
4           ballerina
5     C:    Ten (0.8) [tennis]
6     M:              [Well] they're mostly all
7           queers [anyway]
8  →  S:           [HA HA HA]
9           .hhh Ohh this [is brilliant!]
10    M:                  [not all of] them.
11          [↓No, I wouldn't]=
12    S:    [heh heh heh]
13    M:    =[say, - prob'ly not all of them]
14    C:     [girls like - er- like] tennis mostly ↑don't
15          they
```

Both of these extracts have very similar structures: an extreme case formulation, an NTRI, and a softened ECF. Keith (Extract 6.6) is in the middle of explaining why he objects to women playing rugby. Before long Matt offers a reason for his own objection: 'Always make you think they- they all- all look like dykes don't they?' Notice that here, again, sexuality is made relevant via ECFs and factual, impersonal claims about how 'you' always think they 'all look like dykes' (lines 5–8). Matt is careful not to own his view, by saying 'you think' rather than 'makes me think' (line 5), thus generalizing his opinion to others. *Everyone* is implicated in Matt's (constructed as) typical or commonplace observation about the appearance of women rugby players.

Sue attends to the problematic (and extreme) nature of these remarks with an NTRI in the form of a partial repeat of the prior turn, interspersed with disbelieving laughter particles (lines 10–11 (see Jefferson 1985)). Even before Sue's qualifier (lines 13–14), Matt interrupts, offering a softened 'they prob'ly are not, actually', and an alternative 'it's just that they don't look feminine' (lines 18–19). As before, the extreme case softener is rhetorically robust, yet does not deconstruct the assumptions embedded within the original remark, that there might be something accountable –

165

even newsworthy – about looking like, or being a 'dyke'. It simply refers to a possibility or probability that female rugby players are 'not dykes' – another 'factual' claim. Matt satisfies the interactional demand to repair his (attended to by Sue as derogatory) claim, yet his alternative 'they don't look feminine' allows him to recycle his complaint by referring to gender rather than sexuality. The nature of the complaint has changed, but the degree of the objection has not (i.e. the objection itself remains largely intact). Moreover, and centrally, Matt's original claim is constructed in a way that anticipates a negative uptake. Its internal rhetorical design, and its extremity, simultaneously display Matt's investment in the claim, and builds in his own (easy to soften, should it be necessary) 'get out clause': the potential to soften the ECF.

Extract 6.7 is strikingly similar, highlighting the generality and robustness of disputable proposition management via the move from ECF to ECF softener. Sue (lines 3–4) shows the dinner guests a picture of a male ballet dancer. Here the NTRI is not a partial repeat of the prior turn, as it was in Extract 6.6. The extremity of Matt's disputable proposition, 'mostly all queers anyway' (lines 6–7), is responded to by Sue – in the context of a social science investigation where such comments make interesting data – with spontaneous delight: 'HA HA HA .hhh Ohh this is brilliant!' (lines 8–9). The NTRI not only constitutes what's gone before as hearably extreme, and laughable as such, but is also a reflexive comment on the nature of the interaction *as* a social science investigation, where commenting on sexual identity is worked up as just the type of thing Sue is after.

Matt does not respond to Sue by upgrading his prior statement – or by offering more of the same (as one would expect if Sue's remarks were interpreted as a literal description of 'brilliant' comments). Instead, Matt treats Sue's remarks *as* an NTRI, as attending to something problematic in his prior statement. He softens his original extreme case: 'not all of them' (lines 10 and 13). Again, the extremity of 'mostly all queers' is interactionally rather easy to soften, to show that one has engaged in a repair, without completely undermining the thrust of the original objection. Matt leaves implicit the view that, if *all* of them are not queer, then at least *some* of them will be.

The important thing to note about the extracts in this section, is that by initially describing something in an extreme way, the speaker provides themselves with a ready-made counter to any potential criticism. That is, by making an ECF generalization, one can always counter accusations of prejudice with 'well not all of them', thus avoiding having to attend to the specifics of pretty much *any* objection. One could argue that it is the nature of this structure and the interactional necessity for it in the first place, which demonstrates, *in action*, participants' orientation to the potential uptake of their remarks *as* prejudiced.

Extract 6.8 constitutes a departure from the structure of ECF to ECF softener exemplified in Extracts 6.6 and 6.7. The rhetorical effect, however, is rather similar:

(6.8) [Speer and Potter 2000: 556–7]
```
1    K:    Marilyn Monroe (.) I could never s- (.)
2          visualize that type of lady (.) playing
3          ↑rugby.
4          (0.8)
5    M:    No but [I mean if you were interested]
6    K:           [the- the ones who do are] butch (.)
7          in many ca[ses]
8 →  S:              [Butch?]
9    K:    Butch, (.) quite butch.
10   M:    If you were interested in a girl, (0.6) you
11         know, and she was nice looking and
12         everything, you wouldn't want her to go out
13         and get all smashed ↑up.
```

Rather than suggesting 'most' or 'all' women rugby players are 'butch', Keith says instead that they are butch 'in many cases' (lines 6–7). This is more cautious than an ECF claim about all or most instances. Nevertheless, in order to make such a claim, one simultaneously requires (and Keith displays himself as having) knowledge of the degree of 'butchness' of all cases. Sue offers an NTRI in the form of a partial questioning repeat of the prior disputable utterance: 'Butch?' (line 8). Keith then repeats the derogatory statement. However, this time, he does not qualify the numbers of instances of butch individuals – by saying 'well okay there's only one or two' – which would be the logically parallel softener to 'many cases'. Instead, he refers to and qualifies the *degree* of 'butchness' of any particular individual: they are 'quite butch' (line 9). This construction is particularly hard to counter, since the possibility for exceptions to the rule is built into both utterances. One can always say, 'well I didn't say all of them', and 'I didn't say they're totally, butch – only quite butch', for example. Keith's remarks work as a *display* of responding to Sue's NTRI, yet do not explicitly repair the disputed proposition on its own terms. It is also productively ambiguous, being hearable as either an increase, or a decrease in the strength of the prior claim, a repair or reassertion of the disputable proposition. Again, this leaves much of the legitimacy of his original proposition (on lines 6–7) intact. Because of this ambiguity, and the possibility that it can be heard as a repair, there is little interactional room to get Keith to repair this a second time (with another NTRI such as 'quite butch?', for example). In any case, the repetition in 'Butch, quite butch' makes it a forceful 'end of story' type construction, which closes the discussion down.

Conceding positive features

One rhetorically robust way in which conversationalists manage potentially derogatory statements is with a three-part structure rather like that identified by Antaki and Wetherell (1999) in their conversation analytic article on 'Show concessions'. Antaki and Wetherell argue that 'making a show of conceding by using a three-part structure of proposition, concession and reassertion has the effect . . . of strengthening one's own position at the expense of a counter-argument' (1999: 7). Broadly speaking, this structure consists of:

(i) saying something vulnerable to challenge;
(ii) conceding something [counter-evidence] to that challenge; then
(iii) qualifying that concession and reasserting what one first said.
(see Antaki and Wetherell 1999: 8–9)

Extract 6.9 provides an illustration of this structure in action:

(6.9) [Antaki and Wetherell 1999: 20]
```
→  1    Resp:   there's no way I can influence
→  2            the Federation of Labour         [proposition]
   3            I might [hate them you know      [concession]
   4    Int:            [yeah
   5    Resp:   [willing to go out and shoot the
   6    Int:    [yeah
   7    Resp:   whole lot of them. [But
   8    Int:                       [((explosive laughter))
→  9    Resp:   I can't influence them.          [reprise]
```

Antaki and Wetherell (1999: 20) argue that the respondent is not simply agreeing, or showing that he acknowledges the existence of other points of view. Instead he is 'building up his talk so as to make a *show* of conceding a point'. The three-part structure allows the speaker to draw attention to his concession, and by doing so, 'he is realizing a very particular rhetorical effect' (1999: 20).

It is precisely this three-part structure which is exploited by Mick and Wayne in Extract 6.10, which is taken from a television documentary that was set up to see if 'two homophobic rugby players from Yorkshire' can change their views about gay men after living with them in London's Soho for five days. Mick and Wayne are keeping a video diary, and we join them as they recall their day in Soho:

(6.10) [Speer and Potter 2000: 558]
```
1    M:    ((to camcorder)) Walking down that street
2          today 'n and there were people there- I jus'
3          could have twatted 'em all.
```

```
4   W:      hhh hhh [heh heh] heh .hhh hhh
5   M:              [Horrible].
6           **I mean** like these two kids with Wayne, (0.2)
7           they're like [trying] their 'ardest=
8   W:                   [(   )]
9   M:      =they're re̲ally trying their 'ardest to
10          like (0.4) make us like (.) feel welcome
11          and (0.4) we've had arguments with them,
12          we've had a few arguments with them, (0.8)
13          **but** at end of ↓day (0.8) no matter what they
14          ↓do, (1.0) they're ga̲y ba̲stards.
15  W:      ° hh hh hh hh hh .hhh hhh .hhh°
```

There are two markers which bracket the concession and which signal that it is part of a concession structure: the concession marker 'I mean' (line 6), and the reprise marker 'but' (line 13). The concession marker works both retrospectively – casting what's been said as 'disputable', or 'to cast what has gone before as somehow dangerous to one's presumed impartiality' (Antaki and Wetherell 1999: 13) – and prospectively. It introduces what follows as counter-evidence to the original proposition. The reprise marker, on the other hand, 'signals that the concessionary material is over and heralds that what is to come is in opposition to what has gone before' (1999: 14).

The first part of this structure – the initial 'derogatory' proposition that is 'vulnerable to challenge' – appears on lines 2 and 3 with 'I jus' could have twatted 'em all'. This construction is hearably extreme. It does not sound like the kind of behaviour one man would physically be able to engage in, let alone get away with. Indeed, the term 'twatted' would support the claim that this is a *display* of investment in a view, the strength of Mick's dislike, rather than a literal description of his intentions at the time. 'Twatted' (in contrast to terms such as 'kicked', 'punched' or 'hit') gives Mick's remarks an ironic, not to be taken seriously, tone (and implies that one should not necessarily perceive Mick as dispositionally given to such a reaction (see Edwards 1997: 264–5)). Indeed, the laughter retrospectively constructs these remarks *as* ironic or invested in some way (Edwards 2000).

The show of conceding comes on lines 6–10, with the concession marker 'I mean' and 'they're really trying their 'ardest to like . . . make us like feel welcome'. This concession softens the original, ironized extreme case, and presents Mick and Wayne as reasonable human beings who are able to recognize good hosts. Mick and Wayne have tried to engage with them like 'real blokes', having 'arguments' with them, for example (lines 11–12).

This type of construction is rhetorically quite robust, precisely because of its concessionary format. Making a show of conceding in this way not only draws attention to the very 'disputability' of the original proposition, but also displays an orientation to it *as* problematic. Mick and Wayne demonstrate that they are able to recognize potential opposition to their claims, and they voice (and thus foreclose) that potential opposition in their concessions. While no one challenges Mick and Wayne, then, their 'recognition' of the potential for challenge is built into the design of their utterances.

Having made the concession, Mick complains that, in the final analysis, 'no matter what they do, they're gay bastards' (lines 13–14). Again, as in line 4, the extremity of this claim is oriented to with laughter, which suggests that it was constructed *as* invested or ironic in some way (Edwards 2000). The laughter works with the concession to bolster the extreme claims against attack. This idiomatic reprise (marked with 'but') provides closure to the argument (Drew and Holt 1988) and completes the three-part structure, which undoes the work that the concession does on its own. In its entirety, this construction has 'the rhetorical effect of bolstering the speaker's original proposition against implied (or explicit) challenge, and weakening, or even dismissing, the counter case' (Antaki and Wetherell 1999: 10). The strength of Mick's original claim is thereby enhanced rather than undermined. The rhetorical design of this sequence shows how Mick and Wayne simultaneously display their orientation to the possibility that their views might be heard as problematic, at the same time as managing and working to deflect accusations of prejudice.

Effectively, this extract contains a mixture of rather extreme claims about the speaker's own views: 'I jus' could have twatted 'em all' (lines 2–3), and more distanced (but equally extreme) 'factual' descriptions: 'They're gay bastards' (line 14). These are organized in such a way as to manage the speaker's identity. As Antaki and Wetherell put it: 'The structure attends to some vulnerability of stake or interest (as Edwards and Potter, 1992, call it) in the speaker's starting claim . . . with the twist that it does so while, at the same time, proving the speaker against complaint' (Antaki and Wetherell 1999: 23, 25).

A similar way in which recipients counter the negative claims of others is to assert that, in spite of being gay, 'poofs' or whatever, such individuals also possess other culturally valued characteristics (such as strength, skill, attractiveness, reasonableness, friendliness, and so on). This structure has similarities to some features of 'sexist' and 'racist' talk (see Gill 1993; Van Dijk 1992; Wetherell and Potter 1992). It has the dual effect of managing stake and interest – making the speaker appear more 'liberal' than others, while, again, leaving the presuppositions of the original, disputed claim intact:

(6.11) [Speer and Potter 2000: 559–60]
1   S: what about <u>ballet</u> (.) o↑kay?
2   K: [Oh my God!]

```
3    P:    [For men?]
4    S:    Yep.
5    A:    °Well let Donald have it°.
6    K:    Oh yes(h). See(h) what Donald thinks(h) about
7          th(h)at(h) ha ha .hh .hh He's a RIGHT POOF!
8                [HA HA HA HA]
9    A:          [°.hh .hh .hh .hhh°]
10   P:    [But BY:] JO:VE do they have to be strong.
11   D:    [Yeah]
12   K:    Oh: yeah. [It's a]
13   D:              [Yeah you've] got- you've got to
14         have men in ballet (0.4) to make it really
15         work I think. (0.4) Erm.
16   A:    For-for the lifting
```

We join the interaction at a point where Sue has just shown the dinner guests a picture of a male ballet dancer. Keith exclaims 'He's a RIGHT POOF!' (line 7), to which Pamela responds, 'But BY: JO:VE do they have to be strong' (line 10). As we have already seen, the word 'but' can signal that what is to come is in opposition to what has already been said. In this context, Pamela's statement is constructed 'to be heard as' a display of disagreement with Keith. At the same time, however, its construction (as a concession) implies that the strength of 'poofs', at least, is not self-evident, and needs to be emphasized. Pamela positions herself as more liberal than the other speakers, with an 'awareness' of 'poofs'' redeeming qualities, while cleverly avoiding any reference to sexuality, or criticizing the precise terms of Keith's original claim. There may be a sense, then, in which Pamela's response, and Keith's subsequent agreement, are recipient designed, a possible orientation to the sentiments of the interviewer. Indeed, Keith's emphatic 'Oh: yeah.' (line 12) is evidence that he does not treat Pamela's statement as undermining his earlier claim, but as already taken into account by it.

In all of the extracts considered so far, there is some display (either rhetorically, in the design of the utterance, or by another speaker) that a proposition about sexuality is a challengeable or disputable one. I have argued that this retrospectively works to construct the statements as requiring care or delicacy in the first place, and provides evidence for participants' orientations to prejudice (or, in its more theorized form – heterosexism). However, it is important to remember that the precise meaning of a statement is worked up by speakers in an interaction. Labelling somebody a 'poof' or a 'queen' will not always be treated (by the speakers) as a negative thing, as negativity is not built into certain words. These terms may (not inconceivably) be used as terms of endearment between close friends or partners, for example.

Ironizing 'heterosexist' scripts: a deviant case

Extract 6.12 is taken from *Gaytime TV Special*, a television documentary on the 1998 Gay Games in Amsterdam. It is presented by Richard Fairbrass, an 'out' gay man. Here the words 'queens' and 'poofs' do not seem to be used in a derogatory way:

(6.12) [Speer and Potter 2000: 561].

```
1   RF:            This is a >really curious thing<. (.) You
2                  have erm (.) all these queens here (.) who:
3                  at any other time during the week, >would be<
4                  out clubbing and er, getting all their gear
5                  together and er, having a wonderful time and
6                  .hhh and >everything else< and being queens,
7                  (.) and then you come here, (.) and suddenly
8                  football has turned everybody (.) into a
9                  lager swilling ↑yob. (.) I mean they just (.)
10                 and they all sing the team songs and they
11                 all- they all start 'GO ON MY SON' and er y-
12                 you know it's j'st- where's it all ↑come
13                 from?
14                 ((cameras cut to football match))
15  Man shouts:    'It's a game for men not poofs'
16  RF:            This heterosexuality suddenly came out of
17                 nowhere.
```

Fairbrass sets up a contrast between what he constructs as two seemingly incompatible scripts (Edwards 1994): the script for homosexuality and the script for football playing. While 'queens' ordinarily go out clubbing, 'getting all their gear together', 'having a wonderful time', and 'everything else', and 'being queens' (lines 3–9), footballers, on the other hand, are: 'lager swilling yobs' who 'sing the team songs', and say things like 'go on my son' (lines 12–17). Together, these activities constitute 'this heterosexuality' (line 22). The irony comes in the juxtaposition of these two seemingly incompatible scripts, and in the 'ambiguity, inconsistency, and contradiction' (Mulkay 1988: 3) that Fairbrass indicates their juxtaposition engenders: He says 'this is a really curious thing' and 'where's it all come from?' (lines 1 and 19). In highlighting this incongruity, Fairbrass constructs this as a peculiar and accountable phenomenon: how can football turn queens – whom we typically associate with certain behaviours – into lager-drinking heterosexuals? To emphasize the ridiculousness of this proposition, Fairbrass relies on the very script that he is working to subvert. He makes a mockery of stereotyping and category boundedness by playing up the implausibility in an extreme and scripted fashion, such that the implausibility itself appears ridiculous.

The interjection by the man on the sidelines shouting 'it's a game for men not poofs' (line 21) is rather neatly edited in by the producers of the programme at this particular moment in the sequence. It is juxtaposed within Fairbrass's narrative, coming clearly at the end of his rhetorical question (a transition relevance place), alongside images of gay footballers. The man's comments work *as* irony precisely because he seems to be working to make available the possibility that he is stereotyping gay men, or engaging in some form of sexual reductionism (cf. Schegloff's 'ladies last' in Extract 4.8 in Chapter 4). Instead, however, his interjection, through its ironic placement, works to highlight the social construction of sexuality and the mechanisms through which heterosexuality comes to be seen as normative. Fairbrass's 'this heterosexuality suddenly came out of nowhere' (lines 22–3) works to make *heterosexuality* and not homosexuality accountable – which is precisely the opposite of what is typically held accountable in 'straight' culture. The familiarity and repeatability of the script provides the framework for its own subversion, highlighting its normative but culturally constructed and problematic nature (for more on how irony can be used by speakers to problematize normative understandings of gender, see Speer 2002b).

Chapter summary and discussion

In this chapter I have demonstrated several context-sensitive ways in which interactants attend to and manage 'heterosexist talk'. These findings extend what we know about the constitution of prejudiced talk in general, and heterosexist talk in particular. I want to spend the remainder of this chapter discussing the wider implications of these findings for research on prejudice, attitudes and 'the world in here'.

I have shown how heterosexist talk is not a straightforward emptying out of preformed, stable, homophobic attitudes by the heterosexist person, nor something one can easily identify in specific prejudiced terms or utterances prior to an analysis. When we look at talk that makes sexuality relevant in specific interactional situations, it becomes difficult to divide up individuals into those with heterosexist attitudes and those who are (apparently) more liberal, to divide statements into 'homophobic' versus 'non-homophobic' talk – as is done with the ATLG scale, or to make distinctions between 'cultural' and 'psychological' heterosexism. Global, crudely quantified definitions of what counts as homophobic talk may help us to challenge the most extreme manifestations of heterosexism (such as hate crimes) and can thus be useful weapons in a political struggle, but they tend to be less effective, or even positively misleading, where we are dealing with the sorts of articulate individuals we have seen in these data.

Attitude scales systematically strip off fundamental sequentially sensitive and rhetorically oriented features of discourse. Moreover, they cannot account for the way in which (as with the disclaimer), within any one stretch of talk we may find evidence of heterosexist *and* expressly anti-heterosexist views. Despite this, previous research has said little (if anything) about what members themselves might *treat as* heterosexist in different interactional contexts, where what counts as heterosexism is negotiable and 'up-for-grabs'.

In this chapter, I have tried to understand the role of attitudes and evaluations in their 'home' environment of conversational practices, rather than in the more arcane context of an attitude scale. Rather than starting with the pencil-and-paper measures developed with undergraduate psychology students, a participants' orientations approach highlights heterosexism's mundane, everyday manifestations, and shows how the complicated contours of prejudice need to be understood in their interactional particulars.

Moreover, rather than assuming that we can know in advance of an analysis what a prejudiced statement or utterance looks like, or that members will *not* orient to their talk as problematic, I have shown how, by decomposing heterosexist interaction, and exploring it from a members' perspective, we can see how the issue of what is going to count as prejudiced, derogatory or whatever, is patently and observably an issue for participants as well as analysts.

Although it is clear that in my data heterosexism is *not* a participants' category (e.g. none of the participants – including the moderator, Sue – say 'that was a heterosexist utterance') and participants' talk may or may not always *sound* explicitly derogatory, like the positively scored statements contained in the ATLG scale (Herek 1994), this does not mean that heterosexism and its associated 'trouble' is not relevant to the participants, or oriented to in subtle, less explicit ways. Rather, when we adopt a participants' orientations approach, we can see how prejudicial attitude statements and evaluative descriptions, assessments and so on, are often produced in ways that show a concern for the accountability and identity of the speaker. In fact, there seems to be some interesting work going on in such talk, which displays the speakers' sensitivity to possibly being *heard* as heterosexist or prejudiced.

For example, in the instances discussed here, participants' orientations to the potential for a negative uptake are evident in the internal rhetorical design of their accounts, as well as in their responses to an explicit challenge. Speakers use various conversational and interactional resources to portray themselves as reasonable, rational, unprejudiced, responsive to potential or actual criticism, able to recognize their views as extreme, invested and so on. Thus, interactants do not need to be well versed in sexual identity politics, the analyst's concept of 'heterosexism', or use the words 'heterosexist', 'homophobic' or 'prejudiced', for them to nevertheless manage their talk in a way that is sensitive to its potential uptake, and which forecloses possible counter-arguments and challenges.

The central point I wish to make here, is that it is in their orientations, their attending to potential trouble, that we can find the very constitution of what the participants take to be prejudicial, accountable, 'heterosexist talk'. By repeatedly orienting to their remarks as problematic and as requiring careful management, these participants tell us something important about what is normative and accountable in culture (cf. the discussion of interactional dilemmas in Chapter 4). It may be indicative, for example, that participants are becoming more 'liberal in their views' (Clarke 2005) and, if this is the case, feminists and lesbian and gay psychologists may have reason to feel optimistic that one day, a liberal discourse may give way to a more radical position where heterosexist talk is deemed too problematic to manage and 'voice' at all. Indeed, in culture generally, there is a sense in which disclaimers such as 'I've got nothing against gay people, some of my best friends are gay but . . .' have become stereotyped and accountable things to say in and of themselves.

Extract 6.12 provides a useful illustration of what a more radical discourse may look like. Indeed, the analysis of irony is significant here, for at least three reasons. First, it lends empirically grounded weight to claims that, to date, have been discussed primarily only in the abstract: heterosexist talk is not something that comes 'written into' specific words. What counts as heterosexism is not predetermined, invariable and legislated in advance of interaction (though it *can* be for political or legal purposes: see Butler 1997a, Chapter 3), but is something that takes on its meaning as heterosexist in specific contexts. The labelling of somebody a 'poof' or a 'queen', for example, is not inherently and always negative, as words do not come with their negativity built into them (Wetherell and Potter 1998; cf. Armstrong 1997). They have to be worked up as such. They may or may not become troublesome, prejudicial or otherwise for participants *in situ*, in specific interactional situations, as their meanings are produced and negotiated.

Second, it demonstrates precisely how meanings can be 'reclaimed' and 'resignified' in real-life interactional contexts (cf. Butler 1997a; Speer and Potter 2002). By ironizing their talk, the participants can exploit and at the same time 'denaturalize' commonsense (Marshall and Wetherell 1989: 125). 'Derogatory' utterances can be invoked in a rhetorically gross and ironic way in order to highlight the normativity *and* the futility of just such arguments. Thus terms of abuse (e.g. 'poofs') do not intrinsically support or undermine heterosexist assumptions, but can be used ironically to challenge those assumptions, and be exploited for their variable and indexical usefulness. They can, in other words, be used to both heterosexist *and* egalitarian ends (cf. the discussion of sexist talk in Chapter 2).

Third, since irony works as a *comment* on normativity, it can show how futile prejudice is, and can be exploited to produce a powerful social comment, exposing our heteronormative reality as a social construction (Crawford 1995: 156). Indeed, irony helps speakers to make a complaint about inequality – and in this case – about our heteronormative culture – without actually complaining, problematizing what is taken for granted and highlighting its rhetorical, constructed and constructive nature.

A similar point is made by Rachel Giora (though, like many researchers of sexist and heterosexist talk, she relies primarily on hypothetical examples to support her claims). Giora (1995) notes that irony is a form of 'indirect negation'. By this she means that speakers employ irony in order to comment negatively on some state of affairs without actually doing so in an explicit fashion. While direct negation 'may be vague, it may be face-threatening, and in certain contexts, it may be dull', irony, by contrast, is 'markedly informative if not witty' (Giora 1995: 259, 262). It is for this reason that irony facilitates the achievement of certain 'communicative goals' that would otherwise be 'unattainable by direct negation' (1995: 262). It is no surprise, then, that irony, like humour, has the potential to become a subversive feminist strategy, used to undermine the patriarchal, heteronormative status quo (Crawford 1995: 153). Further analysis of irony in action may prove to be a politically progressive route for future research on heterosexism and a range of other 'isms' (for further examples of irony in action, see Speer 2002b).

Thus a participants' orientations approach is not fundamentally anti-feminist. Instead it provides 'concrete evidence of, the heterosexist world under construction' (Clarke et al. 2004: 17) and an analytically tractable method for detailing the precise mechanisms through which gender and certain forms of hate speech are constituted in speakers' talk, as well as for examining how that speech can be ironized, inverted, resisted, or whatever, in and for specific interactional contexts.

An approach which examines members' orientations does not mean that we cannot *do* feminism, or provide a critique of existing social relations. I am not claiming that heterosexism and other forms of oppression are phenomena which never transcend the local, that the stigma on homosexuality is only a local state of affairs that comes freshly into being each time participants orient to homosexuality in their talk as a delicate matter requiring careful local management (Deborah Cameron, personal communication) or that we cannot, as analysts, specify that such heterosexist interaction has occurred when, or if the interactants do *not* seem to be attending to it as such.

Instead, I am arguing that, when we approach a piece of data, it is important that we *start by* separating out our analyses from our politics. Indeed, there are *two levels to any analysis*. First, there is *what our participants take an interaction to mean* in their observable orientations (as derogatory and offensive, or perfectly acceptable, for example) – orientations that we can access and describe using a technical analysis. Second, there is what we, as feminists with political opinions and views, take the interaction to mean *over and above what the participants can be shown to be attending to in their talk*. An important view I articulate in this book is that we need to have a clear sense of the difference between these 'technical' and 'politicized' levels of analysis, and avoid mixing them up, or subsuming one in the service of the other. If we do confuse the two, and impose our political agendas on the data prematurely, then we may obscure the very sociopolitical features of talk that we seek to explain, and risk an act of what Schegloff (1997) has termed 'theoretical imperialism' – of producing analyses (and politics) that are not empirically grounded, that do not 'bind' to the data and, as such, risk 'ending up merely ideological' (1997: 183).

This point is echoed in Beach's (2000) analysis of 'two guys' stories' about a woman. Beach draws what he calls a 'critically important distinction' between 'observer-imposed and evaluated social order (e.g., "This interaction is clearly sexist") vs. the analytical demonstration that such order is demonstrably relevant (and thus procedurally consequential) for interactional participants' (2000: 401). According to Beach, it is one thing to make one's own (analytic) assessment that a respondent's account is sexist, it is quite another to say that it is recognized and treated as such by the participants. Beach is equivocal about whether his own respondents can be deemed to be doing the latter. My data however, shows that participants can and do recognize that their talk may be problematic.

The resources identified here are not unique to 'prejudice talk' but are common features of all talk (Edwards 2003). Indeed, the arguments in this chapter contribute to wider, ongoing debates concerning the way we analyse phenomena typically understood as rooted in the cognitive-psychological context 'under the skull'. Just as in Chapter 5, where I showed that we do not necessarily need to venture *outside* participants' discourse to explain what is going on within it, in this chapter I have shown how we do not necessarily need to go *beneath* participants' discourse to 'the world in here' to access and understand how members' 'prejudicial attitudes', 'views' and 'beliefs' work. The approach I have advocated here presumes neither cognition nor reality (Edwards and Potter 2001), but shows how descriptions of cognition and context, mind and world, the micro and the macro, are oriented to and invoked in talk to do business. As we have seen, when we approach talk in this way, the crude distinctions between these dualisms dissolve.

7
QUESTIONS, CONCLUSIONS AND APPLICATIONS

This chapter represents the culmination of a journey through a broad terrain. In what follows I will summarize some of the main themes to come out of the book and consider their implications. In particular, I will deal with some unresolved issues and questions that readers might still have about the utility of the approach I have argued for in this book. As in previous chapters, I will organize these questions around the five criteria for a feminist analytic approach set out in Chapter 1.

(i) A constructionist approach

Q: Is a constructionist approach compatible with feminism? Can and should we avoid essentialism?

> And herein lies the critical problem, for there is no single value, moral ideal, or social good that, when fully pursued, will not trammel upon the alternatives and obliterate the social patterns these alternatives support. Pursue justice to its limits, and mercy is lost; favor honesty above all, and personal security is threatened; champion community well-being, and individual initiative may be destroyed. Who then is to establish the hierarchy of the good, and by what right?
>
> (Gergen 1994: 81)

Throughout this book I have argued for a feminist analytic approach that is strongly constructionist in its focus. However, many feminists are ambivalent about constructionism and the associated 'turn to language', and this raises questions about the compatibility of feminism and a constructionist analytic approach. On the one hand, the focus on how language and texts carry and construct meaning, and the argument that all knowledge claims (including claims about gender) are partial, situated and contingent, has been a powerful counter to essentialism. As we saw in Chapters 2 and 3, constructionism has prompted us to ask new questions about the relationship between gender and language, and demonstrates how we might begin to view beyond gender dualism, and current institutional arrangements. Constructionism has challenged the domination of hard science (including psychology) and liberated us from oppressive and apolitical notions of the self, society and power, which have all been redefined (Kitzinger 1987, 1992). It has given a voice to previously silenced minorities, and has heralded a new set of tools in the struggle for emancipation and political choice.

Nevertheless, despite its virtues, some critical psychologists argue that constructionism has generated numerous problems; it has reached an 'impasse' such that 'its strength as a critique is simultaneously its undoing' (Nightingale 1999: xvi). It is deemed to be problematic in two main ways. First, on a theoretical level, it is unclear how we can theorize gendered identity and experience, and develop common political goals, in the context of infinite human variety, and when all knowledge claims are only partial and constructed – and themselves embedded in language (see Gill 1998).

The interpretative gap between object and representation that constructionism depends on is simultaneously its political weakness. For example, we are, as authors, immersed in a reflexive paradox, constructing the phenomena (identity, patriarchy and so on) that we purportedly represent (Gill 1998). This can be termed the 'crisis' of representation and validation. It can lead to a 'potentially infinite interpretative regress', where the researcher becomes immersed in 'analysing their own analysis, and then analysing their own analysis of their own analysis to demonstrate the layers of construction' (Wetherell 2001: 397). How, within such a context, can we make political claims which withstand scrutiny?

Second, while the majority of feminists support the idea that gender is socially constructed, most agree that to *be* feminist one needs a bottom line, an essentialist base from which to ground our politics, and some foundational criteria from which to judge the validity and political adequacy of our claims. How can feminism have meaning if we cannot mobilize collectively around the stable, fixed category of 'woman'? Indeed, it is hard to see how such a foundationalist anti-foundationalism can be reconciled theoretically.

For example, feminism has traditionally needed to have a stable object (patriarchy, men and so on) that is intrinsically negative, measurable and linked up with identity to work with, and against which we can collectively mobilize. There is no room for an 'always indexical' element to identity, as one would never be able to pin it down and capture it for long enough to make claims about the workings of social power. To some extent, then, selective reification of the object of our critique is unavoidable (Woolgar and Pawluch 1985).

For many feminists, it is actually impractical being a constructionist in real life, and essentialist arguments or 'truth claims' are politically necessary in order to drive social change. We may find, for example, that constructionist arguments do not consistently support our cause. Thus, to defend lesbians against the accusation that they are (inherently, by virtue of being lesbian) unfit mothers, we may need to draw on essentialist arguments and statistical analyses (which show that lesbians are 'just like' heterosexuals, or that since they are born, and not made, lesbian, their offspring are unlikely to be recruited to homosexuality (see Clarke 2000)). As Shakespeare (1998; see also Kitzinger 1995: 155) points out, essentialist arguments are not always used to 'underpin social subordination' just as constructionist arguments do not necessarily lead to 'progressive political interventions' and social change (Shakespeare 1998: 171).

The problems outlined here create a dilemma. On the one hand, constructionism has been defined as 'implicitly feminist' in its deconstruction of 'traditional social hierarchies and the totalizing discourse of empirical science' (Gergen 1994: 79). On the other hand, it has been described as anti-feminist in its 'critique of feminist standpoint epistemology' (1994: 7). As the quote from Gergen (1994) which opens this section highlights, taking a position is almost inevitably exclusionary.

One way in which feminists have attempted to manage the dilemma posed by endless deconstruction is to keep their politics separate from their academic life (which avoids rather than overcomes the problem) or treat politics as primary, and use theory and method strategically, depending on their feminist goals. Kitzinger's solution, for example, 'is to be a radical lesbian first, a social constructionist (or essentialist) when it suits my radical feminist purposes, and a "psychologist", as conventionally defined, virtually never' (Kitzinger 1995: 155). This might be termed a form of 'strategic essentialism'. However, from a constructionist perspective, since *all* claims – including constructionist and essentialist ones – are rhetorical, political and strategic, it follows that notions like 'strategic essentialism' become redundant. As I will show later in this chapter, it is entirely consistent – and appropriate – to *be* a constructionist *and* make political claims. Thus, this approach need not lead to a form of immorality, or an absence of critique, but will force us to consider the rhetoric used in claims-making (both our own and those of the 'oppressor') and prevent us from reaching a dangerous and premature form of closure.

(ii) Discourse of mind and world as topic, not resource

Q: If mind and world are constructed in discourse, does this mean that the world and the mind do not exist in empirical reality, and that, in essence, there is 'nothing beyond the text'?

Throughout this book I have argued that the world (the macro-social structural context) and the mind (the cognitive-psychological context) can be retheorized as discursive topic, not resource. Members draw on descriptions which invoke 'facts' about the social world, and descriptions which invoke mental process, thoughts and feelings, in order to produce and reproduce gender in talk, and naturalize or challenge specific understandings of gender.

However, sometimes this argument is taken to mean that 'there is nothing beyond the text' (Cromby and Nightingale 1999: 4) and as encouraging 'a wholesale collapse into discourse idealism, the position that there is nothing but discourse' (Parker 2002: 138; Willig 1999c: 122). In order to avoid this problem, as we saw in Chapters 3 and 5, many discourse analysts influenced by poststructuralism, critical theory and psychoanalysis make a distinction between ways of talking about the world (the discursive or constructed realm) and 'the subjectivities of the actual, living people that are constituted in and from those ways of speaking' (the extra-discursive, material or 'real' world) (Cromby and Nightingale 1999: 4). This position derives from the critical realist belief that 'important aspects of human experience are located outside of language in the "extra-discursive"' (Burr 1999: 113) and that 'discursive constructions of reality are not free-floating' or arbitrary (Willig 2001: 123), but there are underlying 'relatively enduring' and 'intransitive' (Bhaskar 1989) social, economic and material structures and mechanisms that exist in the world outside discourse, which generate 'observable or experienceable phenomena' (Willig 1998: 101; see also Parker 1992, 2002). These phenomena are not *reducible* to discourse, but already constrain 'shape and inform the social constructions we live through and with' (Cromby and Nightingale 1999: 2; Willig 1999c). It is in this way that critical realists aim to develop a form of constructionism that includes 'the real' (Cromby and Nightingale 1999: 3). This, they assert, is a 'grounded' form of social constructionism (Cromby and Nightingale 1999: 10) – a possible candidate for the foundationalist anti-foundationalism mentioned above.

I want to suggest that although this separation of the discursive from the 'extra-discursive' may be politically useful – for example, it allows researchers to talk about the *determination* of one realm by another (Wetherell 2001: 392) – it is, nevertheless, based on the assumption that certain things are 'free from epistemological trouble' (Hepburn 2000: 98), that one can legislate some features of the world into an undisputed, objective, timeless reality, and not others.

However, what critical realists like Burr, Cromby, Nightingale, Parker, Willig and others overlook is that the claim that phenomena are socially constructed in discourse is *not* the same thing as making an ontological statement about the existence, truthfulness or otherwise of those constructions. Constructionism is not a theory of what exists, or a position on what is real, but remains mute on matters of ontology (Gergen 1994: 72).

Thus, exploring how things come to be constructed as they are does not mean that one must deny that those things have any 'reality'. In arguing that we treat the discourse of mind and world as topic, not resource, I am *not* saying that interaction takes place in a social and psychological vacuum, that there are no such things as macro-social structures or cognitive-psychological processes that exist outside, beyond or beneath discourse, that 'society' and the 'psyche' have no effects, or that talk will never tell us anything about facts 'out there in the world' or what is going on 'inside people's heads'.

Likewise, I am not denying the 'reality' of sex and gender categories (cf. Holmes and Meyerhoff 2003a: 10) or claiming that we do not 'have' gender identities, or a 'sense of a gendered self', that sexism, heterosexism and other forms of oppression are 'only' constructions, or that we do not exist in a sociopolitical reality in which women as a group are oppressed by men as a group, or that the stigma surrounding homosexuality is not a 'social fact'.

Instead, the view I have adopted in this book asserts that, since there is no reliable method for accessing 'the truth' about the world or the psyche from participants' talk, and 'all we ever have is access to the words: the discourse' (Wetherell 2001: 394), that we should bracket ontological questions, in favour of exploring how people construct an 'external' reality of social structures, and an 'inner' reality or mental life, and use and orient towards these constructions as they interact with one another. Thus, it is the gendered ontologies of members', not analysts, that is of interest.

(iii) Language as a form of social action

Q: Can an approach which limits itself to the study of talk-in-interaction account for the workings of phenomena that are not discursive – such as silence, and the materiality of the body?

Throughout this book I have argued that discourse is fundamentally action oriented, and that the precise way in which we construct or 'do' gender, depends on the specific action or business that talk is designed to achieve.

One criticism of this approach which relates closely to that discussed in section (ii) above, centres around the extent to which an 'almost exclusive focus on language and discourse' (Cromby and Nightingale 1999: 1) and a 'purely linguistic or textual analysis' (Nightingale and Cromby 1999a: 217) can account for, or enhance our understanding of, the full range of purportedly 'non-discursive' features of our reality that may not be verbalized explicitly in talk, but yet which are politically consequential – such as materiality, embodiment, subjectivity, physical ill health, history, silence and 'the unsaid' (Cromby and Nightingale 1999; Nightingale and Cromby 1999a, 1999b). Many feminist researchers conclude that while constructionist versions of DA may be 'a useful tool in certain circumstances', since they can never go beyond 'a partial, textually contingent analysis' of the functions of a particular stretch of talk (Nightingale and Cromby 1999a: 215), they cannot 'theorize the human condition adequately' (Nightingale 1999: xv).

Take the topics of silence and embodiment. Silence is an important concept in feminist work (De Franscisco 1991; Mahoney 1996; Morgan 1998; Morgan and Coombes 2001; Tannen and Saville-Troike 1985). However, some researchers argue that we 'have yet to focus on the language of silence' (Noble 1999: 191) and that 'silence is a relatively neglected dimension of inquiry into "what's there" in discourse' (West et al. 1997: 137). Some even go as far as to suggest that the phenomenon of silence 'cannot be accessed directly' (Noble 1999: 195). Since it is a non-apprehendable *absence*, it is 'beyond the limits of a discourse approach' (Morgan 1998, discussed in Wetherell and Potter 1998: 377).

Similarly, although there is an increasing focus on theorizing embodiment from a discursive perspective (Braun 1999; Coupland and Gwyn 2003; Malson 1997; Ussher 1997; Wiggins 2002), some feminists argue that 'an appropriate language for theorizing the body beyond the material-discursive divide remains elusive' (Burns 2003: 229), that 'in some social constructionist accounts of subjectivity concerned with resisting essentialist accounts of the body, the body itself threatens to disappear (Burns 2003: 230) and even that 'the person as an experiencing subject has been exorcised from our understanding of human life' (Burr 1999: 113).

In my view, claims that discursive approaches cannot deal with these purportedly 'extra-discursive' phenomena is inaccurate and misleading. In particular, they ignore the significant body of CA research which has dealt with the topics of silence and embodiment in some depth.

First, from its very beginnings, CA has paid considerable attention to silence (see, for example, Sacks et al. 1974; Jefferson 1989). For conversation analysts, silence is not an *absence*. Rather, just as with talk itself, things can be *said and done* with silence. As CA work on preference organization shows (Davidson 1984; Pomerantz 1984), even the briefest silence can be an inferentially rich resource for interactants, and be oriented to as such. Take the interaction in Extract 7.1 below, in which speaker A issues an invitation:

(7.1) [Davidson 1984: 105]
1   A: C'mon down he:re, = it's oka:y,
2   (0.2)
3   A: I got lotta stuff, = I got be:er en stuff 'n

Here, the 0.2 second pause in line 2 does some potent interactional business. Speaker A treats this silence (and their interlocutor's lack of an immediate uptake) as projecting an upcoming declination, or rejection of the invitation. Thus, in line 3, they modify their invitation accordingly, upgrading it to make it more attractive – and thus acceptable – to their co-participant.

The systematic approach to silence in CA shows how 'the unsaid' can be amenable to a discursive analysis (Wetherell and Potter 1998). In fact, the analysis of silence is and should be integral to any CA study. As I have shown in my analyses throughout this book, silences frequently mark troublesome moments in interaction; they are common in members' accounts and in their management of dilemmas, for example, which, I have argued, can provide rich insights into what members treat as problematic, or normative, in culture. In this sense, silence is an incredibly useful resource for understanding the construction and management of gender politics in everyday life, and it would pay dividends if feminists who use discursive approaches pay more attention to it.

Second, within CA there is a growing body of work on the relationship between talk and embodied practices (e.g., gaze and gesture) using videotaped materials (see Goodwin 1980, 2000; Heath 2004). As Heath (2004: 266) argues, 'bodily conduct, objects and artefacts are critical to the practical accomplishment of social action and activity'. By studying 'the body in action', conversation analytic studies can inform the ways in which the vocal, the visual and the material interact (Heath 2004: 279).

Although video is still a relatively under-utilized resource in feminist discursive work, some feminists have begun to use it to analyse embodied practices in institutional settings. Merran Toerien (2004a, 2004b), for example, uses a CA analysis of videotaped materials to analyse body hair removal in the beauty salon.

In contrast to many of the institutional interactions studied by conversation analysts, where the action is accomplished primarily through talk, Toerien demonstrates how, in this setting, 'the key institutionally-defined goal – hair removal – cannot itself be brought off through talk' (Toerien 2004b). Thus, she focuses on how embodied, physical actions, task-directed talk and topic talk 'work to *constitute* the encounter as an institutional one of a particular kind' (Toerien 2004b, emphasis in original), how these different actions may come into conflict, and how they are managed.

Building on social scientific analyses of 'emotion work', Toerien demonstrates 'what is involved in actually *doing* emotion work – in action and *in situ*' (2004b, emphasis in original). She concludes that 'the work of beauty therapy consists of much more than the skilled, physical tasks of, say, waxing, plucking or threading' (2004b). Indeed, the beauty therapist engages in much unpaid relational work.

In sum, CA analyses of embodied practices using video demonstrate that even where communication is non-verbal, it can still be understood discursively, as a form of social practice. As Schegloff (1999a: 561) observes, embodied practices 'do not exist in some other world, or in some special sector of this world. They are intricated into the texture of everyday life'. Researchers can use CA – as Toerien does – to expose such practices, and to explicate how they are 'implicated in the physical, skilled enactment of ideals of femininity'. Indeed it is hard to think of a better approach than CA for accessing and shedding light on such features.

(iv) Analysts' claims are grounded in participants' practices

Q: Can an approach which focuses exclusively on participants' orientations have practical or political applications?

The approach I have advocated throughout this book is concerned to ground analytic claims about the relevance of gender in talk, in the orientations of participants. Arguing against the anti-CA critics, I have shown how this approach can give us access to, and increase our understanding of, a range of purportedly macro-social, ideological and cognitive-psychological features – including gender norms and prejudice.

However, many feminists will remain concerned about the political and practical utility of this approach. Can a participants' orientations approach be reconciled with a desire to make political interventions, or have practical relevance in 'the real world out there'? One might ask, 'so what if participants talk about gender in such-and-such a way? If we can never make inferences beyond the text, then how can we take a position, effect social and political change, and improve the lives of those members whom we research?' One study which provides a neat illustration of the practical and political efficacy of feminist CA is Celia Kitzinger and Hannah Frith's (1999) article 'Just say no?' (see also Kitzinger 2000a, 2002).

Kitzinger and Frith (1999) begin by noting that there is a substantial body of literature which suggests that young women have difficulty in refusing unwanted sex, and that many instances of date rape result from women's failure to communicate clearly to men that they do not want to have sex. In her focus group research with young women between the ages of 16 and 18, Hannah Frith found that women's reports of their experiences bear this out:

(7.2) [Kitzinger 2000a: 176]
You've sat there and all through it you've been thinking 'I don't want to do this, I should have said no, I should have stopped him before, and I can't stop him now, because we're half way through the swing of it all, and I'm just so stupid. Next time I'm just going to sort it all out . . .' But you never do . . . You don't want to hurt their feelings . . . I really try and avoid ever having to be in the situation of having to say to somebody, 'look no I'm sorry' . . . I wouldn't really risk to have a sort of flirty

jokey sort of conversation with someone that I don't know very well in case they suddenly just say, 'OK, how about it', and then it would be like 'uuuuuhhhhhh!'.

Kitzinger and Frith (1999) argue that in the social science, professional and self-help literature, young women who say these kinds of things are diagnosed 'as suffering from low self-esteem, lack of assertiveness . . . or as having internalised traditionally feminine gender role expectations such as passivity, submissiveness, nurturance and acquiescence to male needs' (Kitzinger 2000a: 176). They are viewed as ideal candidates for date rape prevention programmes, which teach women how to avoid victimization by becoming better communicators, and 'to "just say no" clearly, directly and unapologetically' (Kitzinger 2000a: 176).

According to Kitzinger and Frith (1999), the advice given in these refusal skills training programmes contains assumptions about the way refusals get done which is at variance with what CA has shown about how refusals are actually done. For example, the CA literature on how members accept and refuse invitations or offers demonstrates that while acceptances generally involve 'just saying yes', 'refusals very rarely involve "just saying no"' (Kitzinger 2000a: 177). Here are some 'acceptances' discussed by Kitzinger:

(7.3) [Atkinson and Drew 1979: 58]
A: Why don't you come up and see me some[time
B: [I would like to

(7.4) [Davidson 1984: 116]
A: We:ll, will you help me [ou:t
B: [I certainly wi:ll.

Whereas these acceptances are delivered immediately, and without delay, refusals, by contrast, are more complicated phenomena:

(7.5) [Potter and Wetherell 1987: 86]
Mark: We were wondering if you wanted to come over Saturday, f'r dinner.
        (0.4)
Jane: Well (.) .hh it'd be great but we promised Carol already.

(7.6) [Atkinson and Drew 1979: 58]
A: Uh if you'd care to come and visit a little while this morning I'll give you a cup of coffee.
B: hehh Well that's awfully sweet of you. I don't think I can make it this morning. .hh uhm I'm running an ad in the paper and-and uh I have to stay near the phone.

Kitzinger and Frith (1999) argue that refusals are typically indirect, and are marked by delays, prefaces, hedges, palliatives and accounts. As I have shown in my discussion of silence in section (iii), above, a speaker who has issued an invitation may treat a short delay as a strong indication that their invitation will be refused. By contrast, an immediate 'no' may be experienced as 'rude or hostile' (Kitzinger 2000a: 178).

Thus, for Kitzinger, CA 'demonstrates conclusively that it is not necessary to say "no" in order to refuse an invitation or request effectively, and to have a refusal heard *as* a refusal' (2000a: 179). It follows that if women report that they find it difficult to 'give clear, immediate direct "noes" in sexual situations', that is 'because that is not how refusals are normatively done' (2000a: 178). The implications of a CA approach for both the perpetrators of acquaintance rape, and refusal skills training programmes based on the 'just say no' slogan, are far reaching but clear:

> If there is an organized and normative way of doing refusal, which provides for culturally understood ways in which 'maybe later' or 'I do like you but . . .' means 'no', then men who claim not to have understood are claiming to be cultural dopes and playing rather disingenuously on how refusals are usually done and understood to be done . . . the insistence of date rape educators on the importance of just saying no is counter-productive in that it requires women to engage in conversationally abnormal actions and allows rapists to persist in their claim that, if a woman hasn't actually said no (in the right tone of voice with the right body language), then she hasn't actually refused to have sex with him.
> (Kitzinger 2000a: 181)

Although, as Kitzinger and Frith acknowledge, their data look at how young women *talk about* doing refusals, rather than at actual refusals, this provides just one example of how CA-informed analyses can be applied to real world issues and problems (for other examples, see Kitzinger and Peel 2005; Speer and Parsons forthcoming; Tainio 2003). Like the other studies discussed in this book, they demonstrate that there is nothing *intrinsic* to CA which would prevent us from using it to reach politically efficacious outcomes.

In concluding this section, I would, however, like to note two caveats in relation to the increasing drive toward 'application'. First, it is important not to work with too narrow a definition of 'application'. In order to improve practice 'in the world out there', we need to begin by studying in detail that which we *already* do. Understanding for its own sake is typically undervalued, yet without such understanding, we will not be in a position to know what needs changing, or how to change it.

Second, as Potter (1982) pointed out some time ago, the vast majority of research is *potentially* applicable as opposed to *actually* applied. Indeed, it remains to be seen whether Kitzinger and Frith's analyses, or my own analyses of heterosexist talk reported in Chapter 6, will actually have an impact on trainers and educators. It may be that in order to increase the impact and 'real-world applicability' of our work, we need to disseminate it in settings (indeed – in a language) that is actually accessible to practitioners. Practitioners are often very open to what CA analyses can tell them about their current practices, and how they can be improved (Speer and Green forthcoming).

(v) A relativist approach

Q: Is a relativist approach morally vacuous? And is it compatible with a critique of existing social relations?

Throughout this book I have argued that we should treat 'realism', or what counts as real, as an analytic topic (Potter 1996b). Thus, rather than treating sex or gender as a natural fact, we should focus instead on members' 'reality-constructing' work, and explore the rhetorical and discursive resources that participants use to construct sex and gender, *as* real (i.e., as factual, timeless, objective and *beyond construction*).

A number of feminists are of the view that such an approach is fundamentally amoral and unethical, and that we cannot, therefore, reconcile the concerns of both feminism and relativistic forms of analysis. Indeed, relativism is potentially very unsettling for feminism. Feminist psychologists have described it as a 'trap' (Jackson 1998: 61) and as 'a theoretical and political thorn in the poststructuralist flesh' (Willott 1998: 185). Feminism is 'politically dis-membered by relativism' (Ramazanoglu and Holland 2002). It is 'promiscuous and unbridled' (Cromby and Nightingale 1999: 9) and 'nihilistic' (Kitzinger 1992: 247). Moreover, since it has no 'vocabulary of value' (Gill 1995), it offers no grounds for choosing between competing versions, and leads to 'political paralysis' (Wilkinson 1997: 186).

Criticizing the relativistic leanings of much discursive psychology, Sue Wilkinson, in a paraphrase of Jackson (1992), argues that 'if no one set of meanings is more valid than any other, there is no basis . . . for distinguishing between the rape victim's account of sexual coercion and the rapist's account of pleasurable seduction' (Wilkinson 1997: 185). Kenwood (1999: 183) makes a similar claim, arguing that the relativist respects equally 'sexist or racist points of view', and those 'endorsing equality'. Finally, Gillies (1999: 69) argues that the 'extreme relativist position' 'proscribes the holding of any concrete position or interpretation'.

Some feminists, informed by a critical realist perspective, argue that we have a moral and political *obligation* to specify which versions are 'more "true" or "right" than others' (Cromby and Nightingale 1999: 5) and to have some independent, foundational criteria from which to judge the validity and political adequacy of our own and others' claims. Advocates of this form of realism are strongly committed to moral and political activity, and use DA to expose oppressive social practices. Their approach is 'implicit ideology critique' (Parker 1992: 28); they suggest that relativists do not care (about inequality, suffering, making a difference, etc.), while political, critically oriented researchers do.

These criticisms, and the possibilities and limits of relativism more broadly, have been debated in a number of exchanges (see, for example, Edwards et al. 1995; Gill 1995; Grint and Woolgar 1997; Hepburn 2000; Parker 1998, 1999a, 1999c, 2002; Potter 1998b; Potter et al. 1999; Speer 2000). The 'pro-relativist' side of the debate asserts that anti-relativist claims are based on a number of erroneous assumptions and arguments. For example, the critics assume that political activity flows from one's philosophical position, and not from 'political argument and commitment' (Potter 1998b: 31). However, as Potter says, 'relativism is neither claiming nor excluding either of these' (1998b: 31). This view gains support in Alexa Hepburn's (2000) feminist relativist article, where she argues that scepticism regarding objective knowledge foundations does *not* prevent one from taking a committed, politically feminist stance.

A relativist analytic approach does not mean that 'anything goes' (Hepburn 2003: 9), that we cannot apply our feminist political criteria to take sides (with a participant, or a rhetorical strategy, say), adjudicate between competing versions, or make decisions about which versions are more true or more right than others. Indeed, it is entirely possible to be a relativist and to be morally and politically engaged (Wetherell 1999b: 404). As Potter (2004c) points out, 'relativists do not deny the possibility of judgement (as is often claimed), but stress that judgement is bound up with broader human values, cultures, ways of life and political visions in a way that cannot reduce to objective standards'.

Relativists do not assert that political interventions cannot, or should not be made, but actually insist on justifying why one argument or one intervention should be favoured over and above another (Edwards et al. 1995: 39). Indeed, a relativist does not seek 'truth' as the satisfactory end point of analysis, but continually questions the mechanisms that construct something *as* true, and as the most 'appropriate' version.

As Edwards et al. (1995) argue, relativism need not lead to 'moral dissolution'. Rather, its healthy scepticism makes it more, and not less likely to be able to contribute to political debate and argument, and challenge dangerous assumptions:

> It is potentially liberating, dangerous, unsettling, with an appeal that is enduringly radical: nothing ever has to be taken as merely,

> obviously, objectively, unconstructedly, true. Reality can only ever be reality-as-known, and therefore, however counter-intuitive it may seem, produced by, not prior to, inquiry.
>
> (Edwards et al. 1995: 39)

For Potter (1998b: 41), relativism can be 'used most happily against authority, against the *status quo*, against established versions and taken-for-granted realities'. Its political contribution supports a 'freeing up from established systems' and 'promotes a resistance to "settlement"'. It encourages an 'openness' which 'supports critique, plurality, multiplicity of voices, a need for justification'. In this sense, 'relativism does not simply do politics; but political implications can be built out of it' (1998b: 41).

Relativism involves a persistent form of questioning and reflexive self-critique which is particularly conducive to progressive political forms. Thus, it is entirely compatible with Henwood et al.'s (1998: 5) call for a critical perspective which involves the continual 'questioning and reflexive ways of approaching' its subject matter. This questioning and scepticism need not lead us into a political black hole. Instead, unlike realism, which often wants to 'fix' meaning and discourage argument, relativism keeps argument alive (Edwards et al. 1995: 40). Relativism is a morally and politically strong position for feminists to take.

As an approach which questions *all* knowledge claims, relativism is extremely good at exposing the political rhetoric of its own, as well as others', constructions. This need not lead to weakness, an absence of critique (see Wilkinson 1997) or some form of self-referential nihilism, but will prevent us from 'reproducing precisely the assumptions we have set out to criticize' (Potter 1997: 64), of replacing one 'hegemony of the intellectuals' (Schegloff 1997: 167) with another. While some feminists do acknowledge this (see Hepburn 2000), to date, the radical potential of relativism (for feminism) has tended to be asserted rather than demonstrated. An examination of members' 'reality-constructing work' represents a pressing issue for future research.

Concluding thoughts

Throughout this book I have argued for the exciting possibilities of bringing feminism, DP and CA together. I have demonstrated *how* and *why* claims that 'micro-analytic' forms of analysis are theoretically and politically inadequate or limited in some way, are premature.

Nigel Edley (2001b: 137) argues that restricting oneself to a members' perspective 'invites missed opportunities' and 'risks a form of ideological complicity'. However, in my view 'missed opportunities' and 'ideological complicity' come from analysing too little, not from analysing too much. By not taking CA seriously, on its own terms, and by refusing to pay close attention to participants' orientations and practices, we risk producing forms of analysis – and politics – which actually overlook or are insensitive to the concerns of our respondents (Schegloff 1997; Widdicombe 1995). More than this, we may end up simply reflecting and reproducing, rather than developing and extending, current feminist thought; we may avoid challenging or 'unsettling' our politics, and overlook the possibilities for different forms of social organization – the seeds of which may already be evident within the discourse that we study, but which it is not possible to see through our restricted analytic lens.

In her critique of Nicola Gavey's (1989) article 'Feminist poststructuralism and discourse analysis', Sue Widdicombe (1995) makes a related point. She suggests that Gavey's 'analytic rush to identify discourses in order to get on with the more serious business of accounting for their political significance' (1995: 108) blinds her to the 'social functions' of language use, and to the interactional context in which utterances are produced (1995: 63). A critical orientation actually places *limits* on Gavey's analysis, diverting her attention from 'an investigation of the ways in which people themselves fashion their talk to address social and political issues' (Widdicombe and Wooffitt 1995: 64–5), thus making it *less* and not more likely to challenge the status quo. This is significant, because critical discourse analysts often claim to use their research to speak 'on behalf of' or 'give voice to' 'powerless and marginalised groups', but in making their analyses subservient to their politics, 'their analytic concerns do not give those groups a voice'. Indeed, this kind of analysis 'actually seems to deny the significance of what people may be saying and doing with their talk' (Widdicombe and Wooffitt 1995: 65).

Remaining true to participants' orientations is not some 'restrictive' gatekeeping exercise that seeks to starve analytic creativity (Edley 2001b: 136), nor is it an attempt to advocate a 'uni-dimensional' approach (2001b: 138). Instead, it represents an analytic sensitivity that acts rather like a microscope: by changing to a lens of greater magnitude, one gains a deeper understanding of that which is already there. Schegloff (1997: 180) continually points to the importance of 'refracting' the world 'through the prism of disciplined and molecular observation'. By adopting a CA approach, we can render visible phenomena that are typically deemed to be beyond our scope, and which we have hitherto confined to the abstract realm of theorizing: ideology and cognition, 'the world out there' and 'the world in here' *are* analytically tractable and amenable to a CA analysis.

A participants' orientations approach helps ensure that we produce rhetorically persuasive, analytically tractable arguments about the workings of these phenomena, and provides the tools with which we may begin to develop a 'grounded' feminist politics. The power of such an approach lies in its analytic exemplification of how members produce, orient to, account for, naturalize and sustain some gendered norms, ideologies and versions of the world over others. We can use it to silence our anti-feminist critics, and to persuade them of the validity of our claims. Indeed, what better way to convince the sceptics of the real life, everyday existence of oppressive social practices, and the blatant (or, indeed, subtle) inequalities in society, than with a line-by-line demonstration and validation of their workings on the page? To ground our politics in this way provides a rhetorically powerful weaponry in a political struggle, and I urge feminists and others with an interest in ideology and prejudice to take a CA-inspired discursive approach seriously.

CA facilitates the development of feminist research which is 'less opaque and more open to scrutiny' (Bell and Roberts 1984: 9), which avoids appropriating what is said to fit in with our own political agendas, and which enables us to 'make claims that might be valid independent of who makes them' (Merrick 1999: 54). It offers a democratic, 'emancipatory social science' (Oakley 1998: 707) that is entirely consistent with a 'feminist degendering movement' (Lorber 2000). CA gives us the resources to expose and thus denaturalize commonsense. Once we have begun to unravel how members produce current institutional arrangements *as* commonsensical, then we may be in a better position to see what needs to be done to unpick, and transcend those arrangements. Indeed, I know of no other approach which offers a more viable basis from which to drive social change. By using CA, we might finally begin 'to rupture the textual laminations within which Others have been sealed by social scientists' (Fine 1994: 71). This book represents an initial step in that direction.

POSTSCRIPT
THE FUTURE OF FEMINIST CA
METHODOLOGICAL ISSUES

Throughout this book I have dramatized my argument with data examples from both 'naturally occurring' and 'social science' sources. Although it is by no means clear cut 'what counts' as 'natural' data – see the debate between Speer (2002a, 2002c), ten Have (2002), Lynch (2002) and Potter (2002) – most gender and language researchers frequently, if not habitually, study talk generated using conventional social scientific research methods such as interviews and focus groups. As Kitzinger (2000a: 170) observes, very little feminist research is conducted using naturalistic data where gender and sexuality 'just "happen" to be present'.

There are a number of reasons why we have, as feminists, been reluctant to stray far from the use of such 'contrived' materials. Much feminist research deals with topics that are deemed to be too sensitive, private or delicate to be accessed in their 'home' environments, or which might not be mentioned frequently enough by participants to be captured through naturalistic means (e.g., talk about sex, infidelity, sexual harassment, rape and incest, for example). There's an issue here analogous to the one I discussed in relation to Garfinkel's early breaching experiments and the analysis of 'special cases' in Chapter 3. In much research using contrived techniques it seems to be a tacit assumption that since gender is, for most 'ordinary' members, taken-for-granted and thus *background* to interaction, that the researcher must artificially elicit talk *about* gender from participants, just to render it observable – and hence studiable. Indeed, some feminist discourse analysts suggest that contrived sources like interviews and focus groups may 'yield richer data' than naturally occurring talk, 'simply because the topic has been pre-set' (Sunderland 2004: 183).

Although these arguments may, in certain circumstances, and for some research projects, be true (more on this below), my own view is that we need to give serious thought to the extent to which such artificially elicited 'topic talk' that involves putting members in a situation that explicitly requires them to *comment on* gender, is paradigmatic of, or will necessarily give us access to, how members routinely *do* gender in other settings (Deborah Cameron, personal communication).

In much social science data, for example, the presence of an interviewer or focus group moderator means that it is possible to track a 'social science agenda' through it, and this agenda structures the precise concerns that the participants (including the researcher) can be shown to be orienting towards. For example, it is usually the researcher who takes the lead role, who makes gender or sexuality relevant in the first instance, and who allows certain issues and identities to be discussed or elaborated and not others. Likewise, the 'respondent' or 'interviewee' tends to orient to the research interview, by 'doing being an obedient research participant', and giving the interviewer or moderator what they think they want to hear. In some circumstances (and particularly those involving topics around gender and sexuality – where participants' 'prejudice' may be relevant), this leads to a game of 'cat and mouse', where the moderator tries to disguise her 'real' interest, and where the participants simultaneously search for the researcher's 'elusive hypothesis'.

As I have shown in my own research on the use of 'non-directive' and 'participant-centred' techniques (Speer 2002d), even where the researcher tries to avoid imposing her agenda on those she studies, by removing herself as far as possible from the data collection process – as through the use of picture prompts or other stimulus materials – her presence is still very much in evidence, and the data collected, just like the data from other more 'interventionist' techniques, are thereby always collaboratively produced, interactional products. We can never achieve an unmediated access to participants' realities, neutralize the context or disinfect our data of the researcher's presence (Speer and Hutchby 2003a, 2003b) because the knower is always intimately bound up with, and partially constitutive of, what is known. To assume otherwise is to deny the unavoidably social nature of data collection practices. As Holstein and Gubrium (1997: 114) point out, 'any technical attempts to strip interviews of their interactional ingredients will be futile'. Indeed, such worries buy into the very illusion of objectivity and value neutrality that feminists have long since sought to expose and counter. Thus, it is important to remember that views about gender are produced in thoroughly social and interactional contexts, and that the use of non-directive methods does not make those contexts any the less contextual and interactional.

Many feminists acknowledge 'the sterility and impossibility of attempts to launder any research totally of "bias"' (Bell and Roberts 1984: 3), and that prompted or non-interventionist techniques do not 'guarantee against hierarchy . . . nor offer a vision completely untainted by the researcher's agenda' (Campbell and Salem 1999: 86). Instead, they note the importance of developing an ongoing, reflexivity of process – of acknowledging and reflecting critically on the impact that the research context – and particularly that we as researchers – have on our data and our accounts of others' lives (Weatherall et al. 2002: 536). As Kitzinger and Wilkinson

(1996) note, we need to pay attention to the interaction between researchers and participants: 'our work should be not so much about the *Other* as about the *interplay between* the researcher and the Other' (1996: 18, emphasis in original).

Paradoxically, however, despite the importance attached by feminists to reflecting on the processes involved in the doing of research, in practice, such moments of reflexivity tend to be confined to discussions in 'prefaces' and 'postscripts' (Reinharz 1992: 259). Most feminists remain silent about the realities of their research, and rarely set about analysing (as I have tried to do in my analyses in this book) the precise interactional contours of the impact that they have upon it. As Michelle Fine (1992: 218, cited in Merrick 1999: 55) notes, 'the problem is not that we [qualitative researchers] tailor but that so few researchers reveal *how* we do this work'. Thus, many feminist researchers collect their data with a view to analysing how gender or sexuality are 'occasioned' and 'get done' in talk, but fail to explore how their data collection practices themselves impact the 'occasioning' and 'doing' of gender.

In his 'Reply to Wetherell', which I discussed in Chapter 5, for example, Schegloff (1998) argues that Wetherell asks questions of her data which she deems to be beyond the scope of CA, yet ignores the fact that her data are entirely 'researcher prompted', driven by Nigel, the interviewer and '*agent provocateur*' (1998: 415, emphasis in original). 'What is most striking', says Schegloff, 'is the virtually total lack of attention to Nigel and his actions in this analysis' (1998: 415). Likewise, while many feminists are critical of the 'decontextualization' and 'context stripping' associated with 'hygienic research', and suggest that we should *not* edit out our own contributions from the data, in practice, where data are included, they are usually 'cleaned up' and 'polished', any problematic responses being eliminated from the final report.

One reason why the reflexivity that is so commonly advocated by feminists is rarely put into practice to any significant degree, is because many of us do not possess the analytic resources to do this reflexivity very well. As Lather (1988: 575-6) notes, 'developing the skills of self-critique, of a reflexivity which will keep us from becoming impositional and reifiers ourselves remains to be done'. Feminist analyses tend to be theoretically driven rather than data driven, and politics is prioritized over the development or adoption of technically detailed forms of analysis.

A CA approach, as I hope to have demonstrated in this book, offers feminists just such skills and resources. Indeed, CA encourages us to create a form of feminism that is consistent with just the kind of reflexive, respondent-centred, non-hierarchical methodological approach that many of us have been arguing for decades. It challenges us to take a step back and to develop an analytically grounded approach to reflexivity and to the interaction between researcher and researched, to treat members as reflexive participants who orient towards and constitute the research situation, and to attend to exactly how our methods are shaping our data (for more on reflexivity, see Forrester 1999; Hammersley 2003d; Speer and Hutchby 2003a, 2003b).

All this does not mean that existing feminist data collection practices and modes of analysis are wrong or bad, or that we should stop using contrived materials and other 'non-directive' techniques altogether (cf. Potter and Hepburn in press). Indeed, the rhetoric of social science data – just like essentialism – can be a useful tool in certain circumstances (e.g., in a court of law). Nor does it mean that we will never obtain 'naturalistic talk', or gain access to general features of the 'doing' of gender in purportedly 'contrived' materials. Indeed, throughout this book and elsewhere (Speer 2002d), I have shown how, by being sensitive to the ways in which the researcher herself is bound up in the data, we can provide rich insights into respondents' ways of managing the interactional issues and dilemmas their participation throws up, and which in turn provide a route to understanding the workings of normativity in culture. What it *does* mean is simply that we need, as feminists, to give careful thought to the kinds of work that is being accomplished in research contexts, and what the data derived from such contexts can realistically be used *for*.

As conversation analysts themselves have shown, a*ll* data can be natural or contrived depending on what one wants to *do* with it (see, for example, Houtkoop-Steenstra 2000; Widdicombe and Wooffitt 1995). Thus, it is fine if we, as feminists, want to use interview data to explore how gender talk is derived in research contexts, paying close attention to the constructive processes involved (the interview data can be 'naturalized – or treated as natural': see Speer 2002d). However, if one wants to analyse interview talk where participants are asked to *comment on* gender in order to discover how people routinely *do* gender in 'everyday' settings, then such prompted 'gender commentary' may seem contrived, and thus not the best data for our present purposes (see Speer 2002a).

It remains to be seen precisely 'what counts' as an orientation to gender in an interaction (Stokoe and Smithson 2001). Conversation analysts note that gender need not be explicitly mentioned or indexed for it to be oriented to (Schegloff 1997: 182). Likewise, for Hopper and LeBaron (1998), 'the reflexive performances by which speakers gender social scenes remain elusive to scholars in part because spoken indexing of gender (e.g., gendered pronouns, terms of reference or address) may pass without speakers' explicit notice' (Hopper and LeBaron 1998: 60; see also Ochs 1992). Thus, if we are serious about developing our understanding of what counts as an orientation to gender, and what it means to be treated as gendered in an interaction, then we need to give careful consideration to the kinds of methods that we use to analyse 'gender talk'.

What is needed if we are to make well-informed choices about the data we use, and – perhaps more importantly – if we are to produce theoretically sound, analytically tractable justifications *for* those choices, is a more sophisticated understanding of the relationship between method, context and data. We need to be clearer and more consistent about what exactly constitutes the object of our analysis, and to establish why a particular research site is chosen over and above others. In sum, we need to have a greater awareness of how our data collection practices shape the topics to which we wish to gain access.

As I have argued elsewhere (Speer 2002a, 2002c), the key issue that feminists need to consider when embarking on discursive or CA work is how the research context, and its speech exchange system, is *procedurally consequential* for one's topic. Schegloff (1991: 54ff) makes this point clearly in his reference to two laboratory studies, one on self-repair (Levelt 1983) and one I have discussed in previous chapters on interruptions (West and Zimmerman 1983). While the former study was conducted in an experimental setting in which limitations were placed on who could speak, in the latter, experimental setting, there were no such restrictions. Schegloff argues that in the former study the experimental setting *was* consequential for the topic of self-repair, while in the latter it was not.

Likewise, in his analysis of videotaped materials, Drew (1989: 99–100) questions whether the 'intrusion' of a video-camera may have affected his respondents in such a way as to 'contaminate their behaviour' and invalidate his findings. What he argues is that while the camera's presence may indeed alter participants' behaviour – they may laugh and joke more, for example – this is only consequential if one is analysing, say, frequency of laughter. If this is the case, then the results of such an investigation would clearly need to take into account 'the possible disturbance effect of a camera's presence' (1989: 99). If, however, the analytic focus is on how jokes get done, their management and organization, then the disturbance of the camera and participants' knowledge that they are being filmed is not procedurally consequential for the analysis, and is thereby of little consequence.

The CA notion of procedural consequentiality represents one way in which we might begin to reframe the natural/contrived distinction in more sophisticated terms, and to develop a more nuanced understanding of the relationship between our methods and our topics. All this, however, takes us away from the actual *practice* of CA. I want to end with a quote from Schegloff (1999b):

> Readers need to decide what they find most cogent and compelling to do, and then go do it, or prepare themselves further for doing it . . . Whatever it is, *do* it – or try – before *talking* about doing it. And bear in mind that addressing issues of moral and political

> moment does not entail relaxing the imperatives of rigorous analysis, but intensifying them – the more so, the more you believe is at stake.
>
> (Schegloff 1999b: 581, emphasis in original)

There is a very important difference here between *doing* CA and *commenting* on it. To date, most discussions at the feminism–CA nexus have focused on the latter at the expense of the former. I want to get on with the business of attempting to *do* CA, to *demonstrate analytically* what CA can offer feminism. I urge other feminists to do the same.

APPENDIX
TRANSCRIPTION CONVENTIONS

(.)	A pause that is hearable but too short to assign a time to.
(2.0)	The length of a pause or gap, in seconds.
[overlap]	Square brackets indicate the onset and end of overlapping speech.
°quiet°	Degree signs enclose speech that is noticeably quieter than the surrounding talk
Rea::lly	Colons mark elongation of the prior sound.
↑	An upward arrow indicates rising intonation.
↓	A downward arrow indicates falling intonation.
→	Arrows in the left margin point to specific parts of an extract discussed in the text.
LOUD	Capitals mark talk that is noticeably louder than the surrounding speech.
Underline	Underlining marks speaker emphasis.
>faster<	'More than' and 'less than' signs enclose speeded up talk.
=	An equals sign indicates immediate latching of successive talk.
(Brackets)	Single brackets enclose the transcriber's best guess (empty brackets enclose talk that is unclear on the tape).
((laughs))	Double brackets enclose comments from the transcriber.
.hhh	A dot before an h or series of h's indicates an inbreath.
hh	An h or series of h's marks an out-breath.
.	A full stop indicates a stopping intonation.
,	A comma indicates a continuing intonation.
?	A question mark indicates a rising inflection.
-	A dash marks a sharp cut-off of a word or sound.

See Atkinson and Heritage (1984) and Hutchby and Wooffitt (1998) for further information about these transcription symbols.

REFERENCES

Ainsworth-Vaughn, N. (1992) 'Topic transitions in physician–patient interviews: Power, gender, and discourse change', *Language in Society* 21: 409–26.

Alsop, R., Fitzimons, A. and Lennon, K. (2002) *Theorizing Gender*. Cambridge: Polity.

American Psychiatric Association (APA) (1994) *Diagnostic and Statistical Manual of Mental Disorders* (4th edn: DSM-IV). Washington, DC: APA.

Antaki, C. and Wetherell, M. (1999) 'Show concessions', *Discourse Studies* 1(1): 7–27.

Antaki, C. and Widdicombe, S. (eds) (1998a) *Identities in Talk*. London: Sage.

Antaki, C. and Widdicombe, S. (eds) (1998b) 'Identity as an achievement and as a tool'. In C. Antaki and S. Widdicombe (eds) *Identities in Talk* (pp. 1–14). London: Sage.

Antaki, C., Condor, S. and Levine, M. (1996) 'Social identities in talk: Speakers' own orientations', *British Journal of Social Psychology* 35: 473–92.

Armitage, L. K. (2001) 'Truth, falsity, and schemas of presentation: A textual analysis of Harold Garfinkel's story of Agnes', *Electronic Journal of Human Sexuality* 4: 1–12 (http://www.ejhs.org/volume4/agnes.htm).

Armstrong, J. D. (1997) 'Homophobic slang as coercive discourse among college students'. In A. Livia and K. Hall (eds) *Queerly Phrased: Language, Gender, and Sexuality* (pp. 326–34). New York: Oxford University Press.

Atkinson, J. M. (1984) *Our Master's Voices: The Language and Body Language of Politics*. London: Methuen.

Atkinson, J. M. and Drew, P. (1979) *Order in Court: The Organization of Verbal Interaction in Judicial Settings*. London: Macmillan.

Atkinson, J. M. and Heritage, J. (eds) (1984) *Structures of Social Action: Studies in Conversation Analysis*. Cambridge: Cambridge University Press.

Austin, J. L. (1962) *How to do Things with Words*. Oxford: Clarendon Press.

Baker, C. D. (2000) 'Locating culture in action: Membership categorization in texts and talk'. In A. Lee and C. Poynton (eds) *Culture and Text: Discourse and Methodology in Social Research and Cultural Studies* (pp. 99–113). London: Routledge.

Baker, P. (2004) '"Unnatural acts": Discourses of homosexuality within the House of Lords debates on gay male law reform', *Journal of Sociolinguistics* 8(1): 88–106.

REFERENCES

Bakhtin, M. M. (1986) *Speech Genres and Other Late Essays* (trans. by V. W. McGee). Austin, TX: University of Texas Press.

Baron-Cohen, S. (2003) *The Essential Difference*. London: Penguin.

Baxter, J. (2002) 'Competing discourses in the classroom: A poststructuralist discourse analysis of girls' and boys' speech in public contexts', *Discourse and Society* 13(6): 827–42.

Baxter, J. (2003) *Positioning Gender in Discourse: A Feminist Methodology*. Basingstoke: Palgrave Macmillan.

Beach, W. A. (2000) 'Inviting collaborations in stories about a woman', *Language in Society* 29: 379–407.

Bell, C. and Roberts, H. (1984) (eds) *Social Researching: Politics, Problems, Practice*. London: Routledge and Kegan Paul.

Bell, V. (1999) 'On speech, race and melancholia: An interview with Judith Butler', *Theory, Culture and Society* 16(2): 163–74.

Benhabib, S., Butler, J., Cornell, D. and Fraser, N. (eds) (1995) *Feminist Contentions: A Philosophical Exchange*. London: Routledge.

Bhaskar, R. (1989) *Reclaiming Reality: A Critical Introduction to Contemporary Philosophy*. London: Verso.

Billig, M. (1989) 'The argumentative nature of holding strong views: A case study', *European Journal of Social Psychology* 19: 203–23.

Billig, M. (1991) *Ideology and Opinions: Studies in Rhetorical Psychology*. London: Sage.

Billig, M. (1996) *Arguing and Thinking: A Rhetorical Approach to Social Psychology* (2nd edn). Cambridge: Cambridge University Press.

Billig, M. (1999a) 'Conversation analysis and the claims of naivety', *Discourse and Society* 10(4): 572–6.

Billig, M. (1999b) 'Whose terms? Whose ordinariness? Rhetoric and ideology in conversation analysis', *Discourse and Society* 10(4): 543–58.

Billig, M., Condor, S., Edwards, D., Gane, M., Middleton, D. and Radley, A. (1988) *Ideological Dilemmas: A Social Psychology of Everyday Thinking*. London: Sage.

Bing, J. and Bergvall, V. L. (1998) 'The question of questions: Beyond binary thinking'. In J. Coates (ed.) *Language and Gender: A Reader* (pp. 495–510). Oxford: Blackwell.

Black, M. and Coward, R. (1998) 'Linguistic, social and sexual relations: A review of Dale Spender's *Man Made Language*'. In D. Cameron (ed.) *The Feminist Critique of Language: A Reader* (2nd edn, pp. 100–18). London: Routledge.

Boden, D. and Zimmerman, D. H. (eds) (1991) *Talk and Social Structure: Studies in Ethnomethodology and Conversation Analysis*. Cambridge: Polity.

Bodine, A. (1975) 'Androcentrism in prescriptive grammar: Singular "they", sex indefinite "he", and "he or she"', *Language in Society* 4: 129–46.

Bohan, J. (1993) 'Regarding gender: Essentialism, constructionism, and feminist psychology', *Psychology of Women Quarterly* 17: 5–21.

Bologh, R. W. (1992) 'The promise and failure of ethnomethodology from a feminist perspective: Comment on Rogers', *Gender and Society* 6(2): 199–206.

Braun, V. (1999) 'Breaking a taboo? Talking (and laughing) about the vagina', *Feminism and Psychology* 9(3): 367–72.

Bucholtz, M. (1999a) 'Bad examples: Transgression and progress in language and

REFERENCES

gender studies'. In M. Bucholtz, A. C. Liang and L. A. Sutton (eds) *Reinventing Identities: The Gendered Self in Discourse* (pp. 3–24). Oxford: Oxford University Press.

Bucholtz, M. (1999b) 'Series foreword'. In M. Bucholtz, A. C. Liang and L. A. Sutton (eds) *Reinventing Identities: The Gendered Self in Discourse* (pp. vii–viii). Oxford: Oxford University Press.

Bucholtz, M. (2000) 'The politics of transcription', *Journal of Pragmatics* 32: 1439–65.

Bucholtz, M. (2003) 'Theories of discourse as theories of gender: Discourse analysis in language and gender studies'. In J. Holmes and M. Meyerhoff (eds) *The Handbook of Language and Gender* (pp. 43–68). Oxford: Blackwell.

Bucholtz, M. (2004) 'Changing places: *Language and Woman's Place* in context'. In R. Lakoff. *Language and Woman's Place: Text and Commentaries* (revised and expanded edn, ed. M. Bucholtz, pp. 121–8). New York and Oxford: Oxford University Press.

Bucholtz, M., Liang, A. C. and Sutton, L. A. (eds) (1999) *Reinventing Identities: The Gendered Self in Discourse*. New York: Oxford University Press.

Burkitt, I. (1999) 'Between the dark and the light: Power and the material contexts of social relations'. In D. J. Nightingale and J. Cromby (eds) *Social Constructionist Psychology: A Critical Analysis of Theory and Practice* (pp. 69–82). Buckingham: Open University Press.

Burman, E. and Parker, I. (eds) (1993) *Discourse Analytic Research: Repertoires and Readings of Texts in Action*. London: Routledge.

Burningham, K. (1995) 'Attitudes, accounts and impact assessment', *The Sociological Review* 43: 100–22.

Burns, M. (2003) 'Interviewing: Embodied communication', *Feminism and Psychology* 13(2): 229–36.

Burr, V. (1999) 'The extra-discursive in social constructionism'. In D. J. Nightingale and J. Cromby (eds) *Social Constructionist Psychology: A Critical Analysis of Theory and Practice* (pp. 113–26). Buckingham: Open University Press.

Burr, V. (2003) *Social Constructionism* (2nd edn). London: Routledge.

Burridge, J. (2004) '"I am not homophobic but . . .": Disclaiming in discourse resisting repeal of Section 28', *Sexualities* 7(3): 327–44.

Butler, J. (1990a) *Gender Trouble: Feminism and the Subversion of Identity*. New York: Routledge.

Butler, J. (1990b) 'Performative acts and gender constitution: An essay in phenomenology and feminist theory'. In S. Case (ed.) *Performing Feminisms: Feminist Critical Theory and Theatre* (pp. 270–82). Baltimore, MD: Johns Hopkins University Press.

Butler, J. (1993) *Bodies that Matter: On the Discursive Limits of 'Sex'*. London: Routledge.

Butler, J. (1994) 'Against proper objects', *Differences* 6(2–3): 1–26.

Butler, J. (1995) 'Burning acts: Injurious speech'. In A. Parker and E. K. Sedgwick (eds) *Performativity and Performance* (pp. 197–227). London: Routledge.

Butler, J. (1997a) *Excitable Speech: A Politics of the Performative*. New York: Routledge.

REFERENCES

Butler, J. (1997b) *The Psychic Life of Power: Theories in Subjection*. Stanford, CA: Stanford University Press.

Butler, J. (1999) *Gender Trouble: Feminism and the Subversion of Identity (10th Anniversary Edition)*. London: Routledge.

Buttny, R. (1993) *Social Accountability in Communication*. London: Sage.

Cameron, D. (1992) *Feminism and Linguistic Theory* (2nd edn). London: Macmillan.

Cameron, D. (1995) *Verbal Hygiene*. London: Routledge.

Cameron, D. (1997a) 'Performing gender identity: Young men's talk and the construction of heterosexual masculinity'. In S. Johnson and U. H. Meinhof (eds) *Language and Masculinity* (pp. 47–64). Oxford: Blackwell.

Cameron, D. (1997b) 'Theoretical debates in feminist linguistics: Questions of sex and gender'. In R. Wodak (ed.) *Gender and Discourse* (pp. 21–36). London: Sage.

Cameron, D. (1998a) 'Gender, language, and discourse: A review essay', *Signs* 23: 945–73.

Cameron, D. (1998b) 'Lost in translation: Non-sexist language'. In D. Cameron (ed.) *The Feminist Critique of Language: A Reader* (2nd edn, pp. 155–63). London: Routledge.

Cameron, D. (ed.) (1998c) *The Feminist Critique of Language: A Reader* (2nd edn). London: Routledge.

Cameron, D. (1998d) 'Is there any ketchup Vera? Gender, power and pragmatics', *Discourse and Society* 9(4): 437–55.

Cameron, D. (2001) *Working with Spoken Discourse*. London: Sage.

Cameron, D. and Kulick, D. (2003) *Language and Sexuality*. Cambridge: Cambridge University Press.

Cameron, D., McAlinden, F. and O'Leary, K. (1989) 'Lakoff in context: The social and linguistic functions of tag questions'. In J. Coates and D. Cameron (eds) *Women in their Speech Communities* (pp. 74–93). London: Longman.

Campbell, R. and Salem, D. A. (1999) 'Concept mapping as a feminist research method: Examining the community response to rape', *Psychology of Women Quarterly* 23: 65–89.

Carrigan, T., Connell, R. and Lee, J. (1985) 'Towards a new sociology of masculinity', *Theory and Society* 14: 551–604.

Cealey Harrison, W. and Hood-Williams, J. (2002) *Beyond Sex and Gender*. London: Sage.

Clarke, V. (2000) 'Lesbian mothers: Sameness and difference', *Feminism and Psychology* 10(2): 273–8.

Clarke, V. (2005) '"We're all very liberal in our views": Students talk about lesbian and gay parenting', *Lesbian and Gay Psychology Review* 6(1): 2–15.

Clarke, V., Kitzinger, C. and Potter, J. (2004) '"Kids are just cruel anyway": Lesbian and gay parents' talk about homophobic bullying', *British Journal of Social Psychology* 43: 1–20.

Clayman, S. (1992) 'Footing in the achievement of neutrality: The case of news interview discourse'. In P. Drew and J. Heritage (eds) *Talk at Work: Interaction in Institutional Settings* (pp. 163–98). Cambridge: Cambridge University Press.

Clayman, S. and Heritage, J. (2002) *The News Interview: Journalists and Public Figures on the Air*. Cambridge: Cambridge University Press.

REFERENCES

Coates, J. (1986) *Women, Men and Language*. London: Longman.
Coates, J. (1996) *Women Talk: Conversation between Women Friends*. Oxford: Blackwell.
Coates, J. (1997) 'Competing discourses of femininity'. In H. Kotthoff and R. Wodak (eds) *Communicating Gender in Context* (pp. 285–314). Amsterdam: John Benjamins.
Coates, J. (1999) 'Changing femininities: The talk of teenage girls'. In M. Bucholtz, A. C. Liang and L. A. Sutton (eds) *Reinventing Identities: The Gendered Self in Discourse* (pp. 123–44). Oxford: Oxford University Press.
Coates, J. (2003) *Men Talk: Stories in the Making of Masculinities*. Oxford: Blackwell.
Coates, J. and Thornborrow, J. (1999) 'Myths, lies and audiotapes: Some thoughts on data transcripts', *Discourse and Society* 10(4): 594–7.
Connell, R. W. (1987) *Gender and Power*. Cambridge: Polity with Blackwell.
Connell, R. W. (1995) *Masculinities*. Cambridge: Polity.
Cook, J. A. and Fonow, M. M. (1990) 'Knowledge and women's interests: Issues of epistemology and methodology in feminist research'. In J. M. Nielsen (ed.) *Feminist Research Methods: Exemplary Readings in the Social Sciences* (pp. 69–93). Boulder, CO: Westview Press.
Coulter, J. (1979) *The Social Construction of Mind: Studies in Ethnomethodology and Linguistic Philosophy*. London: Macmillan.
Coulter, J. (1989) *Mind in Action*. Cambridge: Polity.
Coupland, J. and Gwyn, R. (eds) (2003) *Discourse, the Body and Identity*. London: Palgrave.
Crawford, M. (1995) *Talking Difference: On Gender and Language*. London: Sage.
Crawford, M. (2000a) 'Editor's introduction: How to make sex and do gender', *Feminism and Psychology* 10(1): 7–10.
Crawford, M. (ed.) (2000b) 'A reappraisal of *Gender: An Ethnomethodological Approach*', *Feminism and Psychology* (special feature) 10(1): 7–72.
Cromby, J. and Nightingale, D. J. (1999) 'What's wrong with social constructionism?' In D. J. Nightingale and J. Cromby (eds) *Social Constructionist Psychology: A Critical Analysis of Theory and Practice* (pp. 1–19). London: Sage.
Danby, S. (1998) 'The serious and playful work of gender: Talk and social order in a preschool classroom'. In N. Yelland (ed.) *Gender in Early Childhood* (pp. 175–205). London: Routledge.
Davidson, J. (1984) 'Subsequent versions of invitations, offers, requests, and proposals dealing with potential or actual rejection'. In J. M. Atkinson and J. Heritage (eds) *Structures of Social Action: Studies in Conversation Analysis* (pp. 102–28). Cambridge: Cambridge University Press.
Davies, B. and Harré, R. (1990) 'Positioning: The discursive production of selves', *Journal for the Theory of Social Behaviour* 20(1): 43–63.
Davis, K. (1988) 'Paternalism under the microscope'. In A. Dundas Todd and S. Fisher (eds) *Gender and Discourse: The Power of Talk* (pp. 19–54). Norwood NJ: Ablex.
Day, D. (1998) 'Being ascribed and resisting membership of an ethnic group'. In C. Antaki and S. Widdicombe (eds) *Identities in Talk* (pp. 151–70). London: Sage.

REFERENCES

De Beauvoir, S. (1952) *The Second Sex*. London: Cape.

De Francisco, V. L. (1991) 'The sounds of silence: How men silence women in marital relations', *Discourse and Society* 2(4): 413–23.

Denny, D. (2000) 'Rachel and me: A commentary on *Gender: An Ethnomethodological Approach*', *Feminism and Psychology* 10(1): 62–5.

Denzin, N. K. (1990) 'Harold and Agnes: A feminist narrative undoing', *Sociological Theory* 8(2): 198–216.

Denzin, N. K. (1991) 'Back to Harold and Agnes', *Sociological Theory* 9(2): 280–5.

Derrida, J. (1976) *Of Grammatology*. Baltimore, MD: Johns Hopkins University Press.

Donaldson, M. (1993) 'What is hegemonic masculinity?', *Theory and Society* 22: 643–57.

Doyle, M. (1995) *The A–Z of Non-Sexist Language*. London: The Women's Press.

Drew, P. (1987) 'Po-faced receipts of teases', *Linguistics* 25: 219–53.

Drew, P. (1989) 'Recalling someone from the past'. In D. Roger and P. Bull (eds) *Conversation: An Interdisciplinary Perspective* (pp. 96–115). Clevedon, UK: Multilingual Matters.

Drew, P. (1995a) 'Conversation analysis: The sequential analysis of intersubjectivity in conversation'. In J. Smith, R. Harré, L. Van Langenhove and P. Stearns (eds) *Rethinking Psychology, Volume 3, Practising Psychology* (pp. 64–79). London: Sage.

Drew, P. (1995b) 'Interaction sequences and "anticipatory interactive planning"'. In E. Goody (ed.) *The Social Origins of Human Intelligence* (pp. 111–38). Cambridge: Cambridge University Press.

Drew, P. (1998) 'Complaints about transgressions and misconduct', *Research on Language and Social Interaction* 31(3–4): 295–325.

Drew, P. and Heritage, J. (eds) (1992a) *Talk at Work: Interaction in Institutional Settings*. Cambridge: Cambridge University Press.

Drew, P. and Heritage, J. (1992b) 'Analyzing talk at work: An introduction'. In P. Drew and J. Heritage (eds) *Talk at Work: Interaction in Institutional Settings* (pp. 3–65). Cambridge: Cambridge University Press.

Drew, P. and Holt, E. (1988) 'Complainable matters: The use of idiomatic expressions in making complaints', *Social Problems* 35(4): 501–20.

Drummond, K. (1989) 'A backward glance at interruptions', *Western Journal of Speech Communication* 53: 150–66.

DuBois, B. (1983) 'Passionate scholarship: Notes on values, knowing, and method in feminist social science'. In G. Bowles and R. Duelli-Klein (eds) *Theories of Women's Studies* (pp. 105–16). Boston, MA: Routledge and Kegan Paul.

Dubois, B. L. and Crouch, I. (1975) 'The question of tag questions in women's speech: They don't really use more of them, do they?' *Language in Society* 4: 289–94.

Eckert, P. and McConnell-Ginet, S. (1992) 'Think practically and look locally: Language and gender as community-based practice', *Annual Review of Anthropology* 21: 461–90.

Eckert, P. and McConnell-Ginet, S. (2003) *Language and Gender*. Cambridge: Cambridge University Press.

Edley, N. (2001a) 'Analysing masculinity: Interpretative repertoires, ideological

REFERENCES

dilemmas and subject positions'. In M. Wetherell, S. Taylor and S. J. Yates (eds) *Discourse as Data: A Guide for Analysis* (pp. 189–228). London: Sage.

Edley, N. (2001b) 'Conversation analysis, discursive psychology and the study of ideology: A response to Susan Speer', *Feminism and Psychology* 11(1): 136–40.

Edley, N. and Wetherell, M. (1995) *Men in Perspective: Practice, Power and Identity*. London: Prentice Hall/Harvester Wheatsheaf.

Edley, N. and Wetherell, M. (1997) 'Jockeying for position: The construction of masculine identities', *Discourse and Society* 8(2): 203–17.

Edley, N. and Wetherell, M. (1999) 'Imagined futures: Young men's talk about fatherhood and domestic life', *British Journal of Social Psychology* 38: 181–94.

Edley, N. and Wetherell, M. (2001) 'Jekyll and Hyde: Men's constructions of feminism and feminists', *Feminism and Psychology* 11(4): 439–57.

Edwards, D. (1991) 'Categories are for talking: On the cognitive and discursive bases of categorization', *Theory and Psychology* 1: 515–42.

Edwards, D. (1994) 'Script formulations: An analysis of event descriptions in conversation', *Journal of Language and Social Psychology* 13(2): 211–47.

Edwards, D. (1995) 'Two to tango: Script formulations, dispositions, and rhetorical symmetry in relationship troubles talk', *Research on Language and Social Interaction* 28(4): 319–50.

Edwards, D. (1997) *Discourse and Cognition*. London: Sage.

Edwards, D. (1998) 'The relevant thing about her: Social identity categories in use'. In C. Antaki and S. Widdicombe (eds) *Identities in Talk* (pp. 15–33). London: Sage.

Edwards, D. (1999) 'Emotion discourse', *Culture and Psychology* 5(3): 271–91.

Edwards, D. (2000) 'Extreme case formulations: Softeners, investment, and doing non-literal', *Research on Language and Social Interaction* 33(4): 347–73.

Edwards, D. (2003) 'Analyzing racial discourse: The discursive psychology of mind-world relationships'. In H. Van den Berg, M. Wetherell and H. Houtkoop-Steenstra (eds) *Analyzing Race Talk: Multidisciplinary Approaches to the Interview*. Cambridge: Cambridge University Press.

Edwards, D. and Potter, J. (1992) *Discursive Psychology*. London: Sage.

Edwards, D. and Potter, J. (2001) 'Discursive psychology'. In A. McHoul and M. Rapley (eds) *How to Analyse Talk in Institutional Settings: A Casebook of Methods* (pp. 12–24). London: Continuum.

Edwards, D. and Stokoe, E. H. (2004) 'Discursive psychology, focus group interviews, and participants' categories'. *British Journal of Developmental Psychology* 22: 499–507.

Edwards, D., Ashmore, M. and Potter, J. (1995) 'Death and furniture: The rhetoric, politics and theology of bottom line arguments against relativism', *History of the Human Sciences* 8(2): 25–49.

Ehrlich, S. and King, R. (1992) 'Gender-based language reform and the social construction of meaning', *Discourse and Society* 3: 151–66.

Ehrlich, S. and King, R. (1994) 'Feminist meanings and the (de)politicization of the lexicon', *Language in Society* 23: 59–76.

Fairclough, N. (1989) *Language and Power*. London: Longman.

Fairclough, N. (1992) *Discourse and Social Change*. Cambridge: Polity.

Fairclough, N. (1995) *Critical Discourse Analysis: The Critical Study of Language*. London: Longman.

REFERENCES

Fairclough, N. and Wodak, R. (1997) 'Critical discourse analysis'. In T. A. van Dijk (ed.) *Discourse as Social Interaction. Discourse Studies: A Multidisciplinary Introduction, Volume 2* (pp. 258–84). London: Sage.

Fein, E. and Schneider, S. (1995) *The Rules: Time-Tested Secrets for Capturing the Heart of Mr Right.* London: Thorsons.

Fenstermaker, S. and West, C. (eds) (2002) *Doing Gender, Doing Difference: Inequality, Power, and Institutional Change.* New York: Routledge.

Ferree, M. M., Lorber, J. and Hess, B. B. (eds) (1999) *Revisioning Gender.* Newbury Park, CA: Sage.

Fine, M. (1992) *Disruptive Voices: The Possibilities of Feminist Research.* Ann Arbor, MI: University of Michigan Press.

Fine, M. (1994) 'Working the hyphens: Reinventing self and other in qualitative research'. In K. Denzin and Y. S. Lincoln (eds) *Handbook of Qualitative Research* (pp. 70–82). London: Sage.

Fish, S. (1994) *There's No Such Thing as Free Speech . . . And it's a Good Thing Too.* Oxford: Oxford University Press.

Fisher, S. (1986) *In the Patient's Best Interest: Women and the Politics of Medical Decisions.* New Brunswick, NJ: Rutgers University Press.

Fishman, P. (1977) 'Interactional shitwork', *Heresies* 2: 99–101.

Fishman, P. (1978) 'Interaction: The work women do', *Social Problems* 25: 397–406.

Forrester, M. A. (1999) 'Conversation analysis: A reflexive methodology for critical psychology', *Annual Review of Critical Psychology* 1: 34–49.

Foucault, M. (1971) 'Orders of discourse', *Social Science Information* 10: 7–30.

Foucault, M. (1972) *The Archaeology of Knowledge.* London: Tavistock.

Frank, J. (1990) 'Gender differences in color naming: Direct mail order advertisements', *American Speech* 65(2): 114–26.

Freed, A. (1992) 'We understand perfectly: A critique of Tannen's view of cross-sex communication'. Paper presented at the Second Berkeley Women and Language Conference, Berkeley, CA: 4–5 April.

Frith, H. (1998) 'Constructing the "other" through talk', *Feminism and Psychology* 8(4): 530–6.

Frith, H. and Kitzinger, C. (1998) '"Emotion work" as a participant resource: A feminist analysis of young women's talk-in-interaction', *Sociology* 32(2): 299–320.

Frosh, S., Phoenix, A. and Pattman, R. (2003) 'Taking a stand: Using psychoanalysis to explore the positioning of subjects in discourse', *British Journal of Social Psychology* 42: 39–53.

Garfinkel, H. (1967) *Studies in Ethnomethodology.* Englewood Cliffs, NJ: Prentice-Hall.

Garfinkel, H. and Wieder, D. L. (1992) 'Two incommensurable, asymmetrically alternate technologies of social analysis'. In G. Watson and R. M. Seiler (eds) *Text in Context: Contributions to Ethnomethodology.* London: Sage

Garfinkel, H. and Wiley, N. (1980) 'Conversation', unpublished transcript. Los Angeles: Sociology Department, University of California.

Gavey, N. (1989) 'Feminist poststructuralism and discourse analysis: Contributions to feminist psychology', *Psychology of Women Quarterly* 13: 459–75.

REFERENCES

Geertz, C. (1988) *Works and Lives: The Anthropologist as Author*. Cambridge: Polity.
Gergen, K. J. (1985) 'The social constructionist movement in modern psychology', *American Psychologist* 40: 266–75.
Gergen, K. J. (1994) *Realities and Relationships: Soundings in Social Construction*. Cambridge, MA: Harvard University Press.
Gergen, M. and Gergen, K. J. (eds) (2003) *Social Construction: A Reader*. London: Sage.
Gibbon, M. (1999) *Feminist Perspectives on Language*. London: Longman.
Giddens, A. (1981) 'Agency, institution and time-space analysis'. In K. Knorr-Cetina and A. V. Cicourel (eds) *Advances in Social Theory and Methodology* (pp. 161–74). London: Routledge.
Giddens, A. (1984) *The Constitution of Society: Outline of the Theory of Structuration*. Cambridge: Polity.
Gilbert, G. N. and Mulkay, M. J. (1984) *Opening Pandora's Box: A Sociological Analysis of Scientists' Discourse*. Cambridge: Cambridge University Press.
Gill, R. (1993) 'Justifying injustice: Broadcasters' accounts of inequality in radio'. In E. Burman and I. Parker (eds) *Discourse Analytic Research: Repertoires and Readings of Texts in Action* (pp. 75–93). London: Routledge.
Gill, R. (1995) 'Relativism, reflexivity and politics: Interrogating discourse analysis from a feminist perspective'. In S. Wilkinson and C. Kitzinger (eds) *Feminism and Discourse: Psychological Perspectives* (pp. 165–86). London: Sage.
Gill, R. (1998) 'Dialogues and differences: Writing, reflexivity and the crisis of representation'. In K. Henwood, C. Griffin and A. Phoenix (eds) *Standpoints and Differences: Essays in the Practice of Feminist Psychology* (pp. 18–44). London: Sage.
Gillies, V. (1999) 'An analysis of the discursive positions of women smokers: Implications for practical interventions'. In C. Willig (ed.) *Applied Discourse Analysis: Social and Psychological Interventions* (pp. 66–86). Buckingham: Open University Press.
Gilligan, C. (1982) *In a Different Voice: Psychological Theory and Women's Development*. Cambridge, MA: Harvard University Press.
Giora, R. (1995) 'On irony and negation', *Discourse Processes* 19: 239–64.
Glenn, P. J. (2003) 'Sex, laughter, and audiotape: On invoking features of context to explain laughter in interaction'. In P. J. Glenn, C. D. LeBaron and J. Mandelbaum (eds) *Studies in Language and Social Interaction: In Honor of Robert Hopper* (pp. 263–74). Mahwah, NJ: Lawrence Erlbaum.
Goddard, A. and Patterson, L. M. (2000) *Language and Gender*. London: Routledge.
Goffman, E. (1977) 'The arrangement between the sexes', *Theory and Society* 4(3): 301–31.
Goffman, E. (1979) *Gender Advertisements: Studies in the Anthropology of Visual Communication*. New York: Harper and Row.
Goffman, E. (1983) 'The interaction order', *American Sociological Review* 48: 1–17.
Goldberg, J. A. (1990) 'Interrupting the discourse on interruptions: An analysis of terms of relationally neutral, power- and rapport-oriented acts', *Journal of Pragmatics* 14: 883–903.

REFERENCES

Goodwin, C. (1980) 'Restarts, pauses and the achievement of mutual gaze at turn-beginning', *Sociological Inquiry* 50: 272–302.

Goodwin, C. (2000) 'Action and embodiment within situated human interaction', *Journal of Pragmatics* 32: 1489–522.

Goodwin, M. H. (1990) *He-Said-She-Said: Talk as Social Organization among Black Children*. Bloomington, IN: Indiana University Press.

Goodwin, M. H. (2001) 'Organizing participation in cross-sex jump-rope: Situating gender differences within longitudinal studies of activities', *Research on Language and Social Interaction* 34(1): 75–106.

Goodwin, M. H. (2002) 'Building power asymmetries in girls' interaction', *Discourse and Society* 13(6): 715–30.

Goodwin, M. H. (2003) 'The relevance of ethnicity, class, and gender in children's peer negotiations'. In J. Holmes and M. Meyerhoff (eds) *The Handbook of Language and Gender* (pp. 229–51). Oxford: Blackwell.

Gough, B. (1998a) 'Men and the discursive reproduction of sexism: Repertoires of difference and tolerance', *Feminism and Psychology* 8(1): 25–49.

Gough, B. (1998b) 'Projecting the gay other: Men, masculinity and the discursive reproduction of homophobia'. In R. Forrester and C. Percy (eds) *Proceedings: International Conference on Discourse and the Social Order*, pp. 28–41. Aston Business School, Birmingham, 16–17 July.

Gough, B. (2001) '"Biting your tongue": Negotiating masculinities in contemporary Britain', *Journal of Gender Studies* 10(2): 169–85.

Gough, B. (2004) 'Psychoanalysis as a resource for understanding emotional ruptures in the text: The case of defensive masculinities', *British Journal of Social Psychology* 43(2): 245–67.

Gough, B. and Edwards, G. (1998) 'The beer talking: Four lads, a carry out and the reproduction of masculinities', *The Sociological Review* 46(3): 409–35.

Gramsci, A. (1971) *Selections from the Prison Notebooks* (ed. and trans. by O. Hoare and G. Nowell-Smith). London: Lawrence and Wishart.

Gray, J. (1992) *Men are from Mars, Women are from Venus: A Practical Guide for Improving Communication and Getting What you Want in your Relationships*. London: Thorsons.

Greer, G. (1970) *The Female Eunuch*. London: Landsborough.

Grint, K. and Woolgar, S. (1997) *The Machine at Work: Technology, Work and Organization*. Cambridge: Polity.

Gumperz, J. (1982a) *Discourse Strategies*. Cambridge: Cambridge University Press.

Gumperz, J. (ed.) (1982b) *Language and Social Identity*. Cambridge: Cambridge University Press.

Habermas, J. (1984) *The Theory of Communicative Action, Volume 1, Reason and the Rationalization of Society*. London: Heinemann.

Hall, K. (1995) 'Lip service on the fantasy lines'. In K. Hall and M. Bucholtz (eds) *Gender Articulated: Language and the Socially Constructed Self* (pp. 183–216). New York: Routledge.

Hall, K. and Bucholtz, M. (eds) (1995) *Gender Articulated: Language and the Socially Constructed Self*. London: Routledge.

Hammersley, M. (1992) *What's Wrong with Ethnography?* London: Routledge.

Hammersley, M. (2003a) 'Conversation analysis and discourse analysis: Methods or paradigms?', *Discourse and Society* 14(6): 751–81.

Hammersley, M. (2003b) 'Doing the fine thing: A rejoinder to Jonathan Potter', *Discourse and Society* 14(6): 795–8.

Hammersley, M. (2003c) 'The impracticality of scepticism: A further response to Potter', *Discourse and Society* 14(6): 803–4.

Hammersley, M. (2003d) 'Analytics are no substitute for methodology: A response to Speer and Hutchby', *Sociology* 37(2): 339–52.

Harding, J. (1998) *Sex Acts: Practices of Femininity and Masculinity*. London: Sage.

Hare-Mustin, R. T. and Maracek, J. (1994) 'Asking the right questions: Feminist psychology and sex differences'. *Feminism and Psychology* 4(4): 531–7.

Harré, R. and Moghaddam, F. (eds) (2003) *The Self and Others: Positioning Individuals and Groups in Personal, Political and Cultural Contexts*. New York: Praeger/Greenwood.

Heath, C. (2004) 'Analysing face-to-face interaction: Video, the visual and material'. In D. Silverman (ed.) *Qualitative Research: Theory, Method and Practice* (2nd edn, pp. 266–82). London: Sage.

Henley, N. (1987) 'This new species that seeks a new language: On sexism in language and language change'. In J. Penfield (ed.) *Women and Language in Transition* (pp. 3–25). New York: State University of New York Press.

Henriques, J., Hollway, W., Urwin, C., Venn, C. and Walkerdine, V. (eds) (1984) *Changing the Subject: Psychology, Social Regulation and Subjectivity*. London: Methuen.

Henwood, K., Griffin, C. and Phoenix, A. (1998) 'Introduction'. In K. Henwood, C. Griffin and A. Phoenix (eds) *Standpoints and Differences: Essays in the Practice of Feminist Psychology* (pp. 1–17). London: Sage.

Hepburn, A. (2000) 'On the alleged incompatibility between relativism and feminist psychology', *Feminism and Psychology* 10(1): 91–106.

Hepburn, A. (2003) *Critical Social Psychology*. London: Sage.

Herek, G. M. (1994) 'Assessing heterosexuals' attitudes toward lesbians and gay men: A review of empirical research with the ATLG Scale'. In B. Greene and G. M. Herek (eds) *Lesbian and Gay Psychology: Theory, Research, and Clinical Applications* (pp. 206–28). Thousand Oaks, CA: Sage.

Herek, G. M. (1995) 'Psychological heterosexism in the United States'. In A. R. D'Augelli and C. J. Patterson (eds) *Lesbian, Gay, and Bisexual Identities over the Lifespan: Psychological Perspectives* (pp. 321–46). New York: Oxford University Press.

Herek, G. M., Kimmel, D. C., Amaro, H. and Melton, G. B. (1991) 'Avoiding heterosexist bias in psychological research', *American Psychologist* 46(9): 957–63.

Heritage, J. (1984) *Garfinkel and Ethnomethodology*. Cambridge: Polity.

Heritage, J. (1987) 'Ethnomethodology'. In A. Giddens and J. Turner (eds) *Social Theory Today* (pp. 224–72). Cambridge: Polity.

Heritage, J. (1988) 'Explanations as accounts: A conversation analytic perspective'. In C. Antaki (ed.) *Analysing Everyday Explanation: A Casebook of Methods* (pp. 127–44). London: Sage.

Heritage, J. (1990–91) 'Intention, meaning and strategy: Observations on constraints in interaction analysis', *Research on Language and Social Interaction* 24: 311–32.

REFERENCES

Heritage, J. (2001) 'Goffman, Garfinkel and conversation analysis'. In M. Wetherell, S. Taylor and S. J. Yates (eds) *Discourse Theory and Practice: A Reader* (pp. 47–56). London: Sage

Heritage, J. (2004) 'Conversation analysis and institutional talk: Analysing data'. In D. Silverman (ed.) *Qualitative Research: Theory, Method and Practice* (2nd edn, pp. 222–45). London: Sage.

Heritage, J. and Maynard, D. W. (eds) (2005) *Communication in Medical Care: Interaction Between Primary Care Physicians and Patients*. Cambridge: Cambridge University Press.

Hester, S. and Eglin, P. (eds) (1997) *Culture in Action: Studies in Membership Categorization Analysis*. Boston, MA: International Institute for Ethnomethodology and University Press of America.

Hewitt, J. P. and Stokes, R. (1975) 'Disclaimers', *American Sociological Review* 40(1): 1–11.

Hilbert, R. A. (1991) 'Norman and Sigmund: Comment on Denzin's "Harold and Agnes"', *Sociological Theory* 9(2): 264–8.

Hollway, W. (1989) *Subjectivity and Method in Psychology: Gender, Meaning and Science*. London: Sage.

Hollway, W. (1994) 'Beyond sex differences: A project for feminist psychology', *Feminism and Psychology* 4(4): 538–46.

Hollway, W. (1995) 'Feminist discourses and women's heterosexual desire'. In S. Wilkinson and C. Kitzinger (eds) *Feminism and Discourse: Psychological Perspectives* (pp. 86–105). London: Sage.

Hollway, W. (1998) 'Gender difference and the production of subjectivity'. In J. Henriques, W. Hollway, C. Urwin, C. Venn and V. Walkerdine (eds) *Changing the Subject: Psychology, Social Regulation and Subjectivity* (reissued edn, pp. 227–63). London: Routledge.

Holmes, J. (1984) 'Hedging your bets and sitting on the fence: Some evidence for hedges as support structures', *Te Reo* 27: 47–62.

Holmes, J. (1995) *Women, Men and Politeness*. London: Longman.

Holmes, J. (ed.) (1999) 'Communities of practice in language and gender research', *Language in Society* (special issue) 28(2): 171–320.

Holmes, J. and Meyerhoff, M. (2003a) 'Different voices, different views: An introduction to current research in language and gender'. In J. Holmes and M. Meyerhoff (eds) *The Handbook of Language and Gender* (pp. 1–17). Oxford: Blackwell.

Holmes, J. and Meyerhoff, M. (eds) (2003b) *The Handbook of Language and Gender*. Oxford: Blackwell.

Holstein, J. A. and Gubrium, J. F. (1997) 'Active interviewing'. In D. Silverman (ed.) *Qualitative Research: Theory, Method and Practice* (pp. 113–29). London: Sage.

Hopper, R. (2003) *Gendering Talk*. East Lansing, MI: Michigan State University Press.

Hopper, R. and LeBaron, C. (1998) 'How gender creeps into talk', *Research on Language and Social Interaction* 31(1): 59–74.

Houtkoop-Steenstra, H. (2000) *Interaction and the Standardized Survey Interview: The Living Questionnaire*. Cambridge: Cambridge University Press.

Hunter, S., Shannon, C., Knox, J. and Martin, J. I. (1998) *Lesbian, Gay, and*

REFERENCES

Bisexual Youths and Adults: Knowledge for Human Services Practice. London: Sage.

Hutchby, I. (1996a) *Confrontation Talk: Arguments, Asymmetries and Power on Talk Radio*. Hillsdale, NJ: Erlbaum.

Hutchby, I. (1996b) 'Power in discourse: The case of arguments on a British talk radio show', *Discourse and Society* 7(4): 481–97.

Hutchby, I. (1999) 'Beyond agnosticism? Conversation analysis and the sociological agenda', *Research on Language and Social Interaction* 32(1–2): 85–93.

Hutchby, I. (2001a) *Conversation and Technology: From the Telephone to the Internet*. Cambridge: Polity.

Hutchby, I. (2001b) 'Technologies, texts and affordances', *Sociology* 35(2): 441–56.

Hutchby, I. (2002) 'Resisting the incitement to talk in child counselling: Aspects of the utterance "I don't know"', *Discourse Studies* 4(2): 147–68.

Hutchby, I. (2003) 'Affordances and the analysis of technologically mediated interaction: A response to Brian Rappert', *Sociology* 37(3): 581–9.

Hutchby, I. and Wooffitt, R. (1998) *Conversation Analysis*. Cambridge: Polity.

Hymes, D. (1962) 'The ethnography of speaking'. In Anthropological Society of Washington, *Anthropology and Human Behavior* (pp. 13–53). Washington, DC: Anthropological Society of Washington.

Hymes, D. (1974) *Foundations in Sociolinguistics: An Ethnographic Approach*. Philadelphia, PA: University of Pennsylvania Press.

Jackson, S. (1992) 'The amazing deconstructing woman', *Trouble and Strife* 25: 25–31.

Jackson, S. (1998) 'Telling stories: Memory, narrative and experience in feminist research and theory'. In K. Henwood, C. Griffin and A. Phoenix (eds) *Standpoints and Differences: Essays in the Practice of Feminist Psychology* (pp. 45–64). London: Sage.

Jagose, A. (1996) *Queer Theory: An Introduction*. New York: New York University Press.

James, D. and Clarke, S. (1993) 'Women, men and interruptions: A critical review'. In D. Tannen (ed.) *Gender and Conversational Interaction* (pp. 231–80). New York and Oxford: Oxford University Press.

Järviluoma, H. and Roivainen, I. (2003) 'Gender in membership categorization analysis'. In H. Järviluoma, P. Moisala and A. Vilkko *Gender and Qualitative Methods* (pp. 69–83). London: Sage.

Jefferson, G. (1984) '"At first I thought": A normalizing device for extraordinary events', unpublished manuscript, Katholieke Hogeschool, Tilburg, Netherlands.

Jefferson, G. (1985) 'An exercise in the transcription and analysis of laughter'. In T. van Dijk (ed.) *Handbook of Discourse Analysis, Volume 3, Discourse and Dialogue* (pp. 25–34). London: Academic Press.

Jefferson, G. (1986) 'Notes on latency in overlap onset', *Human Studies* 9: 153–83.

Jefferson, G. (1989) 'Notes on a possible metric which provides for a "standard maximum silence" of one second in conversation'. In D. Roger and P. Bull (eds) *Conversation* (pp. 166–96). Clevedon, UK: Multilingual Matters.

Jefferson, G. (1990) 'List construction as a task and resource'. In G. Psathas (ed.) *Interaction Competence* (pp. 63–92). Lanham, MD: University Press of America.

Jefferson, G. (2004) 'A note on laughter in "male–female" interaction', *Discourse Studies* 6(1): 117–33.

Jesperson, O. (1922) *Language: Its Nature, Development and Origin*. New York: Allen and Unwin.

Jesperson, O. (1998) 'The woman'. In D. Cameron (ed.) *The Feminist Critique of Language: A Reader* (2nd edn, pp. 225–41). London: Routledge.

Johnson, S. (1997) 'Theorizing language and masculinity: A feminist perspective'. In S. Johnson and U. H. Meinhof (eds) *Language and Masculinity* (pp. 8–26). Oxford: Blackwell.

Johnson, S. and Meinhof, U. H. (eds) (1997) *Language and Masculinity*. Oxford: Blackwell.

Keenan, E. (Ochs) (1989) 'Norm-makers, norm-breakers: Uses of speech by men and women in a Malagasy community'. In R. Bauman and J. Sherzer (eds) *Explorations in the Ethnography of Speaking* (2nd edn, pp. 125–43). Cambridge: Cambridge University Press.

Kendall, G. and Wickham, G. (1999) *Using Foucault's Methods*. London: Sage.

Kenwood, C. (1999) 'Social constructionism: Implications for psychotherapeutic practice'. In D. J. Nightingale and J. Cromby (eds) *Social Constructionist Psychology: A Critical Analysis of Theory and Practice* (pp. 176–89). Buckingham: Open University Press.

Kessler, S. J. and McKenna, W. (1978) *Gender: An Ethnomethodological Approach*. New York: John Wiley and Sons.

Kitzinger, C. (1987) *The Social Construction of Lesbianism*. London: Sage.

Kitzinger, C. (1992) 'The individuated self concept: A critical analysis of social-constructionist writing on individualism'. In G. Breakwell (ed.) *The Social Psychology of Identity and the Self Concept* (pp. 221–50). London: Academic Press.

Kitzinger, C. (1994a) 'Anti-lesbian harassment'. In C. Brant and Y. L. Too (eds) *Rethinking Sexual Harassment* (pp. 125–47). London: Pluto.

Kitzinger, C. (1994b) 'Editor's introduction: Sex differences – Feminist perspectives', *Feminism and Psychology* 4(4): 501–6.

Kitzinger, C. (1995) 'Social constructionism: Implications for lesbian and gay psychology'. In A. R. D'Augelli and C. J. Patterson (eds) *Lesbian, Gay, and Bisexual Identities over the Lifespan: Psychological Perspectives* (pp. 136–61). New York: Oxford University Press.

Kitzinger, C. (1996a) 'Speaking of oppression: Psychology, politics, and the language of power'. In E. D. Rothblum and L. A. Bond (eds) *Preventing Heterosexism and Homophobia* (pp. 3–19). Thousand Oaks, CA: Sage.

Kitzinger, C. (1996b) 'Heteropatriarchal language: The case against "homophobia"'. In L. Mohin (ed.) *An Intimacy of Equals: Lesbian Feminist Ethics* (pp. 34–40). London: Onlywomen Press.

Kitzinger, C. (2000a) 'Doing feminist conversation analysis', *Feminism and Psychology* 10(2): 163–93.

Kitzinger, C. (2000b) 'How to resist an idiom', *Research on Language and Social Interaction* 33(2): 121–54.

Kitzinger, C. (2000c) 'Heterosexism'. In A. E. Kazdin (ed.) *Encyclopedia of Psychology*. New York: American Psychological Association and Oxford University Press.

REFERENCES

Kitzinger, C. (2002) 'Doing feminist conversation analysis'. In P. McIlvenny (ed.) *Talking Gender and Sexuality* (pp. 49–77). Amsterdam: John Benjamins.

Kitzinger, C. (2003) 'Feminist approaches'. In C. Seale, G. Gobo, J. Gubrium and D. Silverman (eds) *Qualitative Research Practice* (pp. 125–40). London: Sage.

Kitzinger, C. (2005) 'Speaking as a heterosexual: (How) does sexuality matter for talk-in-interaction?', *Research on Language and Social Interaction* 38(3).

Kitzinger, C. and Frith, H. (1999) 'Just say no? The use of conversation analysis in developing a feminist perspective on sexual refusal', *Discourse and Society* 10(3): 293–316.

Kitzinger, C. and Peel, E. (2005) 'The de-gaying and re-gaying of AIDS: Contested homophobias in lesbian and gay awareness training', *Discourse and Society* 16(2): 173–97.

Kitzinger, C. and Perkins, R. (1993) *Changing our Minds: Lesbian Feminism and Psychology*. London: Onlywomen Press.

Kitzinger, C. and Wilkinson, S. (1996) 'Theorizing representing the other'. In S. Wilkinson and C. Kitzinger (eds) *Representing the Other: A Feminism and Psychology Reader* (pp. 1–32). London: Sage.

Kitzinger, C. and Wilkinson, S. (1997) 'Validating women's experience? Dilemmas in feminist research', *Feminism and Psychology* 7(4): 566–74.

Kitzinger, C. and Wilkinson, S. (2003) 'Constructing identities: A feminist conversation analytic approach to positioning in action'. In R. Harré and A. Moghaddam (eds) *The Self and Others: Positioning Individuals and Groups in Personal, Political and Cultural Contexts* (pp. 157–80). New York: Praeger/Greenwood.

Knorr-Cetina, K. and Cicourel, A. V. (eds) (1981) *Advances in Social Theory and Methodology*. London: Routledge.

Korobov, N. (2004) 'Inoculating against prejudice: A discursive approach to homophobia and sexism in adolescent male talk', *Psychology of Men and Masculinity* 5(2): 178–89.

Korobov, N. and Bamberg, M. (2004) 'Positioning a "mature" self in interactive practices: How adolescent males negotiate "physical attraction" in group talk', *British Journal of Developmental Psychology* 22: 471–92.

Kramer, C., Thorne, B. and Henley, N. (1978) 'Perspectives on language and communication', *Signs: Journal of Women in Culture and Society* 3(3): 638–51.

Kress, G. (1985) *Linguistic Processes in Sociocultural Practice*. Melbourne, Vic.: Deakin University Press.

Kulick, D. (1999) 'Language and gender/sexuality'. *Language and Culture Mailing list: Online Symposium*. http://www.language-culture.org/archives/subs/kulick-don/index.html

Kulick, D. (2003) 'Language and desire'. In J. Holmes and M. Meyerhoff (eds) *The Handbook of Language and Gender* (pp. 119–41). Oxford: Blackwell.

Kyratzis, A. (2001) 'Children's gender indexing in language: From the separate worlds hypothesis to considerations of culture, context, and power', *Research on Language and Social Interaction* 34(1): 1–13.

Lacan, J. (1989) *Speech and Language in Psychoanalysis* (trans. A. Wilden). Baltimore, MD: Johns Hopkins University Press.

Lakoff, R. (1973) 'Language and woman's place', *Language in Society* 2: 45–79.

Lakoff, R. (1975) *Language and Woman's Place*. New York: Harper and Row.

REFERENCES

Lakoff, R. (1990) *Talking Power*. New York: Basic Books

Lakoff, R. (1995) 'Cries and whispers: The shattering of the silence'. In K. Hall and M. Bucholtz (eds) *Gender Articulated: Language and the Socially Constructed Self* (pp. 25–50). New York: Routledge.

Lakoff, R. (2000) *The Language War*. Berkeley, CA: University of California Press.

Lakoff, R. (2003) 'Language, gender, and politics: Putting "women" and "power" in the same sentence'. In J. Holmes and M. Meyerhoff (eds) *The Handbook of Language and Gender* (pp. 161–78). Oxford: Blackwell.

Lakoff, R. (2004) *Language and Woman's Place: Text and Commentaries* (revised and expanded edn, ed. M. Bucholtz). New York and Oxford: Oxford University Press.

Lather, P. (1988) 'Feminist perspectives on empowering research methodologies', *Women's Studies International Forum* 11(6): 569–81.

Lea, S. and Auburn, T. (2001) 'The social construction of rape in the talk of a convicted rapist', *Feminism and Psychology* 11: 11–33.

Lepper, G. (2000) *Categories in Text and Talk*. London: Sage.

Levelt, W. J. M. (1983) 'Monitoring and self-repair in speech', *Cognition* 14: 41–104.

Livia, A. (2003) '"One man in two is a woman": Linguistic approaches to gender in literary texts'. In J. Holmes and M. Meyerhoff (eds) *The Handbook of Language and Gender* (pp. 142–58). Oxford: Blackwell.

Livia, A. and Hall, K. (1997a) '"It's a girl!" Bringing performativity back to linguistics'. In A. Livia and K. Hall (eds) *Queerly Phrased: Language, Gender, and Sexuality* (pp. 3–18). New York: Oxford University Press.

Livia, A. and Hall, K. (eds) (1997b) *Queerly Phrased: Language, Gender, and Sexuality*. New York: Oxford University Press.

Lloyd, M. (1999) 'Performativity, parody, politics', *Theory, Culture and Society* 16(2): 195–213.

Locke, A. and Edwards, D. (2003) 'Bill and Monica: Memory, emotion and normativity in Clinton's Grand Jury testimony', *British Journal of Social Psychology* 42: 239–56.

Lorber, J. (1994) *Paradoxes of Gender*. New Haven, CT: Yale University Press.

Lorber, J. (2000) 'Using gender to undo gender: A feminist degendering movement', *Feminist Theory* 1(1): 79–95.

Lorber, J. and Farrell, S. A. (eds) (1991) *The Social Construction of Gender*. London: Sage.

Lundgren, E. (2000) 'Ahead of their time, children of their time, in and out of step 20 years later', *Feminism and Psychology* 10(1): 55–61.

Lynch, M. (1993) *Scientific Practice and Ordinary Action: Ethnomethodology and Social Studies of Science*. Cambridge: Cambridge University Press.

Lynch, M. (2000a) 'The ethnomethodological foundations of conversation analysis', *Text* 20(4): 517–32.

Lynch, M. (2000b) 'Response to Wes Sharrock', *Text* 20(4): 541–4.

Lynch, M. (2002) 'From naturally occurring data to naturally organized ordinary activities: Comment on Speer', *Discourse Studies* 4(4): 531–7.

Lynch, M. and Bogen, D. (1991) 'In defense of dada-driven analysis', *Sociological Theory* 9(2): 269–76.

REFERENCES

Lynch, M. and Bogen, D. (1994) 'Harvey Sacks's primitive natural science', *Theory, Culture and Society* 11: 65–104.

McConnell-Ginet, S. (1988) 'Language and gender'. In F. Newmeyer (ed.) *Linguistics: The Cambridge Survey, Volume IV, The Sociocultural Context* (pp. 75–99). Cambridge: Cambridge University Press.

McConnell-Ginet, S. (1989) 'The sexual (re)production of meaning: A discourse-based theory'. In F. W. Frank and P. A. Treichler (eds) *Language, Gender and Professional Writing* (pp. 35–50). New York: Modern Language Association.

McConnell-Ginet, S. (1998) 'The sexual (re)production of meaning: A discourse-based theory'. In D. Cameron (ed.) *The Feminist Critique of Language: A Reader* (2nd edn, pp.198–210). London: Routledge.

McConnell-Ginet, S. (2003) '"What's in a name?" Social labeling and gender practices'. In J. Holmes and M. Meyerhoff (eds) *The Handbook of Language and Gender* (pp. 69–97). Oxford: Blackwell.

McCreanor, T. (1996) '"Why strengthen the city wall when the enemy has poisoned the well?" An assay of anti-homosexual discourse in New Zealand', *Journal of Homosexuality* 31(4): 75–105.

McElhinny, B. (2003) 'Theorizing gender in sociolinguistics and linguistic anthropology'. In J. Holmes and M. Meyerhoff (eds) *The Handbook of Language and Gender* (pp. 21–42). Oxford: Blackwell.

McHoul, A. and Rapley, M. (eds) (2001) *How to Analyse Talk in Institutional Settings: A Casebook of Methods*. London: Continuum.

McIlvenny, P. (2002a) 'Critical reflections on performativity and the "Un/Doing" of gender and sexuality in talk'. In P. McIlvenny (ed.) *Talking Gender and Sexuality* (pp. 111–49). Amsterdam: John Benjamins.

McIlvenny, P. (2002b) 'Introduction: Researching talk, gender and sexuality'. In P. McIlvenny (ed.) *Talking Gender and Sexuality* (pp. 1–48). Amsterdam: John Benjamins.

McIlvenny, P. (ed.) (2002c) *Talking Gender and Sexuality*. Amsterdam: John Benjamins.

McNay, L. (1999) 'Subject, psyche and agency: The work of Judith Butler', *Theory, Culture and Society* 16(2): 175–93.

Mahoney, M. (1996) 'The problem of silence in feminist psychology', *Feminist Studies* 22(3): 603–25.

Maloney, M. and Fenstermaker, S. (2002) 'Performance and accomplishment: Reconciling feminist conceptions of gender'. In S. Fenstermaker and C. West (eds) *Doing Gender, Doing Difference: Inequality, Power, and Institutional Change* (pp. 189–204). New York: Routledge.

Malson, H. (1997) *The Thin Woman: Feminism, Poststructuralism and the Social Psychology of Anorexia Nervosa*. London: Routledge.

Maltz, D. N. and Borker, R. A. (1982) 'A cultural approach to male–female miscommunication'. In J. Gumperz (ed.) *Language and Social Identity* (pp. 196–216). Cambridge: Cambridge University Press.

Mandelbaum, J. and Pomerantz, A. (1990) 'What drives social action?' In K. Tracy (ed.) *Understanding Face-to-Face Interaction: Issues Linking Goals and Discourse* (pp. 151–66). Hillsdale, NJ: Lawrence Erlbaum.

Markova, I. and Foppa, K. (eds) (1991) *Asymmetries in Dialogue*. Hemel Hempstead: Harvester Wheatsheaf.

REFERENCES

Marshall, H. and Wetherell, M. (1989) 'Talking about career and gender identities: A discourse analysis perspective'. In S. Skevington and D. Baker (eds) *The Social Identity of Women* (pp. 106–29). London: Sage.

Martin, P. Y. (1998) 'Why can't a man be more like a woman? Reflections on Connell's *Masculinities*', *Gender and Society*, 12(4): 472–4.

Maynard, D. W. (1991) 'Goffman, Garfinkel, and games', *Sociological Theory* 9(2): 277–9.

Merrick, E. (1999) '"Like chewing gravel": On the experience of analyzing qualitative research findings using a feminist methodology', *Psychology of Women Quarterly* 23(1): 47–57.

Meyers, M. (1994) 'Defining homosexuality: News coverage of the "repeal the ban" controversy', *Discourse and Society* 5(3): 321–44.

Middleton, D. and Edwards, D. (1990) 'Conversational remembering: A social psychological approach'. In D. Middleton and D. Edwards (eds) *Collective Remembering* (pp. 23–45). London: Sage.

Miller, C. and Swift, K. (1976) *Words and Women*. New York: Anchor Press.

Miller, C. and Swift, K. (1980) *A Handbook of Non-Sexist Writing*. London: Women's Press.

Miller, T. (1998) '"Babes" illustrated: The swimsuit issue affair', *International Review for the Sociology of Sport* 33(2): 193–6.

Mills, S. (ed.) (1995) *Language and Gender: Interdisciplinary Perspectives*. New York: Longman.

Mills, S. (1997) *Discourse*. London: Routledge.

Morgan, M. (1998) 'Speaking subjects, discursive worlds: Readings from *Discourse and Social Psychology*', *Theory and Psychology* 8(3): 359–76.

Morgan, M. and Coombes, L. (2001) 'Subjectivities and silences, mother and woman: Theorizing an experience of silence as a speaking subject', *Feminism and Psychology* 11(3): 361–75.

Morrish, E. (1997) '"Falling short of God's ideal": Public discourse about lesbians and gays'. In A. Livia and K. Hall (eds) *Queerly Phrased: Language, Gender, and Sexuality* (pp. 335–45). New York: Oxford University Press.

Mulkay, M. (1988) *On Humour: Its Nature and its Place in Modern Society*. Oxford: Basil Blackwell.

Myers, G. (1998) 'Displaying opinions: Topics and disagreement in focus groups', *Language in Society* 27(1): 85–111.

Nightingale, D. J. (1999) 'Preface'. In D. J. Nightingale and J. Cromby (eds) *Social Constructionist Psychology: A Critical Analysis of Theory and Practice* (pp. xv–xvi). Buckingham: Open University Press.

Nightingale, D. J. and Cromby, J. (1999a) 'Reconstructing social constructionism'. In D. J. Nightingale and J. Cromby (eds) *Social Constructionist Psychology: A Critical Analysis of Theory and Practice* (pp. 207–24). Buckingham: Open University Press.

Nightingale, D. J. and Cromby, J. (eds) (1999b) *Social Constructionist Psychology: A Critical Analysis of Theory and Practice*. Buckingham: Open University Press.

Nilan, P. (1995) 'Membership categorization devices under construction: Social identity boundary maintenance in everyday discourse', *Australian Review of Applied Linguistics* 18(1): 69–94.

Noble, C. (1999) 'Silence: Absence and context'. In I. Parker with the Bolton

REFERENCES

Discourse Network (eds) *Critical Textwork: An Introduction to Varieties of Discourse and Analysis* (pp. 191–200). Buckingham: Open University Press.

Oakley, A. (1998) 'Gender, methodology and people's ways of knowing: Some problems with feminism and the paradigm debate in social science', *Sociology* 32(4): 707–31.

Ochs, E. (1979) 'Transcription as theory'. In E. Ochs and B. B. Schieffelin (eds) *Developmental Pragmatics* (pp. 43–72). New York: Academic Press.

Ochs, E. (1992) 'Indexing gender'. In A. Duranti and C. Goodwin (eds) *Rethinking Context: Language as an Interactive Phenomenon* (pp. 335–58). Cambridge: Cambridge University Press.

Ochs, E. and Taylor, C. (1995) 'The "father knows best" dynamic in dinnertime narratives'. In K. Hall and M. Bucholtz (eds) *Gender Articulated: Language and the Socially Constructed Self* (pp. 97–120). London: Routledge.

Parker, I. (1992) *Discourse Dynamics: Critical Analysis for Social and Individual Psychology*. London: Routledge.

Parker, I. (1997) 'Discursive psychology'. In D. Fox and I. Prilleltensky (eds) *Critical Psychology: An Introduction* (pp. 284–98). London: Sage.

Parker, I. (ed.) (1998) *Social Constructionism, Discourse and Realism*. London: Sage.

Parker, I. (1999a) 'Against relativism in psychology, on balance', *History of the Human Sciences* 12(4): 61–78.

Parker, I. with the Bolton Discourse Network (eds) (1999b) *Critical Textwork: An Introduction to Varieties of Discourse and Analysis*. Buckingham: Open University Press.

Parker, I. (1999c) 'The quintessentially academic position', *History of the Human Sciences* 12(4): 89–91.

Parker, I. (2002) *Critical Discursive Psychology*. Basingstoke: Palgrave Macmillan.

Parker, I. and Shotter, J. (eds) (1990) *Deconstructing Social Psychology*. London: Routledge.

Parsons, T. (1937) *The Structure of Social Action*. New York: McGraw-Hill.

Pauwels, A. (1998) *Women Changing Language*. London: Longman.

Pauwels, A. (2003) 'Linguistic sexism and feminist linguistic activism'. In J. Holmes and M. Meyerhoff (eds) *The Handbook of Language and Gender* (pp. 550–70). Oxford: Blackwell.

Peräkylä, A. (2004) 'Reliability and validity in research based on naturally occurring social interaction'. In D. Silverman (ed.) *Qualitative Research: Theory, Method and Practice* (2nd edn, pp. 283–304). London: Sage.

Plummer, K. (1992) 'Speaking its name: Inventing a lesbian and gay studies'. In K. Plummer (ed.) *Modern Homosexualities: Fragments of Lesbian and Gay Experience* (pp. 3–25). London: Routledge.

Pomerantz, A. (1978) 'Compliment responses: Notes on the co-operation of multiple constraints'. In J. Schenkein (ed.) *Studies in the Organization of Conversational Interaction*. London: Academic Press.

Pomerantz, A. (1984) 'Agreeing and disagreeing with assessments: Some features of preferred/dispreferred turn shapes'. In J. M. Atkinson and J. Heritage (eds) *Structures of Social Action: Studies in Conversation Analysis* (pp. 79–112). Cambridge: Cambridge University Press.

REFERENCES

Pomerantz, A. (1986) 'Extreme case formulations: A way of legitimating claims', *Human Studies* 9: 219–29.

Pomerantz, A. (1990–91) 'Mental concepts in the analysis of social action'. *Research on Language and Social Interaction* 24: 299–310.

Potter, J. (1982) '". . . Nothing so practical as a good theory": The problematic application of social psychology'. In P. Stringer (ed.) *Confronting Social Issues: Some Applications of Social Psychology, Volume 1* (pp. 23–49). London: Academic Press.

Potter, J. (1996a) 'Discourse analysis and constructionist approaches: Theoretical background'. In J. E. Richardson (ed.) *Handbook of Qualitative Research Methods for Psychology and the Social Sciences* (pp. 125–40). Leicester: British Psychological Society.

Potter, J. (1996b) *Representing Reality: Discourse, Rhetoric and Social Construction*. London: Sage.

Potter, J. (1997) 'Discourse and critical social psychology'. In T. Ibáñez and L. Íñiguez (eds) *Critical Social Psychology* (pp. 55–66). London: Sage.

Potter, J. (1998a) 'Discursive social psychology: From attitudes to evaluative practices', *European Review of Social Psychology* 9: 233–66.

Potter, J. (1998b) 'Fragments in the realization of relativism'. In I. Parker (ed.) *Social Constructionism, Discourse and Realism* (pp. 27–45). London: Sage.

Potter, J. (1998c) 'Cognition as context (Whose cognition?)', *Research on Language and Social Interaction* 31(1): 29–44.

Potter, J. (1999) 'Beyond cognitivism', *Research on Language and Social Interaction* 32(1–2): 119–28.

Potter, J. (2002) 'Two kinds of natural', *Discourse Studies* 4: 539–42.

Potter, J. (2003a) 'Discursive psychology: Between method and paradigm', *Discourse and Society* 14(6): 783–94.

Potter, J. (2003b) 'Practical scepticism', *Discourse and Society* 14(6): 799–801.

Potter, J. (2004a) 'Discourse analysis as a way of analysing naturally occurring talk'. In D. Silverman (ed.) *Qualitative Research: Theory, Method and Practice* (2nd edn, pp. 200–21). London: Sage.

Potter, J. (2004b) 'Discourse analysis'. In M. Hardy and A. Bryman (eds) *Handbook of Data Analysis*. London: Sage.

Potter, J. (2004c) 'Relativism'. In M. Lewis-Beck, A. Bryman and T. Futing Liao (eds) *The Sage Encyclopedia of Social Science Research Methods*. London: Sage.

Potter, J. and Hepburn, A. (2003) '"I'm a bit concerned": Early actions and psychological constructions in a child protection helpline', *Research on Language and Social Interaction* 36: 197–240.

Potter, J. and Hepburn, A. (in press) 'Qualitative interviews in psychology: Problems and prospects', *Qualitative Research in Psychology*.

Potter, J. and Wetherell, M. (1987) *Discourse and Social Psychology: Beyond Attitudes and Behaviour*. London: Sage.

Potter, J. and Wetherell, M. (1988) 'Accomplishing attitudes: Fact and evaluation in racist discourse', *Text* 8(1–2): 51–68.

Potter, J. and Wetherell, M. (1989) 'Fragmented ideologies: Accounts of educational failure and positive discrimination', *Text* 9(2): 175–90.

Potter, J. and Wetherell, M. (1995) 'Discourse analysis'. In J. Smith, R. Harré and

REFERENCES

L. van Langenhove (eds) *Rethinking Methods in Psychology* (pp. 80–92). London: Sage.

Potter, J., Wetherell, M., Gill, R. and Edwards, D. (1990) 'Discourse: Noun, verb or social practice?' *Philosophical Psychology* 3(2): 205–17.

Potter, J., Edwards, D. and Ashmore, M. (1999) 'Regulating criticism: Some comments on an argumentative complex', *History of the Human Sciences* 12(4): 79–88.

Praat, A. C. and Tuffin, K. F. (1996) 'Police discourses of homosexual men in New Zealand', *Journal of Homosexuality* 31(4): 57–73.

Puchta, C. and Potter, J. (2002) 'Manufacturing individual opinions: Market research focus groups and the discursive psychology of attitudes', *British Journal of Social Psychology* 41: 345–63.

Ramazanoglu, C. and Holland, J. (2002) *Feminist Methodology: Challenges and Choices*. London: Sage.

Reinharz, S. (1992) *Feminist Methods in Social Research*. New York: Oxford University Press.

Rogers, M. F. (1992a) 'Resisting the enormous either/or: A response to Bologh and Zimmerman', *Gender and Society* 6(2): 207–14.

Rogers, M. F. (1992b) 'They were all passing: Agnes, Garfinkel, and company', *Gender and Society* 6(2): 169–91.

Romaine, S. (2003) 'Variation in language and gender'. In J. Holmes and M. Meyerhoff (eds) *The Handbook of Language and Gender* (pp. 98–118). Oxford: Blackwell.

Rubin, G. (1975) 'The traffic in women: Notes on the "Political Economy of Sex"'. In R. Reiter (ed.) *Towards an Anthropology of Women* (pp. 157–210). New York: Monthly Review Press.

Sacks, H. (1972) 'On the analysability of stories by children'. In R. Turner (ed.) *Ethnomethodology: Selected Readings* (pp. 216–32). London: Penguin.

Sacks, H. (1979) 'Hotrodder: A revolutionary category'. In G. Psathas (ed.) *Everyday Language: Studies in Ethnomethodology* (pp. 7–14). New York: Irvington.

Sacks, H. (1984) 'On doing "being ordinary"'. In J. M. Atkinson and J. Heritage (eds) *Structures of Social Action: Studies in Conversation Analysis* (pp. 413–29). Cambridge: Cambridge University Press.

Sacks, H. (1987) 'On the preferences for agreement and contiguity in sequences in conversation'. In G. Button and J. R. E. Lee (eds) *Talk and Social Organisation* (pp. 54–69). Clevedon, UK: Multilingual Matters.

Sacks, H. (1992) *Lectures on Conversation* (2 vols, G. Jefferson, ed.). Oxford: Blackwell.

Sacks, H. (1995) *Lectures on Conversation* (vols 1 and 2 combined, G. Jefferson, ed.). Oxford: Blackwell.

Sacks, H., Schegloff, E. A. and Jefferson, G. (1974) 'A simplest systematics for the organization of turn-taking for conversation', *Language* 50(4): 696–735.

Schegloff, E. A. (1968) 'Sequencing in conversational openings', *American Anthropologist* 70(6): 1075–95.

Schegloff, E. A. (1979) 'Identification and recognition in telephone conversation openings'. In G. Psathas (ed.) *Everyday Language: Studies in Ethnomethodology* (pp. 23–78). New York: Irvington.

REFERENCES

Schegloff, E. A. (1987) 'Between micro and macro: Contexts and other connections'. In J. Alexander, B. Giesen, R. Munch and N. Smelser (eds) *The Micro-Macro Link* (pp. 207–34). Berkeley, CA: University of California Press.

Schegloff, E. A. (1991) 'Reflections on talk and social structure'. In D. Boden and D. Zimmerman (eds) *Talk and Social Structure* (pp. 44–70). Cambridge: Polity.

Schegloff, E. A. (1992a) 'In another context'. In A. Duranti and C. Goodwin (eds) *Rethinking Context: Language as an Interactive Phenomenon* (pp. 191–227). Cambridge: Cambridge University Press.

Schegloff, E. A. (1992b) 'Repair after next turn: The last structurally provided defense of intersubjectivity in conversation', *American Journal of Sociology* 95(5): 1295–345.

Schegloff, E. A. (1997) 'Whose text? Whose context?', *Discourse and Society* 8(2): 165–87.

Schegloff, E. A. (1998) 'Reply to Wetherell', *Discourse and Society* 9(3): 413–16.

Schegloff, E. A. (1999a) '"Schegloff's texts" as "Billig's data": A critical reply', *Discourse and Society* 10(4): 558–72.

Schegloff, E. A. (1999b) 'Naivete vs sophistication or discipline vs self-indulgence: A rejoinder to Billig', *Discourse and Society* 10(4): 577–82.

Schegloff, E. A. (2001) 'Accounts of conduct in interaction: Interruption, overlap, and turn-taking'. In J. H. Turner (ed.) *Handbook of Sociological Theory* (pp. 287–321). New York: Kluwer Academic/Plenum.

Schegloff, E. A. and Sacks, H. (1973) 'Opening up closings', *Semiotica* 8: 289–327.

Schegloff, E. A., Jefferson, G. and Sacks, H. (1977) 'The preference for self-correction in the organisation of repair in conversation', *Language* 53: 361–82.

Shakespeare, T. (1998) 'Social constructionism as a political strategy'. In I. Velody and R. Williams (eds) *The Politics of Constructionism* (pp. 168–80). London: Sage.

Sharrock, W. and Button, G. (1991) 'The social actor: Social action in real time'. In G. Button (ed.) *Ethnomethodology and the Human Sciences* (pp. 137–75). Cambridge: Cambridge University Press.

Sharrock, W. and Watson, R. (1988) 'Autonomy among social theories: The incarnation of social structures'. In N. G. Fielding (ed.) *Actions and Structure: Research Methods and Social Theory* (pp. 56–77). London: Sage.

Sheldon, A. (1990) 'Pickle fights: Gendered talk in preschool disputes', *Discourse Processes* 13: 5–31.

Shotter, J. (1993) *Cultural Politics of Everyday Life: Social Constructionism, Rhetoric and Knowing of the Third Kind*. Buckingham: Open University Press.

Shotter, J. and Gergen, K. (eds) (1989) *Texts of Identity*. London: Sage.

Sidnell, J. (2003) 'Constructing and managing male exclusivity in talk-in-interaction'. In J. Holmes and M. Meyerhoff (eds) *The Handbook of Language and Gender* (pp. 327–52). Oxford: Blackwell.

Silverman, D. (1998) *Harvey Sacks: Social Science and Conversation Analysis*. Cambridge: Polity.

Smith, D. E. (1978) '"K is mentally ill": The anatomy of a factual account', *Sociology* 12: 23–53.

Smith, D. E. (2002) 'Foreword'. In S. Fenstermaker and C. West (eds) *Doing Gender, Doing Difference: Inequality, Power, and Institutional Change* (pp. i–xv). New York: Routledge.

REFERENCES

Speer, S. A. (1999) 'Feminism and conversation analysis: An oxymoron?', *Feminism and Psychology* 9(4): 471–8.

Speer, S. A. (2000) 'Let's get real? Feminism, constructionism, and the realism/relativism debate', *Feminism and Psychology* 10(4): 539–50.

Speer, S. A. (2001a) 'Participants' orientations, ideology, and the ontological status of hegemonic masculinity: A rejoinder to Nigel Edley', *Feminism and Psychology* 11(1): 141–4.

Speer, S. A. (2001b) 'Reconsidering the concept of hegemonic masculinity: Discursive psychology, conversation analysis, and participants' orientations', *Feminism and Psychology* 11(1): 107–35.

Speer, S. A. (2002a) 'Natural and contrived data: A sustainable distinction?' *Discourse Studies* 4(4): 511–25.

Speer, S. A. (2002b) 'Sexist talk: Gender categories, participants' orientations and irony', *Journal of Sociolinguistics* 6(3): 347–77.

Speer, S. A. (2002c) 'Transcending the natural/contrived distinction: A rejoinder to ten Have, Lynch and Potter', *Discourse Studies* 4(4): 543–8.

Speer, S. A. (2002d) 'What can conversation analysis contribute to feminist methodology? Putting reflexivity into practice', *Discourse and Society* 13(6): 801–21.

Speer, S. A. (2005) 'The interactional organization of the gender attribution process', *Sociology* 39(1): 67–87.

Speer, S. A. and Green, R. (forthcoming) 'Transsexual identities. Constructions of gender in an NHS gender identity clinic', research project, ESRC award no. RES-148-0029.

Speer, S. A. and Hutchby, I. (2003a) 'From ethics to analytics: Aspects of participants' orientations to the presence and relevance of recording devices', *Sociology* 37(2): 315–37.

Speer, S. A. and Hutchby, I. (2003b) 'Methodology needs analytics: A rejoinder to Martyn Hammersley', *Sociology* 37(2): 353–9.

Speer, S. A. and Parsons, C. (forthcoming) 'Gatekeeping gender: Some features of the use of hypothetical questions in the psychiatric assessment of transsexual patients'.

Speer, S. A. and Potter, J. (2000) 'The management of heterosexist talk: Conversational resources and prejudiced claims', *Discourse and Society* 11: 543–72.

Speer, S. A. and Potter, J. (2002) 'From performatives to practices: Judith Butler, discursive psychology, and the management of heterosexist talk'. In P. McIlvenny (ed.) *Talking Gender and Sexuality* (pp. 151–80). Amsterdam: John Benjamins.

Spender, D. (1980) *Man Made Language*. London: Routledge and Kegan Paul.

Spender, D. (1989) *The Writing or the Sex*. New York: Pergamon Press.

Spender, D. (1995) *Nattering on the Net: Women, Power and Cyberspace*. Melbourne, Vic.: Spinifex.

Stanley, L. and Wise, S. (1993) *Breaking out Again: Feminist Ontology and Epistemology*, London: Routledge.

Stokoe, E. (1998) 'Talking about gender: The conversational construction of gender categories in academic discourse', *Discourse and Society* 9: 217–40.

Stokoe, E. (2000) 'Toward a conversation analytic approach to gender and discourse', *Feminism and Psychology* 10(4): 552–63.

REFERENCES

Stokoe, E. (2003) 'Mothers, single women and sluts: Gender, morality and membership categorization in neighbour disputes', *Feminism and Psychology* 13(3): 317–44.

Stokoe, E. (2004) 'Gender and discourse, gender and categorization: Current developments in language and gender research', *Qualitative Research in Psychology* 1(2): 107–29.

Stokoe, E. (2005) 'Analysing gender and language', *Journal of Sociolinguistics* 9(1): 118–33.

Stokoe, E. (in press) 'Doing gender, doing categorisation: Exploring the possibilities of membership categorisation analysis for feminist researchers', *Sociological Review*.

Stokoe, E. and Edwards, D. (2005) 'Mundane morality and gender in familial neighbour disputes'. In J. Cromdal and M. Tholander (eds) *Children, Morality and Interaction*. Hauppague, NY: Nova Science.

Stokoe, E. and Smithson, J. (2001) 'Making gender relevant: Conversation analysis and gender categories in interaction', *Discourse and Society* 12(2): 217–44.

Stokoe, E. and Smithson, J. (2002) 'Gender and sexuality in talk-in-interaction: Considering conversation analytic perspectives'. In P. McIlvenny (ed.) *Talking Gender and Sexuality* (pp. 79–109). Amsterdam: John Benjamins.

Stokoe, E. and Weatherall, A. (eds) (2002) 'Gender, language, conversation analysis and feminism', *Discourse and Society* (special issue) 13(6): 707–864.

Stringer, J. L. and Hopper, R. (1998) 'Generic he in conversation?', *Quarterly Journal of Speech* 84(2): 209–21.

Suhr, S. and Johnson, S. (eds) (2003) 'Political correctness', *Discourse and Society* (special issue) 14(1): 5–110.

Sunderland, J. (2004) *Gendered Discourses*. Basingstoke: Palgrave Macmillan.

Tainio, L. (2003) '"When shall we go for a ride?" A case of the sexual harassment of a young girl', *Discourse and Society* 14(2): 173–90.

Talbot, M. (1992) '"I wish you'd stop interrupting me!" Interruptions and asymmetries in speaker rights in equal encounters', *Journal of Pragmatics* 16: 451–66.

Talbot, M. (1997) '"Randy fish boss branded a stinker": Coherence and the construction of masculinities in a British tabloid newspaper'. In S. Johnson and U. Hanna Meinhof (eds) *Language and Masculinity* (pp. 173–87). Oxford: Blackwell.

Talbot, M. (1998) *Language and Gender: An Introduction*. Cambridge: Polity.

Talbot, M. (2000) '"It's good to talk?" The undermining of feminism in a British Telecom advertisement', *Journal of Sociolinguistics* 4(1): 108–19.

Tannen, D. (1990) *You Just Don't Understand! Women and Men in Conversation*. London: Virago.

Tannen, D. (1994a) 'Interpreting interruption in conversation'. In D. Tannen, *Gender and Discourse* (pp. 53–83). Oxford: Oxford University Press.

Tannen, D. (1994b) *Talking from 9 to 5*. New York: William Morrow.

Tannen, D. (1994c) 'The relativity of linguistic strategies: Rethinking power and solidarity in gender and dominance'. In D. Tannen, *Gender and Discourse* (pp. 19–52). Oxford: Oxford University Press.

Tannen, D. (1997) 'Women and men talking: An interactional sociolinguistic approach'. In M. R. Walsh (ed.) *Women, Men and Gender* (pp. 82–90). New Haven, CT and London: Yale University Press.

Tannen, D. (1999) 'The display of (gendered) identities in talk at work'. In M. Bucholtz, A. C. Liang and L. A. Sutton (eds) *Reinventing Identities: The Gendered Self in Discourse* (pp. 221–40). New York: Oxford University Press.

Tannen, D. (2003) 'Gender and family interaction'. In J. Holmes and M. Meyerhoff (eds) *The Handbook of Language and Gender* (pp. 179–201). Oxford: Blackwell.

Tannen, D. and Saville-Troike, M. (eds) (1985) *Perspectives on Silence*. Norwood, NJ: Ablex.

Te Molder, H. and Potter, J. (eds) (2005) *Conversation and Cognition*. Cambridge: Cambridge University Press.

ten Have, P. (1999) *Doing Conversation Analysis: A Practical Guide*. London: Sage.

ten Have, P. (2002) 'Ontology or methodology? Comments on Speer's "natural" and "contrived" data: A sustainable distinction?' *Discourse Studies* 4(4): 527–30.

ten Have, P. (2004) *Understanding Qualitative Research and Ethnomethodology*. London: Sage.

The Harry Benjamin International Gender Dysphoria Association (HBIGDA) (2001) *Standards of Care for Gender Identity Disorders* (sixth version). Minneapolis, MN: HBIGDA.

Thornborrow, J. (2002) *Power Talk: Language and Interaction in Institutional Discourse*. London: Longman.

Thorne, B. (1993) *Gender Play: Girls and Boys in School*. Buckingham: Open University Press.

Thorne, B. and Henley, N. (eds) (1975) *Language and Sex: Difference and Dominance*. Rowley, MA: Newbury House.

Tiefer, L. (2000) 'Agreeing to disagree: Multiple views on gender laws and transsex', *Feminism and Psychology* 10(1): 36–40.

Todd, A. D. (1989) *Intimate Adversaries: Cultural Conflict between Doctors and Women Patients*. Philadelphia, PA: University of Pennsylvania Press.

Toerien, M. (2004a) 'Talking hair removal: Negotiating between emotion work and hair removal tasks in the beauty salon', BSA Annual Conference, University of York, 22–24 March.

Toerien, M. (2004b) 'Doing hair removal in the beauty salon: A feminist conversation analytic study', unpublished PhD thesis, University of York.

Uchida, A. (1992) 'When "difference" is "dominance"', *Language in Society* 21: 547–68.

Unger, R. (1979) 'Toward a redefinition of sex and gender', *American Psychologist* 34: 1085–94.

Ussher, J. (ed.) (1997) *Body Talk: The Material and Discursive Regulation of Sexuality, Madness and Reproduction*. London: Routledge.

van Dijk, T. A. (1987) *Communicating Racism: Ethnic Prejudice in Thought and Talk*. Newbury Park, CA: Sage.

van Dijk, T. A. (1992) 'Discourse and the denial of racism', *Discourse and Society* 3(1): 87–118.

van Dijk, T. A. (1993) 'Principles of critical discourse analysis', *Discourse and Society* 4(2): 249–83.

REFERENCES

van Dijk, T. A., Ting-Toomey, S., Smithson, G. and Troutman, D. (1997) 'Discourse, ethnicity, culture and racism'. In T. A. van Dijk (ed.) *Discourse as Social Interaction* (pp. 144–80). London: Sage.

Verkuyten, M. (1998) 'Attitudes in public discourse: Speaker's own orientations', *Journal of Language and Social Psychology* 17: 302–22.

Walker, S. (1994) *Hate Speech: The History of an American Controversy*. London: University of Nebraska Press.

Watson, G. (1994) 'A comparison of social constructionist and ethnomethodological descriptions of how a judge distinguished between the erotic and the obscene', *Philosophy of the Social Sciences* 24(4): 405–25.

Weatherall, A. (2000) 'Gender relevance in talk-in-interaction and discourse', *Discourse and Society* 11(2): 286–8.

Weatherall, A. (2002a) *Gender, Language and Discourse*. London: Routledge.

Weatherall, A. (2002b) 'Towards understanding gender and talk-in-interaction', *Discourse and Society* 13(6): 767–81.

Weatherall, A., Gavey, N. and Potts, A. (2002) 'So whose words are they anyway?', *Feminism and Psychology* 12(4): 531–9.

Weedon, C. (1997) *Feminist Practice and Poststructuralist Theory* (2nd edn). Oxford: Blackwell.

West, C. (1979) 'Against our will: Male interruptions of females in cross-sex conversation', *Language, Sex, and Gender* (Annals of the New York Academy of Sciences), 327: 81–97.

West, C. (1992) 'Rethinking "sex differences" in conversational topics', *Advances in Group Processes* 9: 131–62.

West, C. (1995) 'Women's competence in conversation', *Discourse and Society* 6(1): 107–31.

West, C. (1998) 'Not just doctor's orders: Directive-response sequences in patients' visits to women and men physicians'. In J. Cheshire and P. Trudgill (eds) *The Sociolinguistics Reader: Gender and Discourse* (pp. 99–126). London: Arnold.

West, C. and Fenstermaker, S. (2002a) 'Accountability and affirmative action: The accomplishment of gender, race and class in a University of California Board of Regents meeting'. In S. Fenstermaker and C. West (eds) *Doing Gender, Doing Difference: Inequality, Power, and Institutional Change* (pp. 141–68). New York: Routledge.

West, C. and Fenstermaker, S. (2002b) 'Accountability in action: The accomplishment of gender, race and class in a University of California Board of Regents', *Discourse and Society* 13(4): 537–63.

West, C. and Garcia, A. (1988) 'Conversational shift work: A study of topical transitions between women and men', *Social Problems* 35: 551–75.

West, C. and Zimmerman, D. (1983) 'Small insults: A study of interruptions in cross-sex conversations between unacquainted persons'. In B. Thorne, C. Kramarae and N. Henley (eds) *Language, Gender and Society* (pp. 102–17). Cambridge, MA: Newbury House.

West, C. and Zimmerman, D. (1987) 'Doing gender', *Gender and Society* 1: 125–51.

West, C. and Zimmerman, D. (1991) 'Doing gender'. In J. Lorber and S. Farrell (eds) *The Social Construction of Gender* (pp. 13–37). Newbury Park, CA: Sage.

West, C., Lazar, M. and Kramarae, C. (1997) 'Gender in discourse'. In T. A. van

Dijk (ed.) *Discourse as Social Interaction. Discourse Studies: A Multidisciplinary Introduction*, Volume 2 (pp. 119–43). London: Sage.

Wetherell, M. (1995) 'Romantic discourse and feminist analysis: Interrogating investment, power and desire'. In S. Wilkinson and C. Kitzinger (eds) *Feminism and Discourse: Psychological Perspectives* (pp. 128–44). London: Sage.

Wetherell, M. (1998) 'Positioning and interpretative repertoires: Conversation analysis and post-structuralism in dialogue', *Discourse and Society* 9(3): 387–412.

Wetherell, M. (1999a) 'Discursive psychology and psychoanalysis: Theorising masculine subjectivities'. Paper presented at the Millenium World Conference of Critical Psychology, University of Western Sydney, 30 April–2 May.

Wetherell, M. (1999b) 'Beyond binaries', *Theory and Psychology* 9(3): 399–406.

Wetherell, M. (2001) 'Debates in discourse research'. In M. Wetherell, S. Taylor and S. J. Yates (eds) *Discourse Theory and Practice: A Reader* (pp. 380–99). London: Sage.

Wetherell, M. (2003) 'Paranoia, ambivalence and discursive practices: Concepts of position and positioning in psychoanalysis and discursive psychology'. In R. Harré and F. Moghaddam (eds) *The Self and Others: Positioning Individuals and Groups in Personal, Political and Cultural Contexts*. New York: Praeger/Greenwood.

Wetherell, M. and Edley, N. (1998) 'Gender practices: Steps in the analysis of men and masculinities'. In K. Henwood, C. Griffin and A. Phoenix (eds) *Standpoints and Differences: Essays in the Practice of Feminist Psychology* (pp. 156–73). London: Sage.

Wetherell, M. and Edley, N. (1999) 'Negotiating hegemonic masculinity: Imaginary positions and psycho-discursive practices', *Feminism and Psychology* 9(3): 335–56.

Wetherell, M. and Potter, J. (1988) 'Discourse analysis and the identification of interpretative repertoires'. In C. Antaki (ed.) *Analysing Everyday Explanation: A Casebook of Methods* (pp. 168–83). London: Sage.

Wetherell, M. and Potter, J. (1992) *Mapping the Language of Racism: Discourse and the Legitimation of Exploitation*. London: Harvester Wheatsheaf.

Wetherell, M. and Potter, J. (1998) 'Discourse and social psychology: Silencing binaries', *Theory and Psychology* 8(3): 377–88.

Wetherell, M., Stiven, H. and Potter, J. (1987) 'Unequal egalitarianism: A preliminary study of discourses concerning gender and employment opportunities', *British Journal of Social Psychology* 26: 59–71.

Wetherell, M., Taylor, S. and Yates, S. J. (eds) (2001a) *Discourse as Data: A Guide for Analysis*. London: Sage.

Wetherell, M., Taylor, S. and Yates, S. J. (eds) (2001b) *Discourse Theory and Practice: A Reader*. London: Sage.

Widdicombe, S. (1995) 'Identity, politics and talk: A case for the mundane and the everyday'. In S. Wilkinson and C. Kitzinger (eds) *Feminism and Discourse: Psychological Perspectives* (pp. 106–27). London Sage.

Widdicombe, S. (1998a) '"But you don't class yourself": The interactional management of category membership and non-membership'. In C. Antaki and S. Widdicombe (eds) *Identities in Talk* (pp. 52–70). London: Sage.

Widdicombe, S. (1998b) 'Epilogue: Identity as an analysts' and a participants'

REFERENCES

resource'. In C. Antaki and S. Widdicombe (eds) *Identities in Talk* (pp. 191–206). London: Sage.

Widdicombe, S. and Wooffitt, R. (1995) *The Language of Youth Subcultures: Social Identity in Action*. London: Harvester Wheatsheaf.

Wiggins, S. (2002) 'Talking with your mouth full: Gustatory *Mmms* and the embodiment of pleasure', *Research on Language and Social Interaction* 35(3): 311–36.

Wiggins, S. and Potter, J. (2003) 'Attitudes and evaluative practices: Category vs. item and subjective vs. objective constructions in everyday food assessments', *British Journal of Social Psychology* 42: 513–31.

Wilkinson, S. (1997) 'Prioritizing the political: Feminist psychology'. In T. Ibáñez and L. Íñiguez (eds) *Critical Social Psychology* (pp. 178–94). London: Sage.

Wilkinson, S. (1999) 'Focus groups: A feminist method', *Psychology of Women Quarterly* 23: 221–44.

Wilkinson, S. and Kitzinger, C. (eds) (1995) *Feminism and Discourse: Psychological Perspectives*. London: Sage.

Willig, C. (1998) 'Social constructionism and revolutionary socialism: A contradiction in terms?' In I. Parker (ed.) *Social Constructionism, Discourse and Realism* (pp. 91–104). London: Sage.

Willig, C. (ed.) (1999a) *Applied Discourse Analysis: Social and Psychological Interventions*. Buckingham: Open University Press.

Willig, C. (1999b) 'Beyond appearances: A critical realist approach to social constructionist work'. In D. J. Nightingale and J. Cromby (eds) *Social Constructionist Psychology: A Critical Analysis of Theory and Practice* (pp. 37–51). Buckingham: Open University Press.

Willig, C. (1999c) 'Discourse analysis and sex education'. In C. Willig (ed.) *Applied Discourse Analysis: Social and Psychological Interventions* (pp. 110–24). Buckingham: Open University Press.

Willig, C. (2001) *Introducing Qualitative Research in Psychology: Adventures in Theory and Method*. Buckingham: Open University Press.

Willott, S. (1998) 'An outsider within: A feminist doing research with men'. In K. Henwood, C. Griffin and A. Phoenix (eds) *Standpoints and Differences: Essays in the Practice of Feminist Psychology* (pp. 174–90). London: Sage.

Willott, S. and Griffin, C. (1997) '"Wham bam, am I a man?" Unemployed men talk about masculinities', *Feminism and Psychology* 7(1): 107–28.

Wittgenstein, L. (1953) *Philosophical Investigations*. Oxford: Blackwell.

Wodak, R. (ed.) (1989) *Language, Power and Ideology: Studies in Political Discourse*. Amsterdam: John Benjamins.

Wodak, R. (1997) '"I know we won't revolutionize the world with it, but . . .": Styles of female leadership in institutions'. In H. Kotthoff and R. Wodak (eds) *Communicating Gender in Context* (pp. 335–70). Amsterdam: John Benjamins.

Wodak, R. (2003) 'Multiple identities: The roles of female parliamentarians in the EU parliament'. In J. Holmes and M. Meyerhoff (eds) *The Handbook of Language and Gender* (pp. 671–98). Oxford: Blackwell.

Wood, B. (1998) 'Stuart Hall's cultural studies and the problem of hegemony', *British Journal of Sociology* 49(3): 399–414.

Wood, L. A. and Kroger, R. O. (2000) *Doing Discourse Analysis: Methods for Studying Action in Talk and Text*. London: Sage.

REFERENCES

Wooffitt, R. (1992) *Telling Tales of the Unexpected: The Organization of Factual Discourse*. London: Harvester Wheatsheaf.

Wooffitt, R. (2005) *Conversation Analysis and Discourse Analysis: A Comparative and Critical Introduction*. London: Sage.

Woolgar, S. and Pawluch, D. (1985) 'Ontological gerrymandering: The anatomy of social problems explanations', *Social Problems* 32(3): 214–27.

Wowk, M. T. (1984) 'Blame allocation, sex and gender in a murder interrogation', *Women's Studies International Forum* 7(1): 75–82.

Wowk, M. T. (forthcoming) 'Another sociological chimera: Kitzinger's feminist conversation analysis'.

Zimmerman, D. H. (1992) 'They were all doing gender, but they weren't all passing: Comment on Rogers', *Gender and Society* 6(2): 192–8.

Zimmerman, D. H. and West, C. (1975) 'Sex roles, interruptions and silences in conversation'. In B. Thorne and N. Henley (eds) *Language and Sex: Difference and Dominance* (pp. 105–29). Rowley, MA: Newbury House.

INDEX

action orientation 23–4, 81, 110, 134, 182; *see also* social action
adjacency pairs 98–9
adjectives 33
agency: Butler 63, 64, 65, 78–80, 82, 88; critical 64; ethnomethodology 80, 81, 88; linguistic 66, 81
'Agnes' case 68–71, 85
analytic techniques 24, 126; ethnomethodology 86; sex differences research 53–7, 59; *see also* data collection; methodological issues
anecdotal data 53, 54, 56
Antaki, C. 13, 115, 168, 169, 170
anti-foundationalism 86, 179, 181
argument 102–4, 121
Armstrong, J. D. 157–8
assertiveness training 36, 43
Atkinson, J. M. 186
ATLG *see* Attitudes Towards Lesbians and Gay Men scale
attitudes 16, 153–7, 173–4
Attitudes Towards Lesbians and Gay Men (ATLG) scale 153, 154, 155, 173, 174
Austin, John 66, 81

Bakhtin, M. M. 162
Baron-Cohen, S. 44–5
Beach, W. A. 177
Bell, C. 192, 194
Billig, Mick 19, 111
Bologh, R. W. 71, 76
Borker, R. A. 42
'bracketing' 2, 3, 59, 72, 120, 126–7

Bucholtz, M. 36, 37, 54, 75, 83–4
Burkitt, I. 79
Burns, M. 183
Burr, V. 79, 181
Butler, Judith 60, 61–7, 71, 75–88, 135; anti-foundationalism 86; constructionist approach 75–6, 77, 83, 84; context 81–2; discourse 78–80, 86, 87, 88; Maloney/Fenstermaker critique of 85–6

CA *see* conversation analysis
Cameron, Deborah 10, 13, 31–2, 36, 37, 45, 67
Campbell, R. 24, 194
categorization analysis *see* membership categorization analysis
CDP *see* critical discursive psychology
child development 12
Clarke, V. 175, 176
cognition 48, 109; conversation analysis 105, 191; discursive psychology 16, 17, 104–5
cognitive psychology 22, 107
cognitive realm 28, 128, 177; conversation analysis 4, 5, 97; discourse as topic 22, 180, 182
cognitivism: Butler 80, 88; conversation analysis 105; ideological dilemmas 111; sex differences research 47–9, 57, 58
colour terms 33, 37
commonsense 111, 192
communicative styles 12, 32, 42, 43, 44, 45
communities of practice 11
Connell, R. W. 129, 130

229

INDEX

constructionist approach 20, 21–2, 59, 125, 178–80; Butler 75–6, 83, 84; conversation analysis 91, 124; critical realism 181; limitations of 182–3; sex differences research 45–7, 58; *see also* gender, social construction of

context 2, 22, 148; Butler 81–2; 'container' theory of 46; conversation analysis 100–2, 115; ethnography of communication 12; ethnomethodology 82–3; hate speech 65–6; indexicality 23, 100; sex differences research 49–53, 58–9; sexist language 10, 11, 38

conversation analysis (CA) 3–5, 9, 15–18, 90–125, 190–2; action orientation 23–4; analytic example 94–6; applicability of 188; Butler influence on 87–8; cognition 105; constructionism 91, 124; critiques of 3, 18–20, 127–8, 149, 151–2; 'doing' 198; dominance framework 41; embodiment 184–5; ethnomethodology influence on 87–8; feminist research 17–18, 19, 20, 27–8, 126; hegemonic masculinity 134–5; ideological dilemmas 111–14; ideologically loaded nature of 3; interruptions 51; membership categorization analysis 117; methodological issues 196, 197; normative patterns 149; orienting to gender 115–16; participants' orientations 19, 114–15, 126, 127, 149, 151, 152; power and asymmetry in talk 102–4; prejudicial attitudes 155; procedural consequentiality 197; reflexivity 195–6; refusals 185, 186–7; relativism 120; silence 183–4; social institution of interaction 98–100; social institutions in interaction 98, 100–2; twin focus of 97–8; variability of discourse 109–11; Wetherell-Schegloff debate 127; *see also* discursive psychology; talk

Coulter, J. 104

Crawford, Mary 32, 44

critical discursive approaches 9, 14–15, 27, 191; heterosexism 157; reification of discourse 79, 101; Schegloff 93, 94, 96, 126–7; Wetherell-Schegloff debate 126–7; *see also* poststructuralism

critical discursive psychology (CDP) 15, 130

critical realism 181, 188–9

critical theory 9, 14, 15, 18, 181

Cromby, J. 79, 181, 182–3, 188

DA *see* discourse analysis

data collection 5–6, 24, 193–4, 195, 196, 197; ethnomethodology 85, 88; sex differences research 53–6, 59; *see also* methodological issues

date rape 10, 185–6, 187

Davidson, J. 183, 186

Davis, K. 104

De Beauvoir, Simone 60

deficit framework 32–7, 38

derogatory terms 10, 50, 81, 119–20, 157–8, 171, 175; *see also* hate speech Derrida, Jacques 63, 66, 86

determinism: Butler 61, 64, 75, 79, 80, 88; contextual 101; discursive 148; hegemonic masculinity 142, 143; linguistic 41

difference framework 32, 42–5

disclaimers 156–7

discourse: action orientation 182; Butler 62–4, 66–7, 78–80, 82, 86, 87, 88; gendered 7; hegemonic masculinity 134, 135, 147–9; heterosexism 158; political nature of 7; regularities 111, 135, 150; reified 78, 79, 88, 101, 147; rhetorical organization of 120–4; sex differences 47–9, 58; as social practice 23, 82; as topic 20, 22–3, 97, 180–2; variability of 109–11; *see also* discursive psychology; language

discourse analysis (DA) 3–4, 18; critical discursive approaches 14–15; critical realism 189; data sources 193; language use 13–14

discrimination, linguistic 35

discursive psychology (DP) 3, 4, 16–18, 20, 90; action orientation 23–4; anti-cognitivism 104–5, 124; attitudes and evaluations 153–5; cognitive-psychological realm 97; constructionism 27, 91; feminist analytic approach 28, 124, 126;

230

INDEX

membership categorization analysis 117; relativism 120, 188; rhetorical analysis 121; variability of discourse 110; Wetherell 129; *see also* conversation analysis
dominance framework 32, 37–41
Donaldson, M. 129, 130
DP *see* discursive psychology
Drag 64–5
Drew, Paul 17, 162, 186, 197

ECFs *see* extreme case formulations
Eckert, P. 11
Edley, N. 28, 128–9, 130–5, 141, 147–8, 149, 190
Edwards, Derek 17, 117–19, 163, 164, 189–90
Ehrlich, S. 11
embodiment 183, 184–5
emotion work 184
emotions 33
empathy 43, 45
equality, linguistic 35–6
essentialism 21, 25, 28, 88, 124; constructionist approaches 84, 179–80; determinism 75; sex differences research 45, 46, 58, 59, 60; 'strategic' 180
ethnicity 12
ethnography of communication 9, 12–13
ethnomethodology 9, 15–16, 27, 60–1, 67–74, 75–89; analytic approach 86; constructionism 76–8; context 82–3; critiques of 71, 84–5, 86; discourse 86; indexicality 23; limitations of 88, 89, 90; participants' practices 84–5; relativism 86–7; structure-agency dualism 80–1
extreme case formulations (ECFs) 163–4, 165, 166, 167

Fairbrass, Richard 172–3
femininity: constructionist approaches 84; embodied practices 185; normative 122, 123
feminism: Butler 67, 75–6, 83, 88; constructionist approach 178–80, 182–3; conversation analysis 4, 17–20, 27–8, 90–125, 127–8, 191–2, 198; critical discursive approaches 14, 15, 27; critique of Garfinkel 71; data collection 24, 193, 194, 195, 196; essentialism 21, ethnomethodology 71, 73–4, 76; heterosexism 152; interpretation of utterances 1–2; irony 176; membership categorization analysis 119; participants' orientations 3, 149–50, 151, 176, 177, 185; performativity 67, 88; postmodern 78; poststructuralist 60–7, 74–89; radical 128; reflexivity of research 195; reification of discourse 79; relativism 188–9, 190; research on gender and language 7–20, 31–2; resistance 104; sex differences 31, 32; silence 183, 184; Spender 40, 41, 58; 'two-cultures' model 44
Fenstermaker, S. 74, 82, 85–6
Fine, Michelle 192, 195
Fishman, Pamela 40
folklinguistics 30–1, 36, 57
Foucault, Michel 62, 64, 78, 86, 99
Frankfurt School 14, 15
Frith, Hannah 19, 185–6, 187
functionalism 16, 81, 102

Garfinkel, Harold 15, 60, 67–71, 74, 80, 88; constructionism 76, 77–8; context 82–3; gender attribution process 72, 73, 106; participants' practices 84–5; relativism 86, 87
Gavey, Nicola 191
gay men: Attitudes Towards Lesbians and Gay Men scale 153, 154, 155, 173, 174; derogatory words 10, 50, 119–20; *see also* heterosexism; homosexuality
Gaytime TV Special 172–3
gender: Butler 61–3, 64–5, 66–7, 75–6, 87; constructionist approaches 21–2, 59, 60, 83–4, 178–9; conversation analysis 28, 90, 96–7, 124; essentialism 45; ethnomethodology 61, 67–74, 76–8, 83, 84, 87, 88; interpretation of utterances 1–2; membership categorization analysis 18, 119; methodological issues 193, 194, 196; non-cognitivist analysis 105–9; orienting to 3, 115–16; 'reality analysis' 120; reification of 46, 58; research on gender and language 3, 7–20, 27, 28; sex

INDEX

differences 30–59; sex distinction 61–2; social construction of 13, 41, 62, 70–1, 74, 76–7, 179; transsexualism 70; 'variables and effects' model 45–7, 58; *see also* femininity; masculinity; sex; women
gender attribution process 72–3, 105–9
genderlect 42, 43
Gergen, K. J. 21, 178, 180
Gibbon, M. 32
Giddens, Anthony 104
Gill, R. 188
Gillies, V. 188
Giora, Rachel 176
Goddard, A. 41, 51
Goffman, E. 15, 74
Goodwin, Marjorie Harness 13
gossip 30, 44
Gramsci, Antonio 129
Gubrium, J. F. 194
Gumperz, John 12

Hall, K. 63
Hammersley, M. 17, 25
hate speech 65–6, 81, 176; *see also* derogatory terms
'he/man' language 9, 39
Heath, C. 184
hedges 34, 37
hegemonic masculinity 28, 128, 129–50
hegemony 129, 130, 149
Henwood, K. 190
Hepburn, Alex 181, 189
Herek, G. M. 153, 154
Heritage, John 17, 77, 86–7, 98, 99, 100–1
heteronormativity 59, 82, 176
heterosexism 7, 29, 151–77, 182; Attitudes Towards Lesbians and Gay Men scale 153, 154, 155, 173, 174; conceding positive features 168–71; cultural 153, 160; discounting 159–60; irony 172–3, 175–6; lack of understanding 160–2; language 9, 10; participants' orientations 29, 128, 151, 158–73, 174–7; psychological 153, 160; relativist approach 26; softening the blow 162–7; *see also* homophobia; homosexuality
heterosexuality 1, 26, 123; Butler 62, 64, 75, 76; hegemonic masculinity 130; ideological dilemmas 112–14; ironizing heterosexist scripts 172, 173; 'man-made' language 39; *see also* sexuality
hierarchy 43, 53
Holland, J. 188
Holmes, Janet 37
Holstein, J. A. 194
homophobia 152, 157–8, 168, 173; hegemonic masculinity 130; ideological dilemmas 112, 113, 114; *see also* heterosexism
homosexuality 112–14, 146; Attitudes Towards Lesbians and Gay Men scale 153, 154, 155, 173, 174; stigma on 176, 182; *see also* gay men; heterosexism; lesbians; sexuality
Hopper, R. 116–17, 196
Hutchby, Ian 84–5, 102–4, 162
Hymes, Dell 12

identity 1, 27, 87, 125, 179; activity-relevant 96; Butler 78–9; cognitive-psychological context of 128; constructionist approach 60; conversation analysis 91, 115, 124; discursive psychology 16, 91, 124; gender attribution process 106, 107, 108, 109; hegemonic masculinity 28, 129, 130–1, 139, 141, 145–7; ideological dilemmas 113, 114; Wetherell and Edley's 'synthetic approach' 135
identity politics 76, 150
ideological dilemmas 109, 111–14
ideology 4, 111, 149, 191, 192
indexicality 23, 51, 81, 82–3, 100
inequalities 45, 74, 192
interactional sociolinguistics 9, 12–14
internet 41
interruptions: analytic example 93, 94, 95, 96; sex differences research 39, 40, 41, 50, 51–3
intersexed persons 68–71
intimacy 44, 53
irony 169, 170, 172–3, 175–6
italics 34
iterability 63–4, 66

Jackson, S. 188
Jagose, A. 62
Jefferson, Gail 6, 15, 91, 96
Jesperson, Otto 31, 36

232

INDEX

Keenan, Elinor (Ochs) 13
Kenwood, C. 188
Kessler, S. J. 60, 71, 72–4, 80, 88; constructionism 76–8; context 82–3; gender attribution process 72–3, 106; participants' practices 84–5; relativism 86
King, R. 11
Kitzinger, Celia: critiques of conversation analysis 18–19; ethnomethodology 76; heterosexism 151, 152–3, 188; refusals 185–6, 187; relativism 26, 188; research methodology 24, 193, 194–5; 'strategic essentialism' 180
knowledge: confidence in one's own 48, 49; relativist approach 25, 26, 190
Kulick, D. 77

Lakoff, Robin 9, 32–7, 40, 41, 44, 47; cognitivism 47–8, 49; context 50; data collection 53–5, 56; realist approach 57, 58; Spender critique of 37, 38; 'variables and effects' model 46
language: Butler 67; cognitive processes 47–9; constructionist approach 21, 178–9; critical discursive approaches 14–15; deficit framework 32–7, 38; difference framework 32, 42–5; dominance framework 32, 37–41; form/function separation 41; hate speech 65–6; interactional sociolinguistics 12–14; 'man-made' 38–9; 'neutral' 33, 36; research on 3, 7–20, 27; sex differences 3, 30–59, 78; sexist 9–12; as social action 20, 23–4, 49–53, 81–3, 109, 182–5; 'variables and effects' model of 45–7, 58; *see also* discourse; linguistics; meaning; talk
Lather, P. 195
laughter 91, 96
LeBaron, C. 116–17, 196
legislation 65
lesbians: Attitudes Towards Lesbians and Gay Men scale 153, 154, 155, 173, 174; derogatory words 10, 50, 119–20; essentialist arguments 180; *see also* heterosexism; homosexuality
liberalism 175

'linguistic discrimination' 35
linguistics: critical 14, 15; feminist 31–2, 36; folklinguistics 30–1, 36, 57; sexist language 10; *see also* language; sociolinguistics
Livia, A. 54, 63
Lorber, J. 192
Lundgren, E. 77, 83

McConnell-Ginet, S. 11
McElhinny, B. 115
macho masculinity 131–2, 134, 141
McIlvenny, P. 18, 67, 82
McKenna, W. 60, 71, 72–4, 80, 88; constructionism 76–8; context 82–3; gender attribution process 72–3, 106; participants' practices 84–5; relativism 86
McNay, L. 81
macro realm 20, 28, 114, 177; conversation analysis 4, 5, 19, 97, 98, 102, 124, 128; discourse as topic 22, 180, 182; ethnomethodology 80, 88; mainstream sociology 101; male dominance 58; poststructuralism 101–2; Wetherell and Edley's 'synthetic approach' 135; *see also* social structure
Maloney, M. 82, 85–6
Maltz, D. N. 42
'man-made' language 38–9
Marx, Karl 135
masculinity: constructionist approaches 84; as a determined 'mind-set' 141–3; as 'extreme' 136–8; hegemonic 28, 128, 129–50; as a 'hive mind' 144–5; as inauthentic 140–1; as a 'mask' 143–4; as 'self-confidence' 138–40
MCA *see* membership categorization analysis
meaning: blocking of women's meanings 39–40; context 2, 50, 53, 58–9, 82–3; fluidity of 10, 11, 66; hate speech 65–6; indexicality 23, 100; message/metamessage 43; resignification of 64, 66, 82, 175; 'semantic rule' 51; social construction of 10; tag questions 50–1; women-centred 40; *see also* language
membership categorization analysis (MCA) 18, 74, 90, 117–20, 152

Merrick, E. 192
message 43
metamessage 43
methodological issues 24–5, 53–7, 125, 193–8; *see also* analytic techniques; data collection
Meyers, M. 157
micro realm 20, 22, 28, 177; conversation analysis 4, 5, 19, 97, 98, 102, 124; ethnomethodology 80, 88; mainstream sociology 101; male dominance 41, 58; poststructuralism 101–2; Wetherell and Edley's 'synthetic approach' 135
Mills, S. 79
mind 20, 22–3, 180–2; Butler 78–80; conversation analysis 97; discursive psychology 104, 105; sex differences research 47–9; *see also* cognition; cognitivism
motherhood 39

names 35
next turn repeat initiator (NTRI) 164–5, 166, 167
Nightingale, D. J. 79, 179, 181, 182–3, 188
Noble, C. 183
norms: conversation analysis 16; gender 4, 109; oppressive 7; socialization 22
'noticings' 117
NTRI *see* next turn repeat initiator

Oakley, A. 192
objectivity 24, 25, 194

Parker, I. 79, 181
Parsons, Talcott 16, 81, 99
participants' orientations 18, 25, 114–15, 126, 185, 191–2; critiques of conversation analysis 3, 19, 149, 151, 152; dismissed as anti-feminist 20; hegemonic masculinity 28, 128–9, 134–6; heterosexism 29, 128, 151, 158–73, 174–7; politics 150; Schegloff-Wetherell debate 127
participants' practices 20, 24–5, 185–8; conversation analysis 114–15; ethnomethodology 84–5; sex differences research 53–7, 59

patriarchy 1, 7, 24, 125; hegemonic masculinity 129; patriarchal order 38; radical feminist challenging of 128; 'semantic rule' 51; stereotyped assumptions 59; *see also* sexism
Patterson, L. M. 41, 51
peer pressure 143, 144
performativity 14, 15, 61–3, 67, 82, 83, 88
Plummer, Ken 152
political correctness 11
politics 3, 176–7, 191, 192; constructionism 179, 180; critical discursive analysis 15; participants' orientations 150; relativism 189, 190; Spender 58
Pomerantz, Anita 15, 17, 94–5
pop psychology 44
positioning: critical discursive approaches 14, 15; masculinity 131, 132, 133, 147, 148
postmodernism 7, 78
poststructuralism 9, 14, 15, 18, 27; Butler 60–7, 75–88; constructionist approach 75–6, 83–4; context 81–2; discourse 78–80, 181; hegemonic masculinity 129, 135, 147, 149; limitations of 88, 89, 90; macro-micro contexts 101–2; queer theory 76
Potter, Jonathan: cognition 109; discourse analysis 13; discursive psychology 16, 17, 105; heterosexism 10, 152, 159, 161, 162–7, 168–70, 172; realism 121; refusals 186; regularity in discourse 111; relativism 25, 189, 190; research applicability 188
power 41, 53, 102–4; critical discursive approaches 14, 15; critiques of conversation analysis 19; hegemony 129; interruptions 93
prejudice 152, 155–7, 194; futility of 176; gender attribution process 107, 108; participants' orientations 151, 162–6, 170, 171, 174, 185; *see also* heterosexism; homophobia; racism; sexism
procedural consequentiality 3, 16, 197
psyche 64, 78, 79–80, 88
psychoanalysis 9, 14, 15, 18; Butler 60, 64, 79–80; discourse 181

INDEX

psychology: cognitive 22, 107; feminist 18; heterosexism 152–3; language as a resource 97; *see also* discursive psychology

quantitative sociolinguistics 12
queer theory 67, 76

racism: concessionary talk structure 170; denials of prejudice 156; relativism 188; reproduction of 155; rhetorical mechanisms 121
radio 102–4
Ramazanoglu, C. 188
rape 10, 185–6, 187
realism 25, 188, 190; critical 181, 188–9; rhetorical analysis 120–1; sex differences research 57–8, 59
reflexivity 26, 54, 194, 195
refusals 185, 186–7
relativism 20, 25–6, 188–90; conversation analysis 120; ethnomethodology 86–7
repetition 63–4
research 7–20, 27, 28; applicability of 188; conversation analysis 15–18; critical discursive approaches 9, 14–15; essentialism 21; interactional sociolinguistics 9, 12–14; methodological issues 24–5, 53–7, 125, 193–8; sex differences 3, 21, 27, 30–59, 60, 75; sexist language 9–12; *see also* analytic techniques; data collection; ethnomethodology
rhetorical analysis 120–4
rising intonation 33
Roberts, H. 192, 194
Rogers, M. F. 71
Rosen, Alexander 68
rugby 110–11, 122–4, 162–7
rules of conversation 94–6, 99–100

Sacks, Harvey 15, 17, 18, 90, 102, 117
Salem, D. A. 24, 194
Schegloff, Emmanuel 2–3, 15, 18, 19, 150, 197–8; analytic example 91–6; embodied practices 184–5; 'hegemony of the intellectuals' 190; identity 115; ideological dilemmas 112; Lakoff analysis of 37; macro contexts 135; orienting to gender 115–16; participants' orientations 25, 127, 152, 191; procedural consequentiality 197; 'theoretical imperialism' 177; Wetherell debate with 126–7, 195
science 72, 74
self-confidence: language use 34, 48, 49; masculinity 138–40
'semantic rule' 51
sex: gender distinction 61–2; intersexed persons 68–71; relativist approach 26; social construction of 62, 71, 77; transsexualism 70; 'variables and effects' model 45–6; *see also* gender
sex differences 3, 21, 27, 30–59, 60; Butler 75, 78; constructionist approach 45–7, 58; context of language 49–53, 58–9; conversation analysis contrast with 91, 96, 97; critiques of 77; deficit framework 32–7, 38; difference framework 32, 42–5; discourse of mind and world as topic 47–9; dominance framework 32, 37–41; macro-micro contexts 101, 102; participants' practices 53–7, 59; realist approach 57–8, 59
sexism 7, 9–12, 13, 151, 182; concessionary talk structure 170; context 50, 51; critique of Garfinkel 71; data collection 54, 55; denials of prejudice 156; Jesperson 31, 36; 'man-made' language 38, 39; observer recognition of 177; relativism 26, 188; reproduction of 155; rhetorical mechanisms 121, 122; Schegloff 37; Spender critique of deficit framework 38; *see also* heterosexism; patriarchy
sexuality 1, 29; Butler 62; ethnomethodology 87; Garfinkel 69, 70, 76, 86; ideological dilemmas 112–14; 'man-made' language 39; masculinity 145; social construction of 173; *see also* gay men; heterosexism; heterosexuality; homosexuality; lesbians
Shakespeare, T. 180
Sharrock, W. 101
signs 63
silence 40, 183–4
Silverman, David 17, 86
Smith, Dorothy 78, 83, 121–2

235

INDEX

Smithson, J. 19–20, 151–2, 156
social action 20, 23–4, 109, 182–5; Butler 81–2; conversation analysis 98, 102; discursive psychology 91; sex differences research 49–53; *see also* action orientation; context
social change 7, 31, 192; essentialist arguments 179–80; linguistic change 36, 40; membership categorization analysis 119–20
social class 12
social institution of interaction 98–100
social institutions in interaction 98, 100–2
social structure 22, 47, 182; Butler 63, 78; conversation analysis 16, 100–1, 102, 149; critical discursive approaches 14–15; ethnomethodology 80, 83, 88; poststructuralism 79; sexuality 69, 70; *see also* macro realm
socialization 12, 22, 34
sociolinguistics 3, 27, 87; essentialism 21, 28; interactional 9, 12–14; 'two-cultures' model 44; *see also* linguistics
sociology 22, 78, 87, 97, 101
solidarity 53, 76
speech acts 66, 81–2
Spender, Dale 9, 32, 37–41, 44, 47; cognitivism 48; context 50, 51; data collection 55–6; double standards 58; realist approach 57, 58; tag questions 51; 'variables and effects' model 46
stereotypes 40, 45, 54, 59, 117; critique of Garfinkel 71; folklinguistics 30, 31, 36, 57; masculine 132
Stokoe, Elizabeth 18, 19–20, 119–20, 124, 151–2, 156
Stoller, Robert 68
structural functionalism 16, 81, 102
structure 64, 65, 78–80, 88; *see also* social structure
Sunderland, J. 193
surgery 68, 69
symmetry 43, 53

tag questions 33, 37, 48, 50–1
talk 2–3, 16, 17, 18, 28, 177; anecdotal utterances 53, 54; cognitivism 49; gender creeping into 116–17; heterosexist 29, 158–73, 174, 175; idealized data 56; orienting to gender 115–16; power and asymmetry 102–4; realist approach 57, 58, 59; research methodology 196; social structure relationship 100–2; transcription conventions 199; 'variables and effects' model of 47; *see also* conversation analysis
talk radio 102–4
Tannen, Deborah 32, 42–5, 47; cognitivism 48–9; context 50, 53; data collection 56; interruptions 51–3; realist approach 57, 58; 'variables and effects' model 46
TCU *see* turn construction unit
three-part concessionary structure 168–70
Toerien, Merran 184, 185
topic shifts 41
transcription conventions 199
transsexualism 70, 72–3, 83, 85
turn construction unit (TCU) 94
turn-taking 94–5, 96, 98–100
'two-cultures' model 42–5

Uchida, Aki 45

variability of discourse 109–11
'variables and effects' model 45–7, 58, 93–4
variationist research 3, 12, 21, 28
'verbal hygiene' 10
video 184, 197

Watson, R. 101
Weatherall, A. 32
West, C.: ethnomethodology 74, 85–6; interruptions 51, 52, 53; Schegloff critique of 93; sex differences research 40, 41; silence 183
Wetherell, Margaret: discourse analysis 13, 182; discursive psychology 16, 17, 129; hegemonic masculinity 28, 128–9, 130–5, 141, 147–8, 149; realism 121; refusals 186; regularity in discourse 111; relativism 25; researcher's self analysis 179; Schegloff debate with 126–7, 195; three-part concessionary structure 168, 169, 170
Widdicombe, Sue 115, 191

Wilkinson, Sue 24, 128, 188, 194–5
Willig, Carla 79, 181
Willott, S. 188
Wittgenstein, L. 104
women: blocking of meanings 39–40; difference framework 32, 42–5; dominance framework 37, 38–40, 41; representation in language 32–3, 34–5, 37; silencing of 38, 39, 40, 41; subordinate status of 32, 34, 35, 47; use of language 31, 32, 33–4, 35–6, 37; 'woman' category 76; *see also* femininity; feminism; gender; sexism
Wooffitt, R. 84–5, 102, 103, 104, 162, 191
Wowk, M. T. 76

Zimmerman, D. H.: ethnomethodology 70, 74, 76, 86–7; interruptions 51, 52, 53; male-female laughter 96; Schegloff critique of 93; sex differences research 40, 41